CLASS, CITIZENSHIP,
AND
SOCIAL DEVELOPMENT

CLASS, CITIZENSHIP, AND SOCIAL DEVELOPMENT

Essays by T. H. Marshall

WITH AN INTRODUCTION BY
SEYMOUR MARTIN LIPSET

The University of Chicago Press
Chicago and London

Class, Citizenship, and Social Development was originally published in England with the title *Sociology at the Crossroads*, by Heinemann Educational Books, Ltd. This edition is published by arrangement with Heinemann Educational Books, Ltd., and Doubleday & Company, Inc.

The University of Chicago Press, Chicago 60637
The University of Chicago Press, Ltd., London

Introduction Copyright © 1964 by Doubleday & Company, Inc.
Copyright © 1963 by T. H. Marshall
All rights reserved. Published 1964
University of Chicago Press Edition 1977
Printed in the United States of America
87 86 85 84 83 82 81 80   6 5 4 3 2

ISBN: 0–226–50702–5

INTRODUCTION

For many decades sociology was criticized for having departed from the historical concerns of its nineteenth-century founders. This departure was characterized by a shift from a macroscopic to a more microscopic focus on society, from studies of social change and aspects of total societies, viewed in a historical and comparative perspective, to the study of interpersonal relations, the structure of small groups, and the analysis of the decision-making process, accompanied by an emphasis on improving the quantitative methodology appropriate to these topics. This change suggested to its critics that modern sociology had lost contact with its original intellectual traditions. The writings of men like Max Weber, Alexis de Tocqueville, Robert Michels, and Vilfredo Pareto were apparently of contemporary interest only insofar as they had attempted to specify formal functional relationships and social psychological processes of the type that interested latter-day sociologists.

In the last decade, however, the situation has changed again. In American sociology, once viewed by many European scholars as ahistorical and concerned only with problems for which advanced statistical techniques are appropriate, there has been a significant revival of historical and comparative sociology. At a number of major sociology departments, a sizable number of recent tenure appointees are involved in the analysis of social change and with historical and comparative sociology, while a number of important older scholars have turned or returned to the analysis of total societies viewed in a comparative context, or to historical work. This revival has taken many forms, including interest in the sociology of science, concern with the determinants of change in intellectual life, interest in the evolution of national values, and many others. The growth of interest in such problems is so recent that many with an interest in sociology, including some in the profession itself, are unaware of the extent to which leading sociologists and departments have become involved in these fields of inquiry.

Perhaps the most significant source of renewed interest in historical and comparative sociology has been the emergence of a body of inquiry which, lacking a better label, has been called the sociology of development. This term refers to interest in the processes that affect changes within total societies and nations. As a field of research, it parallels the work of economists on problems of economic development. And just as economists concerned with economic development have recognized that much of what is conventionally termed economic history is actually the study of economic development, and that generalizations concerning economic development which are relevant to contemporary "developing economies" can be tested by reference to the past history of developed economies, so sociologists interested in problems of societal modernization and nation building in Africa and Asia have come to recognize that the "old states" of the world have much to tell us about these processes. In sociology as in economics, interest in comparative development has involved a renewed concern with historical analysis.

This emergence of serious and extensive interest in historical and comparative sociology places T. H. Marshall, the author of this book, in a curious position. When the major essay in the volume, "Citizenship and Social Class," was first presented as the Alfred Marshall lectures at Cambridge in February 1949, many would have said that it was an example of the old-fashioned type of sociology that had characterized European scholarship before World War II, but had been supplanted in the United States by more systematic and quantitative approaches—approaches that were then being rapidly adopted in Europe as well. I recall my surprise, when attending the Second World Congress of Sociology held at Liege in 1953, to find that many of the younger Europeans there regarded such men as Max Weber, Emile Durkheim, and Robert Michels as outmoded, representatives of the prescientific era of sociology. And much of the presentation and discussion of papers among this group involved quantitative studies of relatively small problems.

Less than a decade later, in the summer of 1962, the Fifth World Congress of Sociology, under the presidency of T. H. Marshall, met in Washington, D.C., with the "Sociology of Development" the principal topic for analysis. Far from being a representative of the past, Marshall had proved to be a precursor of the future. His earlier book, *Citizenship and Social Class*, did not have an American edition in 1950. In 1964 this larger work is being printed by Doubleday, one of the largest trade houses in the country, clearly suggesting a judgment that this type of sociology now has a sizable market.

The re-emergence of historical and comparative sociology does not reflect any general feeling that the emphases on quantitative techniques, rigorous methodology, and systematic theory, which characterized the postwar period, were misguided. If there is any criticism of these efforts, it is only that they had the temporary effect of narrowing the focus of concern from macroscopic (total society) to microscopic (small unit) problems. In a sense, the swing back to the macroscopic involves an effort to relate the new methodological and theoretical developments to the analysis of total social systems and social change. Much of the logic of inquiry developed and tested with respect to experimental and microscopic sociology has proven applicable to macroscopic research.

In analyzing problems of societal development in the modern era, it is now recognized that the "old states" endured many problems and processes that are somewhat similar to those now characteristic of the states of Asia, Africa, and Latin America as they attempt to establish stable legitimate authority and to industrialize. Hence any effort to study developments in the latter nations must proceed, in part, from generalizations derived from comparable processes in Europe or North America; e.g., about the formulation of national identity, the way in which societies admit new strata to participation in the polity, or the way in which "modern" values are incorporated in a developed society. It is ironic that only a few years ago the very concept of development would have been regarded by many sociologists as deriving from the erroneous and utopian notion of inevitable progress or unilinear social evolution. While it was considered legitimate to speak of an *economy* as more or less developed, in referring to its level of productivity, one could not speak of *societies* in the same sense without implying a value preference.

Today sociologists once more recognize that it is both possible and necessary to discuss the preconditions for the development of modern society. To speak of social modernization is simply to refer to what appear to be the social processes and relationships inherent in a modern industrial society; thus the use of the concept social modernization neither implies a value preference nor assumes a necessary evolutionary process.

Modernization appears to involve modes of social relationships in which there is a greater emphasis on universalism as distinct from particularism, on equality in contrast to elitism, on individual achievement rather than ascription (hereditary status), on specificity (interaction on the basis of specific attributes) rather than diffuseness (interaction on the basis of one general trait). The very concept of social modernization refers to the social conditions characteristic of an urbanized, economically advanced society, in which there has been a great deal of social differentiation, division of labor, and social change, in contrast to the institutions of a traditionalist rural or preindustrial society, with its relative lack of differentiation and its emphasis on social stability. (These are, of course, ideal-typical statements; both developed and underdeveloped societies vary considerably among themselves.)

In nations that have democratized politically as they have moved from economic underdevelopment to development, there is a greater need to move along the lines of social development presented above than in those states that have not adopted such political institutions. If nations "develop" along one dimension—the economic, for example—but resist change in the political or social dimensions, serious tensions may result. Germany is an example of a country that developed economically and allowed freedom of class organization but resisted change in the political and social sphere, and values and rights corresponding to a premodern society persisted. I will not elaborate on the causal process here, but it has been argued that much of the tension in German political life reflected the strains created when the demands of new strata for rights inherent in a developed economy were resisted by the old dominant classes, who sought to preserve the social relations characteristic of a preindustrial society. It has also been suggested that the failure of most Catholic nations to develop as rapidly as Protestant ones economically, or to sustain stable democracies to the same extent before World War II, reflects the fact that the Catholic Church has helped to preserve social values congruent with medieval feudalism and in opposition to advanced industrialism or egalitarian democracy.

Many of T. H. Marshall's writings have been concerned with the emergence of a modern class structure based on the divisions inherent in industrial society in his native Britain. This was the first country to experience the industrial revolution, and, more significantly from a sociological point of view, it is one of the few nations that have successfully admitted the new classes of industrial society—first the bourgeoisie and later the workers—into the polity, while preserving the monarchy's and the aristocracy's traditional status and aura of legitimacy. In most of the European nations, the aristocracy resisted granting rights to the new strata, a reaction that often had the effect of inhibiting economic growth or precipitating revolution. In Britain alone of the major European countries, economic development was paralleled by peaceful changes in the social and political structure that made a stable democracy possible.

The key concept in Marshall's thinking on these matters is

the notion of citizenship. Citizenship for him is a status that involves access to various rights and powers. In premodern times citizenship was limited to a small elite, and to a considerable extent social development in European states has consisted of the admission to citizenship of the new strata of industrial society.

For Marshall, the concept of citizenship has three components: civil, political, and social. The civil aspects of citizenship arose with the emergence of the bourgeoisie in the eighteenth century and involve a set of individual rights—liberty, freedom of speech, equality before the law, and the right to own property. Political rights, the access to the decision-making process through participation in the choice of parliament by universal manhood suffrage, emerged in the nineteenth century and reflect in part the demands of the working classes for citizenship. Social rights—welfare, security, and education—have become a major component in the definition of citizenship in the twentieth century.

Perhaps the most important aspect of the concept of citizenship in Marshall's view is its assumption of equality. Equality ". . . is a status bestowed on those who are full members of the community. All who possess the status are equal with respect to the rights and duties with which the status is endowed. . . . [S]ocieties in which citizenship is a developing institution create an image of an ideal citizenship against which achievement can be measured and towards which aspiration can be measured." But if citizenship rights, which arose with capitalism and industrialization, imply equality, the class structure is a system of inequality. Hence, argues Marshall, citizenship and class create ". . . a conflict between opposing principles." Modern industrial democratic society is historically unique in seeking to sustain a system of contradictory values. All previous societies had systems of stratification which assumed inequality; they also denied citizenship to all except a small elite. Once full and equal citizenship was established, the privileges of the elite inevitably came under attack. Political citizenship was preceded or followed by industrial citizenship—the representation of workers within factories by trade-unions.

The equalitarian emphasis in citizenship has fostered a successful attack on the many aspects of class inequality. In particular, it has sharply reduced hereditary privilege; there is now much more emphasis on personal achievement. The school system, as the principal mechanism of occupational placement, increasingly serves to provide for each individual "the equal right to display and develop differences, or inequalities; the equal right to be recognized as unequal."

In stressing the revolutionary character of citizenship, the creation of a status in which all men are equal, Marshall has revived an idea common among nineteenth-century thinkers, leftists and rightists alike, that equal suffrage and hereditary class privilege are incompatible. Conservatives feared and socialists welcomed the suffrage as the means that would encourage the majority of non-property-holders or possessors of little power to reduce the wealth and power of the dominant classes. As Tocqueville wrote in the early 1850s:

> How should the poor and humble and yet powerful classes not have dreamt of issuing from their poverty and inferiority by means of their power. . . . The people had first endeavoured to help itself by changing every political institution, but after each change it found that its lot was in no way improved, or was only improving with a slowness quite incompatible with the eagerness of its desire. Inevitably, it must sooner or later discover that that which held it fixed in its position was not the constitution of the government but the unalterable laws that constitute society itself; and it was natural that it should be brought to ask itself if it had not both the power and the right to alter those laws, as it had altered all the rest. And to speak more specially of property, which is, as it were, the foundation of our social order— all the privileges which covered it and which, so to speak, concealed the privilege of property having been destroyed, and the latter remaining the principal obstacle

to equality among men, and appearing to be the only sign of inequality—was it not necessary, I will not say that it should be abolished in its turn, but at least that the thought of abolishing it should occur to the minds of those who did not enjoy it.[1]

On the left, Karl Marx himself became an early exponent of the proposition that in a political democracy the right to vote means a significant share in power. As he put it in discussing Britain in 1852, for the "working class, universal suffrage means political power, for the proletariat forms the great majority of the population. . . ."[2] And in 1869 in re-editing *The Eighteenth Brumaire of Louis Napoleon,* he deliberately omitted the criticisms he had written almost two decades earlier against universal suffrage.[3] Toward the end of the nineteenth century, Friedrich Engels, Marx's great collaborator, was to put the identification between working-class politics and democracy in even stronger terms: "If one thing is certain it is that our Party and the working class can only come to power under the form of the democratic republic."[4]

In a real sense, as Marshall argues, as "citizenship and the capitalist class system have been at war . . . the former has imposed modifications on the latter." A great deal of democratic politics involves the efforts of the lower strata to equalize the conditions of existence and opportunity. And over time political change has been in this direction. Conservative parties such as the American Republicans, the British Tories, or the continental Christian Democrats now support policies that, but a few decades ago, they described as

[1] *The Recollections of Alexis de Tocqueville* (London: The Harvill Press, 1948), p. 84.
[2] Letter by Karl Marx to the New York *Tribune,* August 25, 1852, cited in George Lichtheim, *Marxism* (London: Routledge and Kegan Paul, 1961), p. 99.
[3] J. P. Mayer, "Introduction," to *The Recollections of Alexis de Tocqueville,* op. cit., p. xxi.
[4] Karl Marx and Friedrich Engels, *Correspondence 1846–1895* (New York: International Publishers, 1935), p. 486.

rank socialism. There can be little doubt "that the preservation of economic inequalities has been made more difficult by the enrichment of the status of citizenship."

In the essay written shortly after World War II, "Citizenship and Social Class," from which these quotes have been taken, Marshall raises as one of the problems of an equalitarian society the possibly adverse effects of the emergence of what Michael Young was later to dub the "meritocracy," an elite whose claim to high status is based on its superiority rather than on inheritance or luck.[5] If occupational status is largely a function of educational ability, then inequality in the form of status differentiation secures a basic "stamp of legitimacy, because it has been conferred by an institution designed to give the citizen his just rights." But though the assumption that status differentiation within the bureaucracies of industry and government is linked to intellectual ability justifies some inequality of reward, the emphasis on equality implicit in citizenship asserts that inequality should not be very great.

The tension between equality and inequality then is inherent in the very fabric of modern industrial democratic society. The conflict, however, does not mean that one or the other must triumph, or that the strain will destroy or even necessarily weaken the social fabric. Rather, Marshall argues: "Apparent inconsistencies are in fact a source of stability, achieved through a compromise which is not dictated by logic." In other words, the predominant character of modern industrial democracy as a free and evolving society is in part a result of the chronic tensions between the pressures toward inequality inherent in complex society and the emphasis on equality that is endemic to democracy.

In recent years some students of the politics of the New States have suggested that the "politics of equality" are central to modernizing societies regardless of whether they are liberal-democratic or totalitarian. Thus Lloyd Fallers suggests that both types involve politics that are "populistic," in ide-

[5] See Michael Young, *The Rise of the Meritocracy* (London: Thames and London, 1958).

ology if not in practice. "They differ from traditional authoritarianisms precisely in feeling the necessity to *require* the people to participate by actively consenting to political acts. . . . Second, modern politics, whether liberal-democratic or totalitarian, are egalitarian in the sense that one of the principal objects and justifications of politics is assumed to be a constant improvement in the social and economic welfare of the common man. . . . Finally, modern politics are egalitarian in that the state, again whether it is totalitarian or liberal-democratic, assumes responsibility for furthering equality of opportunity."[6] And he concludes that all these aspects of modern politics follow directly from "the processes of structural differentiation and cultural modernization," that a commitment to science and technology and to economic growth, which implies structural differentiation of occupational roles, inevitably breaks down traditionalistic particular ties and presses for equalitarianism.

Although Marshall does not discuss this point of view (to a considerable extent it has emerged since his main work on equality was written), he does address himself to certain dangers inherent in policies that assume, as do the ideologies of modernizing authoritarianisms, that socio-economic equality is possible and reject the assumption that democratic rights for the masses are essential to reduce the pressures toward stabilizing the bases of inequality inherent in all stratification systems.

As he points out, "some children are more able than others, . . . some occupations demand qualities that are rarer than others and need longer and more skilled training to come to full maturity, and . . . they will therefore probably continue to enjoy higher prestige." The advocacy of complete socio-economic equality confronts limits inherent in social rela-

[6] Lloyd Fallers, *Equality, Modernity and Democracy in New States* (Mimeographed, Committee for the Study of New Nations, University of Chicago, 1962), pp. 77–8; see also Edward Shils, "The Military in the Political Development of New States," in John Johnson, ed., *The Role of the Military in Underdeveloped Countries* (Princeton University Press, 1962), pp. 9–10.

tions, and the ignoring of these limits might result in the creation of a more invidious system of social differentiation. If we "recognize some measure of economic inequality as legitimate and acceptable," it will be possible to combat "rigid class divisions, and . . . anything which favours the preservation or formation of sharply distinguished culture patterns at different social levels."

In any effort to understand the present, some sense and knowledge of history is necessary. All too often, sociologists, and other intellectuals as well, tend to see some aspect of the modern as unique. The general consensus, that life today is different from that of the previous generation or even from that of a century or more ago, is often accepted unquestioningly as fact.

Marshall does sociology a distinct favor in revealing the extent to which, for almost a century, it has been common every few years to proclaim a social revolution involving the sharp improvement of the worker's status.

"From the 1880's to the 1940's people were constantly expressing amazement at the social transformation witnessed in their lifetime, oblivious of the fact that, in this series of outbursts of self-congratulation, the glorious achievements of the past became the squalid heritage of the present." But in spite of the progress that leads one generation to proclaim the significance of the social improvements that have occurred within its lifetime, only a few years later others are arguing that the present conditions of the poor, of the lowly, are intolerable, that they cannot possibly be tolerated by free men who believe in equality. And, as Marshall indicates, such phenomena do not "mean that the progress which men thought they made was illusory. It means that the standards by which that progress was assessed were constantly rising, and that ever deeper probing into the social situation kept revealing new horrors which had previously been concealed from view."

This historical perspective leads Marshall to question whether the concept of the Affluent Society will have any longer life than some of its predecessors. In the very book that gave the concept currency, Galbraith pointed to the existence in America of large pockets of poverty in groups that are relatively invisible—the aged, families without a male head, the chronically ill, the badly educated, the unskilled, and large segments of the rural population. Although a nearly forgotten topic in the early postwar years, when the poor had supposedly been eliminated as a social category by the Welfare State reforms of the Labor government and the New Deal, with the assistance of full employment, concern for the poor has now returned with a vengeance. In both the United States and Britain, scholars and journalists have rediscovered the existence of a significant stratum of poverty, and the political left has returned to an attack on the causes of such poverty.

In large measure the newly discovered poor are now described as the "culturally deprived." They are the people who have grown up in rural or urban slums, are badly educated, and have lived their lives in cultural as well as economic poverty. Their families, which are larger than those of the more well-to-do, are exposed to the vicious reinforcing cycle of poverty, so that the dream of the equal opportunity for all to mount the educational, and consequently the occupational, ladder is still restricted. The problem, as Marshall noted long before others, becomes one of breaking down these cultural barriers through deliberate social action. Here is the most recent example of the conflict between the principles of equality inherent in citizenship and the forces endemic to complex stratified society that serve to maintain or erect cultural barriers between the classes. The latter operate as a consequence of the differential distributions of reward and access to culture and must be combated continually if they are not to dominate.

Although T. H. Marshall has made important contributions to sociology's conceptual framework, his theoretical innovations are perhaps not as widely acknowledged as they should be because he has not presented his analytic framework as part of a general theory. This reflects a deliberate choice, the result of a policy he recommends to contemporary sociology as a whole, and not only to himself. In his inaugural

lecture, on being appointed professor at the London School
of Economics (the first essay in this book), Marshall coun-
seled a strategic orientation for the discipline, which has become widely accepted in the United States through its
independent advocacy here by Robert K. Merton. As Marshall
puts it, what sociology needs is "sociological stepping stones
in the middle distance," or, as Merton stated it, theories of
the middle range.[7] Marshall, in this first L.S.E. lecture, elo-
quently presented a program for sociology, which deserves a
wide hearing:

> I do not recommend the way to the stars; sociologists
> should not, I think, expend all their energies climbing in
> search of vast generalizations, universal laws, and a total
> comprehension of human society as such. They are more
> likely to get there in the end if they don't try to get there
> now. Nor do I recommend the way into the sands of
> whirling facts which blow into the eyes and ears until
> nothing can be clearly seen or heard. But I believe there
> is a middle way which runs over firm ground . . . [S]o-
> ciology can choose units of study of a manageable size—
> not society, progress, morals, and civilization, but spe-
> cific social structures in which the basic processes and
> functions have determined meanings.[8]

[7] Robert K. Merton, *Social Theory and Social Structure* (Glencoe:
The Free Press, 1957), pp. 9–10.
[8] The idea of middle distance or middle range theory has a long
intellectual history, as Karl Mannheim points out in a note to his
own discussion of *principia media* (middle principles). John Stuart
Mill used the concept in his *System of Logic* and indicated that he
derived it from Bacon. Mannheim first employed the concept in the
German edition of *Mensch und Gesellschaft im Zeitalter des Umhaus*
(1935). Morris Ginsberg also discussed *principia media* in his *Sociology* (1934), as did Adolf Löwe in *Economics and Sociology*
(1935). For Mannheim's discussion see *Man and Society in an Age
of Reconstruction* (New York: Harcourt Brace and Co., 1950), pp.
173–90. It is interesting to note that the most important exponent
of general system theory, Talcott Parsons, wrote a detailed critique
of an emphasis on *principia media* before he published his own conceptions. See his review of *Economics and Sociology*, by Adolf Löwe,
American Journal of Sociology, 43 (1937), pp. 477–81. Merton also

The fact that Marshall believes that sociology can best be developed by seeking generalizations applicable to specific structures and settings, rather than by formulating general theories, does not mean that he joins those critics who see all efforts to develop ahistorical hypotheses about complex societies as ill-taken. As he stated in his lecture inaugurating the teaching of sociology at Cambridge University in 1960, the "central concern of sociology . . . is the analytical and explanatory study of social systems. . . . To me . . . it seems obvious that, if society were not systematic, there could be no social science. And I would go further and add that if the fundamental elements of which social systems are made were not essentially the same in all societies (though differently combined), and if the possible ways of using these fundamental elements were not limited in number, the social sciences, so-called, would be devoid of all general theory. And sociology, which depends more than any other discipline on comparative study, would be the hardest hit of all."

But, as he also notes in the same lecture, "careful studies in depth of limited areas of selected social systems" are the best way to develop an understanding of the nature of social systems. And he suggests, as I have already noted, the need for "detailed study of so-called underdeveloped—or 'developing'—countries . . . [which] uses for purposes of comparison . . . our historical knowledge of what are now the 'advanced' civilizations."

In seeking to make use of historical materials for comparative analysis, sociologists have frequently been criticized by historians for not really analyzing historical situations in depth, for not really seeking to understand the causal process in chronological perspective. If this criticism is legitimate, then efforts at comparative sociology are truly pointless, for

calls attention to the precursors of this approach in his "The Role-Set: Problems in Sociological Theory," *British Journal of Sociology*, 8 (1957), pp. 108–9; and in his "Introduction" to Allen Barton, *Social Organization Under Stress: A Sociological Review of Disaster Studies* (Washington: National Academy of Sciences—National Research Council Publication 1032, 1963), p. xxxi.

no comparative sociologist can hope to become as expert on the societies or historical periods relevant to his problem as are those who spend their entire lives on a given nation or period. And it must be admitted that sociologists concerned with historical materials have erred in two directions. Some have rushed in to generalize about historical epochs with little knowledge, while others have been so intimidated by the need to document that they have become, in effect, sociological historians rather than comparative sociologists.

These excesses are not, however, inherent in comparative historical research. Sociologists, Marshall well argues, must take historians at their word and rely on them as experts.

[S]ociologists must inevitably rely extensively on secondary authorities, without going back to the original sources. They do this partly because life is too short to do anything else when using the comparative method, and they need data assembled from a wide historical field, and partly because original sources are very tricky things to use. . . . It is the business of the historian to sift this miscellaneous collection of dubious authorities and to give to others the results of their careful professional assessment. And surely they will not rebuke the sociologist for putting faith in what historians write.

It does appear to some that efforts to generalize, relying on extensive comparisons and secondary sources for data, cannot be scientific, and, therefore, macroscopic comparative sociology cannot claim to be a science. This view has been voiced both by those sociologists who would limit the discipline to problems that permit the application of rigorous quantitative methods and by non-sociologists who reject the possibility of a "science of society." Marshall rejects the arguments of both. As he says: "Science . . . is knowledge acquired by the collection and analysis of information through the scrupulous use of procedures sufficiently systematic to enable the work done by one man to be repeated by another, and their results to be combined or compared, so that in this way the body of knowledge may grow." Clearly we may apply

the logic of science to the study of social systems with as
much justification as we apply it to the analysis of individuals
and institutions. No two individuals develop in precisely the
same way; that is, have the same history, but this does not
prevent psychologists, physiologists, neurologists, or others
from making generalizations about individual behavior by
comparing instances in which the circumstances of development have been similar. As the political scientist Karl
Deutsch and a group of historians working with him on problems of history and comparative method point out:

> Since historical cases can best be compared in only some
> of their aspects, and practically never in all of them, any
> comparison means the sacrifice of a great deal of detail,
> much of it important information. Yet to draw limited
> comparisons from only partly comparable data is of the
> essence of human thought. Throughout our lives we all
> apply selected memories from the past to our decisions
> in the present and to our expectations for the future. If
> we elaborate this time-honored practice into a research
> project and call it the "case method," we can hope to be
> more explicit in the techniques we use, in the assump-
> tions we make, and in the data we leave out.[9]

To be sure, there are relatively few societies to compare,
so that hypotheses about the operation of a specific variable
in their evolution are bound to be less subject to explicit verification than are generalizations about the operation of variables in individual development, where many more cases can
be studied and compared. Because of the relatively small
number of national cases and because social systems are complex units, we will always have to rely upon historical case
studies as one of our basic methods. However, the historical
case method as used by a sociologist can contribute to the
development of general theory, both by drawing out gener-

[9] K. W. Deutsch, S. A. Burrell, R. A. Kann, M. Lee, Jr., M. Lich-
terman, R. E. Lindgren, F. L. Loewenheim, R. W. Van Wagenen,
Political Community and the North Atlantic Area (Princeton:
Princeton University Press, 1957), p. 15.

alizations that can be applied to all similar cases and by testing, and elaborating, hypotheses previously formulated on a
more general level. There is no necessary conflict between an
interest in developing scientific hypotheses and a concern
with historical specificity. "Much may be gained by using
analytical concepts to guide our historical inquiry, and by using the results of historical inquiry to modify our concepts
regarding present day problems."[10]

Although the logic and methods of science can and should
be used in historical and comparative sociology, it is obvious
that much sociological work, though fruitful, cannot validate
hypotheses with the rigor normally associated with the concept of a science. As Marshall observes, "sociological explanation does consist, in the last resort, of the application to the
problem in question of the collective wisdom of the discipline
through the judgment of individual scholars." In this regard,
it is important to recognize that one of the most important
methods of macroscopic social science is the method of the
dialogue. By looking at the same problem from different theoretical perspectives, we increase knowledge about social
processes. Different conceptual frameworks lead men to high-
light certain aspects that others ignore. Often what appear to
be contradictory findings merely reflect the fact that different
scholars have used varying concepts. It should be clear in
dealing with studies of complex systems that, no matter how
rigorous the methodology employed, in elaborating or presenting a thesis that involves interrelating structural variables
such as national values, class, personality, and the like, most
social scientists are still engaged basically in presenting an
argument which they then "validate" by showing that there is
more supporting than contradictory evidence available.

Most of the concepts we use in comparative and historical
sociology are necessarily very imprecise, and consequently
leave a great deal of room for the analyst unwittingly to find
reasons for selecting those indicators that best fit the conceptual framework he is using. In reading the work of others,

[10] ibid., p. 14.

we are normally inclined to accept their findings as both valid and reliable, as long as they agree with our predispositions. Disagreement, however, results in efforts to reanalyze the evidence and to locate data that may demonstrate that previous work has drastically oversimplified, or simply ignored, much relevant material.

A meaningful scientific dialogue, of course, requires certain basic levels of agreement concerning the rules of the discussion. Where problems are stated in fundamentally different terms as between orthodox Marxist and empirically and behaviorally-oriented social scientists, no effective scientific dialogue is possible. One must agree concerning the levels of hypotheses and the nature of evidence. Thus the method of the dialogue results in replication and the growth of knowledge. This "method" has, of course, been the very meaning of scholarship in history. The social sciences, however, with their sense of employing the same approaches to the verification of hypotheses as the natural sciences, have been reluctant to recognize that dialogue or controversy may remain a principal means of scientific verification of hypotheses in their disciplines as well.

T. H. Marshall has contributed greatly to the sociological dialogue. He has kept alive the perspective that society requires conflict—a view that sees change as an endemic and continuous aspect of all major social systems and that implies a conception of the role of the scholar that calls for his relating the knowledge and insights of sociology to the issues of the day. While primarily concerned with problems basic to the discipline, Marshall has not hesitated, as some of the essays in this book clearly indicate, to apply the conclusions of sociology to contemporary social problems. Since American sociology has moved increasingly in recent years toward a detailed consideration of the topics that have concerned Marshall for most of his working life, it is fitting that this collection of his essays on matters sociological and social is now made readily available in this country.

Seymour Martin Lipset

PREFACE

In choosing the material for this volume of essays I have tried to include everything of substance that I have written on the subjects which have claimed most of my attention since I turned from history to sociology some thirty years ago. I have selected what seemed to me to be worth preserving from among articles I had already published and added three papers which appear here for the first time, as Chapters II, XIII and XV of this book.

The first part of the book contains some general reflections on sociology, its achievements and prospects, its strength and its weaknesses, its opportunities and responsibilities. Every sociologist is bound at some time to contribute to the interminable discussion of these questions, and I did so first in my inaugural lecture at the London School of Economics in February 1946, which appears here as Chapter I. Chapter II was deliberately written as a sequel to it, and originated as a public lecture given in Cambridge in November 1960, to celebrate the introduction of sociology into the syllabus of the Economics Tripos. Chapter III is the Hobhouse Memorial Lecture for 1959 and was composed while I was serving with UNESCO in Paris. It is included in the latest volume of these lectures published by the Athlone Press in 1962, and I am indebted to the London School of Economics for permission to reproduce it here.

The second and longest part of the book is devoted to the subject on which I did most work while I was teaching sociology, namely social stratification. I cannot now remember what led me to choose it, as it was not then as popular a subject among sociologists as it has since become. My first effort in this field appeared in the *Sociological Review* in January, 1934 under the title 'Social Class—a Preliminary Analysis'. I have not included this. It seemed to me, when I re-read it, to be not only 'preliminary' but naïve, and so out of date, especially in its terminology, that it was more likely to confuse than to enlighten. I acted on the principle that one should only re-publish work which one can re-read without blushing. Chapter IV, the longest in the book, is based on the Marshall Lectures delivered in Cambridge in 1949. This and Chapters VI and VII are reprinted, with the consent of the Cambridge University Press, from the volume published by them in 1950 with the title *Citizenship and Social Class*. Chapter VI had previously appeared in *The Canadian Journal of Economics and Political Science* for August 1939, and Chapter VII in the volume entitled *Class Conflict and Social Stratification* which I edited for the Le Play House Press in 1938.

Chapter V is a paper presented to the Third World Congress of Sociology in 1956 and published in the *Transactions*, Volume III. The general theme of the Congress was 'Social Change', and I acted as chairman of the section on social stratification. The paper was an attempt to sum up the points made by the various participants and to make some original contributions. Chapter VIII appeared as the first article in the 1953 issue of the *Yearbook of Education*, which was devoted to the study of the status of teachers. It was my task to elucidate the concept of status. Chapter IX was written in 1954 for the *Ghurye Felicitation Volume* to celebrate the sixtieth birthday of Professor Ghurye of Bombay. Chapter X is an address I gave to the Institute of Labour Management (as it was then called) in 1945, which was published in the Institute's journal. The origin of Chapter XI, which is only a fragment of a symposium, is explained in a note on page 248.

The papers in the third part of the book are the fruit of

my growing interest in modern social policy, which was first expressed in the latter part of *Citizenship and Social Class*. It was stimulated by my experience as Head of the Social Science Department of the London School of Economics and my period of service with the Control Commission in Germany in 1949–50, during which I had to consider how to present post-war British society to the Germans. This involved trying to identify the essential characteristics of the Welfare State. Chapter XII is the Galton Lecture for 1953, published in the *Eugenics Review*, Volume XLV, Number 2. Chapters XIII and XV are lectures not hitherto published. The first was delivered at the University of Leeds in January 1961, and the second at a conference of the British Sociological Association at Brighton in March 1962. Chapter XIV is an article written for *The European Journal of Sociology* in 1961 which appeared in Volume II, Number 2. These three papers deal with very much the same subject, and there is inevitably some overlapping between them. I have made some amendments in order to reduce this, but have not tried to eliminate it altogether. The last chapter is a review article of Lord Beveridge's book *Voluntary Action*, and appeared in *The Political Quarterly* for January–March, 1949. I wish to acknowledge my indebtedness to the editors of the journals or other publications in which these papers originally appeared.

T. H. *Marshall*

November 1962

CONTENTS

PART THREE
SOCIAL WELFARE

PART ONE

SOCIOLOGY TODAY AND TOMORROW

CHAPTER I

SOCIOLOGY AT THE CROSSROADS

As I look back at those days in October of last year when we reassembled in this building,[1] and I fought my way through a seething mob in the entrance hall and climbed the stairs to find my room, my colleagues, or something to eat, two images recur to my mind. One is a poster in the third floor passage bearing in large letters the sinister words 'Sociology Squash'. As I shied like a startled horse and crept shuddering past it I felt that in some way which I could not as yet fully understand it presaged the shape of things to come. The other is the sad plight of my colleague Professor Ginsberg, almost literally submerged as wave after wave of students broke against his door and tumbled into his room. These phenomena have a bearing on my subject this afternoon. They provide the setting against which we must examine the two questions: Where does sociology stand today? and Along what road should it travel into the future? Or, in other words, Why do these throngs press upon us? What are they looking for, and what are we going to give them that will satisfy their craving?

But we must not jump too hastily to conclusions. A body of people streaming along a road may be moved either by attraction or by repulsion. There is all the difference between a football crowd on its way to a match and a company of refugees. It is not impossible that these students are running

[1] This inaugural lecture was delivered at the London School of Economics, 21 February 1946.

away from something, rather than, eagerly and with a clear sense of purpose, running towards something. They may have arrived at sociology by a process of elimination. They thought, perhaps, that economics would prove too abstract and geography too concrete, history too wide and statistics too narrow, law too dry and political science too spicy for their taste. Sociology might possibly offer a more genial climate and a more appetizing diet. At least it was worth trying.

But, even if that were the explanation, it would mark a significant change in the public mind. For I shall be the first to admit that sociology has not enjoyed too good a reputation in this country and that even now it is still regarded in some quarters with a certain amount of suspicion. As I sat in this hall just two weeks ago to this hour and heard the words 'sociologist' and 'sociological' uttered from the platform, I thought I caught a faint trace of that inflexion of the voice which implies that their use renders other derogatory epithets superfluous. Now I am fully in accord with Professor Ashton when he condemns the bad work done by sociologists in the past on the ground that it was unhistorical. But I would register a protest at once if anyone expressed his condemnation of the bad work done by historians or economists by calling it sociological. I am not accusing Professor Ashton of this, but there was a time when such a use of words was not unthinkable. The reputation of sociology suffered, I think, partly from the company it was obliged to keep. There were among its devotees too many of those earnest people who come with heart wide open and brain half closed, inspired equally by a deep faith in the fundamental goodness of things and a firm determination to make them very much better. I am not suggesting that its friends were mainly of this kind, but the type was conspicuous enough to lend itself to unfriendly caricature, and possibly to influence the exponents of the subject. Sociologists are often accused of being woolly, but nothing is more conducive to woolly thinking than the knowledge that one is addressing a flock of sheep. But times have changed.

The evidence of this change is not to be found only in the registers of the London School of Economics. This influx of students is not an aimless migration; it is a symptom of a wider movement. If you go among those groups of men and women who are today exploring, often with an urgent practical object in view, the problems which beset contemporary society, or among those whose approach to these problems is one of action rather than of research alone, you will meet again and again with the realization that sociology is not only desirable but essential for their work. The call is there; the question is whether and how it can be answered. Has sociology in fact got a special contribution of its own to make, a body of knowledge, an angle of vision, a discipline and a method, or is it just a hotch-potch of fragments drawn from other fields? Can we feed this hungry host from our own stocks, or must we import food from the territories occupied by the other social sciences—a little economic theory, a sprinkling of statistics, some law, a modicum of psychology, and a few slices of good nourishing history, all mixed together to make a savoury stew? Is that the position? Well, if it were the position, sociology would indeed be at the crossroads occupying a suicide's grave. But I am convinced that it is not the position.

It is true, of course (if I may change my metaphor), that all the social sciences extract their data from the same rich mine. They differ in their selection and in the use they make of what they extract. But they do not slink away from the pithead with their booty hidden under their cloaks to work in isolation until they are ready to put the finished product on the market. There is exchange all along the line. When the final assembling takes place there are fitted into place some pieces manufactured from the raw materials by the science itself, some received as semi-manufactured goods, and some as the finished products of other sciences. It may well be that sociology makes more extensive use of these semi-manufactured and finished articles than do other branches of the social sciences, but this does not mean that it has no purpose, no discipline, no integrating principle of its own, nor that it builds from borrowed designs or, still worse, without any design at all. It is, I believe, not a pirate but a partner in a common task which cannot be fully accomplished without its aid. It is the realization of this truth that has caused the rapid awakening of interest in sociology in this country in recent years and in other countries at an earlier date.

It has frequently been stated that the distinctive task of sociology is synthesis. It has also been said that synthesis is urgently needed in the present stage of our knowledge of society. Neither proposition implies that analysis is unnecessary or outmoded. A science that did not itself engage in analysis would lack discipline and assurance in handling its materials, and it would incidentally be ill-fitted to serve as a vehicle for education, in which training in analysis must play a major part. And an age which rejected analysis in its eagerness to see things whole would soon get out of step with the march of events. The two processes are in fact inseparable, and the opinions I have cited refer to a balance of emphasis, the one in relation to a time sequence and the other to a division of labour.

That analytical techniques developed rapidly in the nineteenth century is a commonplace. That we are now busy trying to redress the balance is sufficiently clear. I am a little tired of those who attack the classical economists and their successors for their preoccupation with such fascinating abstractions as economic man and perfect competition, and pass judgement on a methodological device as though it claimed to be a final interpretation of reality. But it has to be admitted that even the best methods are open to abuse, especially in the hands of semi-skilled practitioners.

A physicist would be unlikely to apply conclusions drawn from observing the behaviour of bodies in a vacuum to conditions in the outside world without allowing for the resistance of the air, but mistakes almost as crude as this may be made by over-eager adventurers in the social sciences. The passage from pure theory to reality in the social sciences is apt to fall into two stages, and it is possible for the first process to be completed and the second omitted. An economist is unlikely to draw practical conclusions from theories of perfect competition without adding relevant assumptions and making allowances for the imperfections that exist in the economic system he is investigating. The danger is, I think, that he will allow only for those facts and forces which carry the label 'economic' sufficiently prominently on their persons to show that they are addressed to him. But the indivisibility of social life is such that classifications of this kind cannot safely be made; and a large part of the knowledge needed to apply economic theory to reality is not economic knowledge at all—it is social, political, legal and psychological. And, whereas the relevant economic facts may be fitted in in terms of economic theory, the other social facts are but dead matter unless manipulated in terms of a body of theory which is not economic but, over a wide area of the field, sociological. One specialist in the social sciences cannot treat neighbouring specialists as the craftsman treats the boy who hands him the materials and parts as he needs them for his job. They must work together in partnership, or, if that is not always possible, at least in series. As Professor Hicks once said:

> The economist, in running away with the problem, does not in the end want to keep it to himself. He always seeks to refer it back to some 'datum', that is to say to something which is extra-economic . . . he always wants to hand over the problem to some sociologist or other—if there is a sociologist waiting for him. Very often there isn't.[2]

That is better than nothing, though it is not what I should call a very warm invitation to collaborate, and it has a sting in its tail—'Very often there isn't.' That, I am afraid, is true, and I do not imagine that Professor Hicks used the words 'waiting for' in the sense in which Mrs Wootton was waiting for Professor Hayek.

Another field in which analysis made rapid progress was that of psychology, and the very word 'analysis' is part of the title of one of the most vigorous schools of thought within the science. But experience, in which war service in selection and

[2] J. R. Hicks: *The Social Sciences: Their Relations in Theory and in Teaching* (1936), p. 135.

rehabilitation has, I think, played a part, has brought home to many of the practitioners the need for synthesis in terms of social psychology. If you wish to clothe in flesh and blood that strange procession of ghostly figures that flit through the pages of psycho-analytic literature—the Ego, the Super-ego, and the Id: Oedipus, Narcissus and Polycrates—you must insinuate them into the living tissues, not only of individual man in the consulting-room, but also of social man in town and village, in club and factory. At the same time industrial psychology has been turning its attention more and more from motion studies and fatigue measurement to the human elements in industrial co-operation.

The task of synthesis has been forced upon us by events in various ways. In the last quarter of a century the world has seen a violent clash of contemporary civilizations moving simultaneously in different directions. The contrast was not between the old and the new, the static and the dynamic, but between what appeared to be distinct species of human society, each with its own vital principle. Many who tried to grasp the meaning of this phenomenon and to gauge its consequences became sociologists despite themselves. Fascism and Communism cannot be explained in terms of politics or economics alone, and of those who concentrated their attention on one aspect only, some came to the conclusion that they were diametrically opposed and others that they were fundamentally the same. The disagreement owed much, no doubt, to political predispositions, but it can only be resolved by synthesis; extreme judgements follow naturally from partial or one-sided examination. Totalitarian society—that at least is obvious—must be 'totally' studied.

A similar pressure is being exerted by developments within our own society. It is visible wherever there is planning, for however limited and specialized a plan may appear on paper it can only be translated into action through impact on individuals, groups and communities in which the complex forces of social life meet and interact. And so we find that those who are preparing for the day when the reconstruction of our towns and countryside can begin in earnest are talking

about 'neighbourhood units' and 'community spirit' and looking to sociology to help them to discover the realities which
lie behind these concepts. Nor is it an accident that social
security measures are today being integrated into a single
comprehensive scheme which pays due respect to the unity,
not only of the individual life, but of the family. But let me
add that, when I point this connexion between sociology and
planning, I do not imply that the sociologist is by definition
a socialist. I am only drawing attention to the indisputable
fact that planning is taking place on an increasing scale and
arousing a growing interest in and demand for sociological
investigations.

And there are other activities of a similar quality which do
not so readily leap to the mind as examples of planning. In
medicine, for instance, it has been a common complaint in
recent years that specialization led to the treatment of the
disease rather than of the patient, and that this must be
rectified by reassembling, as it were, the individual man in
his social setting. At the same time the movement has gone
on from individual therapeutics, through public health, to
social medicine. Criminology, too, has reacted against the
purely legal analysis of crime and the philosophic approach to
punishment in favour of a deeper study of the social causes
of crime and the effects of punishment on the criminal and
on society. Or consider what has been happening in education. We used to find the class of schoolchildren treated as
an undifferentiated mass, with a single mind and a single
voice, chanting its lessons in unison. At the other end of the
scale was the view that each child should be regarded as a
unique personality from which the teacher must draw out and
develop the gifts planted there by nature—and the more the
child could be got by itself the better. The choice seemed to
lie between a heap of stones and a battery of test-tubes. But
today we see the class as a living group with an educative force
of its own, and recognize that the development of a child that
is to become a social being must take place within the field
of action and reaction that such a group creates. The nature
of these intra-group relations is one of the main objects of

sociological study. There is also the problem of integrating life in the school with life outside. If a sharp dichotomy exists, the child must change roles with the skill of a professional actor as he passes from home to classroom, to playground and back to the home. This analysis of the child—if I may use the phrase—is yielding to a synthesis which has, I believe, already affected the attitude of children towards their schools. Finally there is the biggest problem of all, the adjustment of education to meet the needs of life in a changing society. It is, therefore, by no means inappropriate that an eminent sociologist should have been appointed to the Chair of Education in the University of London.

The story is repeated if we look at the problem of poverty. In early small-scale communities the pauper was a person known to his neighbours and could be judged by them in the light of his misfortunes and his misdeeds. As society grew in scale and complexity paupers, like schoolchildren, were treated as an undifferentiated mass. Then came analysis, splitting this mass up into categories according to the causes and consequences of poverty. This was a great step forward, but the analysis inevitably rested on abstraction. A further process of re-integration was necessary, on two levels. First the causes identified by their immediate impact on poverty had to be traced backwards and outwards through their antecedent causes and their interrelations with other social forces. This work is going on but much still remains to be done. To take two small examples: unemployment is a major cause of destitution, but do we know as much as we might about the social obstacles to geographic and occupational mobility which may separate the supply of labour from the demand? Old age is a cause of poverty, but when does it begin? We are proposing to encourage people to lengthen their working life, but I doubt whether we have collected all the available data needed to show what such a measure really involves. And secondly, re-integration is needed at the level of the individual or family, by studying each particular case, or type of case, to see where the categories overlap and what other extraneous circumstances must be taken into account. And finally, we find that some of the facts fall into groups of a different kind where they are fused into a single whole with other elements which did not appear in our original calculations. We pass from the study of types of unemployment to the study of depressed areas, communities dominated by unemployment but not composed entirely of the unemployed. Or, having discovered the category of poverty caused by large families, which swells the proportion of pauper children, we go on to examine the effect of the extreme poverty of some children on the community life of the school, and study the question in a new group setting. It would be easy to multiply examples; I have not, for instance, mentioned what is perhaps the most obvious—the passage from statistical to sociological demography, from reproduction rates to the social and economic factors affecting the age at marriage and the size of families. But I think I have said enough to show how the pressure of events is urging us more and more towards research whose main object is to achieve synthesis in various forms and at various levels, to re-integrate, as it were, groups and individuals that have been split by the abstractions of earlier analysis. I have dwelt on this theme at some length because I felt it enabled me to give in the most practical way an idea of the kind of subject to which I feel sociology should devote its attention, the general direction of the path it should follow from the crossroads at which it now stands. And I hope I have made it clear that this rearrangement of categories into social groups, this movement from abstraction towards reality, is only the first step. The groups have then to be studied, and this involves detailed analysis of a different kind on principles and with the aid of concepts and theories suited to the matter in hand. The oscillation between the two methods must never stop.

But, you may well ask, are these in fact the problems that sociology has been studying? Has not the passion for synthesis carried it, not nearer to reality, but further and further away from it, up into the clouds of vast general speculations? It is true, as Professor Ginsberg says, that one of the roots of sociology 'is the philosophy of history, which in modern times

has generally been an attempt in the grand manner to interpret the whole course of human history as part of a wider
philosophical world view'.[3] The search may be for universal
laws of historical development, for general principles of social
psychology, or for the fundamental meaning and value of social life. To say that the valiant assaults made on these great
problems are so much waste of time would be an impertinence;
but to say that research and speculation on these high levels
should not be the main preoccupation of sociologists in general is only common sense. Few have the knowledge or the
energy to carry such studies to the point at which anything
approaching valid results can be obtained—and short cuts can
lead only to confusion and error. Few have the detachment
needed to judge the evidence they assemble without the aid of
assumptions and beliefs formulated before the search began.

Professor Toynbee maintains, and has shown, that the historian can overcome the 'deep impress from the dominant
institutions of the transient social environment in which the
thinker happens to live',[4] but the philosopher is, perhaps,
even more sorely tried. For it is a hard thing to demand of
a man of high purpose and keen perception of the world
around him that he should walk back through history with an
open mind groping for a faith. Influences of these kinds are
hard to shake off. No one can fail to note the contrast between the quiet optimism of Hobhouse's picture of social
progress and the tortured doubts of many who today are
probing the wounds of a decaying civilization. 'If the experiences of the past ten years,' writes Lewis Mumford, 'have
made the colours of the final volume somewhat more sombre
than the earliest one, they have not altered the original design . . . These books were written during a period of rapid
social disintegration.'[5] And Dr Moreno concludes his book,
Who Shall Survive?, with the words: 'The question is therefore not only the survival or passing of the present form of
human society but the destiny of man. As all races suffer in

[3] M. Ginsberg: *Sociology*, p. 25.
[4] A. J. Toynbee: A *Study of History*, Vol. 1, p. 16.
[5] *The Condition of Man*, Preface.

this respect from a common insufficiency, they are going to live or perish together.'[6]

And it is striking, too, from what different angles these vast and pregnant questions can be approached. Comte presents his philosophic law of the three stages, Mumford offers a highly subjective picture of the pageant of human history, and in particular of human thought, while Le Play sought the clues to modern civilization in detailed studies of peasant families, and Moreno starts his quest for an answer to his cosmic question by putting a group of newborn infants on the nursery floor, noting their movements towards one another and plotting them on a chart. But wide generalizations and the interpretation of concrete social phenomena lie far apart. From whichever end one starts, the journey is long and arduous, and the travellers are sorely tempted, in their impatience to arrive, to take at some point or other a bold leap over intervening space, landing on the other side dazed and bewildered, having lost a large part of their baggage in their flight. What they need is, so to speak, stepping-stones in the middle distance, and it is one of the great merits of Hobhouse's work that he attempted to provide them by his analysis and classification of social institutions. But this is a matter to which I shall return later. At the moment I wish only to point out that one path from the crossroads leads towards universal laws and ultimate values. We might call it the way to the stars and, although few at any one time can profitably follow it, it should never be barred. Even the failure of a powerful mind attempting the impossible may be more fruitful than the successes of lesser minds in grasping things that are within reach of all.

And there is another temptation which may induce sociologists to dwell too long in the realms of abstraction. It is the fascinating game of elaborating concepts. It is true that without concepts there can be no research but only an aimless assembly of facts. It is also true that, if the concepts are ill-chosen, inadequately defined, inconsistent with one another,

[6] J. L. Moreno: op. cit., p. 366.

or used in different senses by different inquirers, research will not be fruitful. So there is still work to be done in clarifying and standardizing concepts, but I think this should aim at simplification rather than at elaboration. This does not mean, I am afraid, that sociology can be content to use the simple language of ordinary speech. Sociologists are sometimes accused of writing long books which merely express common ideas in uncommon language, and I cannot lay my hand on my heart and swear that this never happens. It is disquieting, for instance, to find the act of shutting a door described as 'overt non-symbolic attitudinal behaviour'.[7] But one should remember the peculiar difficulties of a science that deals with the familiar objects of daily experience around which cluster a host of ambiguities and unconscious assumptions embedded in the language of the man in the street. The words have been spoiled for scientific use and one is forced to look for something better. As Whitehead says of philosophy: 'The existence of such perplexities arising from the common obviousness of speech is the reason why the topic exists. Thus the very purpose of philosophy is to delve below the apparent clarity of common speech.'[8] Sociology is faced by a similar dilemma.

But the over-elaboration of concepts may lead into a bog from which there is no easy way of escape. As Professor Burgess says: 'Many early and even some contemporary social scientists appear to consider a conceptual analysis of society as if it were a substitute for research. This survival of the tradition of the social philosopher has retarded the development of sociological research.'[9] This is a hard saying, but there is more than a little truth in it, and it is not only philosophers who are tempted to indulge in these allegedly barren exercises. A concept is an abstraction, and the sociologist wishes to be practical. It seems easier to move the concept slowly towards reality by building into it more and more qualifications and assumptions relevant to conditions in the real world than to test its usefulness by genuine empirical

[7] Cited in G. A. Lundberg: *Social Research*, p. 213.
[8] A. N. Whitehead: *Adventure of Ideas*, p. 285.
[9] *American Journal of Sociology*, May 1945, p. 475.

research; and it is easier to use facts for illustration than for demonstration. And for the teacher this method has the attraction of enabling him to enjoy the sense of power gained by tying the student's brain into knots and then disentangling it again—which may be a salutary process, provided one does not forget how to perform the second half of the trick. Concepts are made for use, not for show. There was a compelling persuasiveness about the famous cry, 'Give us the tools and we will finish the job.' One may be forgiven for responding less eagerly to the scholar, be he sociologist or anything else, who says, 'Give me a job, and I will spend the rest of my life polishing the tools.'

But I must return to the crossroads. I have spoken of one of the paths that meet there, which I called the way to the stars. There is another which might be called the way into the sands. It leads to the expenditure of great energy on the collection of a multitude of facts with sometimes an inadequate sense of the purpose for which they are being collected. It has been more popular in the United States than in this country, and George Lundberg says of it:

> The pronounced empirical trends in recent sociology have raised the question as to whether theory is not being neglected. There has been warrant for this concern during the recent era of extensive and expensive surveys without either hypotheses or theories, and there is still reason to emphasize the point.[10]

There are several reasons, I think, why these activities should be somewhat intemperately pursued. One is the vast number of sociologists in America looking for something to do. It has been computed that there were in 1940–4 in the United States 441 institutes with departments of sociology together offering 5,260 courses in the subject (not counting anthropology and social work), of which only about 9 per cent. were courses in principles, general sociology and so forth.[11] The rest, presumably, dealt with specific topics. Well, these

[10] *American Journal of Sociology*, May 1945, p. 503.
[11] ibid., pp. 535 and 545.

courses must be fed with data and their students must be provided with exercises. Another reason is the ambition to bring the social sciences more into line with the natural sciences by making greater use of quantitative methods. Now it is one thing to say that measurement should be used whenever the relevant data can be measured; it is quite another thing to hold that everything that is measurable is worth measuring—and that is a state of mind into which it is very easy to slip. A third reason is the excitement engendered by the feeling that sociology has methods of its own—the survey, the questionnaire, the opinion poll—by which it can gather data which slip through the net of the other sciences. Here again, it is good that these methods should be used where they are useful, but it is foolish to imagine that small facts are worth more than big because it takes finer tackle to catch them. Sociology can find a better patron saint than Autolycus, that 'snapper-up of unconsidered trifles', and some of us may still prefer to spend time over such gross and obvious things as law, justice, authority and citizenship, instead of joining the merry hunt after the laws that determine whether men lean their right or left side against the bar when drinking, and what social conditions determine the rate at which they empty their glasses.

And there is yet a fourth and perhaps a more significant reason. It arises from the point to which I have already referred, the extent to which sociologists are being called on to help in the preparation of plans for action. It is, I believe, most desirable that they should respond to the call, but they must be careful not to prostitute their services. Facts are essential for any social plan, but the planners are apt to be in a hurry and to know, or think they know, already what it is they are after. Scientific induction is a slow and difficult process, and it is much quicker and easier to bring order into the data by marrying them to principles of policy and canons of administration adopted in advance. By such methods one may get results, but one does not get sociology.

I suggested earlier that the general or theoretical sociologist may become a slave to his concepts. Similarly, I believe, the passionately empirical sociologist may become a slave to his methods. It may seem very heretical to say that one may be too much of a perfectionist about methods—but I will say it nevertheless. By a perfectionist I do not mean one who regards the slovenly misuse of methods as the worst crime in the academic calendar; I am with him all the way. I mean rather one who looks with cold disapproval on those who, having found within the context of the present body of our knowledge a subject that urgently demands exploration, embark on their research without being able to guarantee in advance that the methods at the moment at their disposal are adequate to lead them to a final and unchallengeable solution of their problem. Methods, like concepts, can only be perfected in use, and they must be constantly revised and refurbished in the light of experience. This is a long business, extending as a rule through several generations of researchers, and great services are rendered by those who travel but do not arrive at the ultimate goal. Without these hopeful experiments no science could have been developed— nor could you even teach a child to walk. Destructive criticism of the honest adventurer is the bane of a young science, but he must be honest; he must, that is to say, use the best methods available and use them fairly.

Where the perfectionist is a devotee of the quantitative methods used in the natural sciences, he is often liable to disparage qualitative analysis which tries to discover meaning by close observation of social processes in action. He is also inclined to exaggerate the value of quantitative material and imagine that the mere accumulation of statistical tables can provide sociological knowledge. He is quite right when he refuses to try by statistical manipulation to make figures do what they are incapable of doing, but he is apt to attribute to the knowledge of quantitative facts an ultimate value which it does not possess. Undoubtedly such facts are a real contribution to our study of society. They reveal the proportions of our problems, save us from blunders, and help us to formulate useful hypotheses. But they are not sociology. If I may cite, in elucidation of this point, the important con-

tributions made by the Director of the School[12] to my subject, I would say that, although sociologists find *The Social
Structure of England and Wales* invaluable, they extend an
even warmer welcome to *The Professions*, with its qualitative
picture of an influential social group. Or take the example of
poverty, an institution that permeates the whole of our social
life. From what I said earlier it will be clear that a sociologist
is not satisfied by an analytical study of the law of property.
He wants more than that. A psychologist may offer him a
thesis on the acquisitive instinct or on anal fear and property
obsessions. Then a statistician provides figures showing the
distribution of property. The picture gets clear and more social, but it is not a synthesis and does not even contain the
material for making a synthesis. For that the sociologist must
explore the part played by property in the life of the individual citizen and his family, in the formation of groups, and in
the distribution of political and economic power. And one way
of gaining understanding of the quality of these functions
may be to conduct some of those microcosmic studies which
Professor Ashton recommended to the attention of historians.

But, if the purist may think that his job is finished when
the figures have been collected, the enthusiast pushes reck-
lessly on. He collects figures in armfuls and throws them into
his machine, expecting the answer to his problem to come out
when he turns the handle. He longs to hand over his problem
to some statistician or other—if there is a statistician waiting
for him. Very often there is. But fortunately statisticians, like
psychologists, have become increasingly aware of their responsibility as social scientists, and when that is the case the
sociologist can have no more powerful ally than the statistician. I have as yet, unfortunately, had little time to delve
deeply into the volumes on Yankee City produced, on the
basis of five years of intensive research, by Lloyd Warner and
Paul Lunt, but my first impressions are not quite as encouraging as I had hoped. They begin by speaking of the dichotomy in social science between those who treat the individual

[12] Sir Alexander Carr-Saunders.

as ultimate and those who treat human behaviour as a group phenomenon. This sounds to me a little out of date, and suggests the old device of setting up a guy to knock it down practised by those who do not feel too sure of their own ground. And they go on: 'The Yankee City research, on the whole, has been inspired by the belief in a scientific collection of facts, not for their own sake, but for the purpose of later scientific generalization in an effort to understand their nature.'[13] I don't like 'on the whole', and the word 'later' seems to indicate a certain indifference as to the kind of generalization for which the facts may be used. And these fears are not entirely dispelled as one reads on. The conceptual basis of the research seems to be vague and jejune, and the results so far achieved correspondingly meagre. The central theme is social stratification, but I have been unable to discover exactly how the authors determined the boundaries of the six classes they have identified, and assigned every member of the population to one and in no case to more than one. But some of the methods used are interesting.

In the second volume they develop a technique of positional analysis.[14] It goes roughly like this. The relationship between any two persons is affected by their social rank; the attitude may be one of superiority, equality, or inferiority. The position of anyone in a group depends on the number of classes represented and his own place in the social scale. This reveals the complex of his class relations within that group. Given six classes and assuming that every possible combination of them is found, it is easy to arrive at the total number of possible positions by logical deduction from one premise and two assumptions. But in fact every possible combination is not found, and the variety of combinations differs in different types of group or institution. And so we pass from logical deduction to an empirical study of Yankee City. The institutions, or social structures, are divided into seven categories—family, clique, Church, association, etc.—and, when all the known facts are fitted into this framework, it is found

13 *The Social Life of a Modern Community*, pp. 11, 12.
14 *The Status System of a Modern Community*.

that there are 89 distinct positions. Further analysis yields some interesting results. It shows which forms of class mixture are most characteristic of each institution, and what kinds of interclass relationship are met with by the members of the different classes in their various activities. The facts are not always what one might have expected, and the method proves its value by bringing them to light. But it is not a very rich harvest. And I very much doubt whether the method justifies the 86 pages of figures in which the results are summarized at the end of the volume. I am not sure what any future investigator is expected to do with them.

If I find fault with the work, it is not so much for what it has done, which is of real value, as for what it has not done. One feels that the immense labour expended should have enabled the authors to get nearer to the heart of the matter. Their subject is 'The Social Life of a Modern Community', and that is something which cannot be fully expressed in figures and diagrams. Their special theme is the role of social classes, which is supremely a matter of the quality of relationships. And it is evident that they collected a vast amount of material which might throw light on this problem, but they have made little systematic use of it, and they do not seem to realize that the elaborate plotting and counting of positions is no substitute for qualitative study. They could have considerably enhanced the value of their work if they had adopted the simple methods of studying institutions prevalent in this country, and they might have enhanced it still further by using the methods of social psychology.

Now, in saying this, I am not attacking statistical methods of social investigation. As I have already said, the statistician is one of the most powerful allies the sociologist can have. He needs his help to extract relevant quantitative material from a complex body of data, as in the case of the distribution of property that I mentioned earlier. He needs him to perfect techniques of sampling, without which no large-scale social survey is possible. He must use his apparatus for working out correlations between related phenomena, and also for constructing rating scales and measuring devices without which correlations of certain types of phenomena cannot be made. And this brings me to one of the more controversial issues in sociological method—the measurement of attitudes and mental qualities and the use of sociometric scales.

The belief that these are newfangled methods deviating sharply from the paths of orthodoxy is, I think, based on a misconception for which some of their advocates are perhaps partly responsible. In fact the very term 'attitude measurement' is misleading, for what is measured is not a state of mind, but its manifestation in certain selected forms of behaviour. Nobody would object to the calculation of a marriage rate on the grounds that love is a passion that defies the measuring rod. Nobody would condemn the study of crime rates because they do not measure criminal propensities. Market research is constantly measuring attitudes and preferences as expressed in buying habits, and some equally objective indices can be found in behaviour expressing race prejudice and class-consciousness. But, whereas the salesman is interested only in one form of behaviour—buying—the sociologist who studies race prejudice is interested in all the various forms of behaviour that express the attitude, and some of them are too subtle to be observed and classified. Also, those which can be classified and recorded must be weighted in order to produce a single index, and that is where the major difficulty arises. When verbal expression is used as the index of an attitude or preference, there is a further complication. Not only do words and phrases carry different weight for different people—one man's 'blast' is another man's 'damn'—but the testimony may be consciously or unconsciously falsified, as everyone knows who has tried to draft a questionnaire. But experience and experiment have yielded many devices for reducing these obstacles, and I believe that, within limits, these methods can be used to add to our knowledge of human behaviour. They are not perfect and they will never be quantitatively exact. They may not, in many cases, measure in the true sense of the word at all but only rate, or arrange in order of magnitude. But that is very much better than nothing. They may not give us the whole truth, but only take us a few steps nearer to it. How much that advance is worth can only be discovered by trying.

I fear I have ranged over a very wide field and have left sociology standing at the crossroads where I found her. Which road is the poor lady to take? I do not recommend the way to the stars; sociologists should not, I think, expend all their energies climbing in search of vast generalizations, universal laws, and a total comprehension of human society as such. They are more likely to get there in the end if they don't try to get there now. Nor do I recommend the way into the sands of whirling facts which blow into the eyes and ears until nothing can be clearly seen or heard. But I believe there is a middle way which runs over firm ground. It leads into a country whose features are neither Gargantuan nor Lilliputian, where sociology can choose units of study of a manageable size—not society, progress, morals, and civilization, but specific social structures in which the basic processes and functions have determined meanings. The knowledge we have gained about the larger subjects should be used to illumine our more modest researches, rather than as a focal point to which we should continuously direct our attention. I think, too, that the most fruitful, though not the sole, field of work is to be found in more or less contemporary society. Again the wider view is illuminating. But I venture to suggest that, in the present stage of our knowledge, its chief value lies in education rather than in research. The contrasting of widely different cultures helps the student to clear his mind of assumptions implicit in his judgement of familiar social phenomena and makes him question things which he is inclined to take for granted. It also suggests subjects for investigation by a true comparative method, and tentative hypotheses with which to approach them.

The search for what I have called stepping-stones in the middle distance has been pursued by many of those who have embarked on sociological inquiry. Durkheim faced the dilemma of discovering a middle way between a vague and abstract philosophy and purely descriptive monographs, and found it in the concept of social types or species.[15] Hobhouse grouped his empirical studies round the structure and functions of social institutions. Max Weber perfected the device of the 'ideal type' by which units of any size could be chosen and norms constructed against which the variations found in the world of reality could be seen and measured. Professor Mannheim advocates the employment of 'middle principles' which he defines as 'universal forces in a concrete setting as they have become integrated out of the various factors at work in a given place and at a given time'.[16]

I think the most urgent task of sociology today is to study these limited phenomena within the 'concrete setting' of contemporary civilization. The new methods of which I have spoken, some already proved and others still on trial, offer us the means to do this in a way denied to our predecessors. In choosing topics it is natural that we should be influenced by the nature of the practical problems that face us. Sociology need not be ashamed of wishing to be useful. There are real advantages in relating research to current issues. In the first place, it is stimulating and purposeful, and less likely to lead to random investigations. In the second, facilities may be available which are lacking in other cases. Much of the data now needed can be collected only by public authorities, and when the needs of the moment urge them to action social scientists can reap the benefit. At the same time co-operative or parallel studies by social scientists may greatly increase the value of official inquiries. There is naturally a tendency for public authorities to direct their attention where things have gone wrong, and to fail to make those comparative studies of things in good order without which valid general conclusions cannot be drawn. American sociologists have been accused of following this mistaken lead. Elton Mayo writes: 'In so far as attention is devoted merely to those areas in which the social controls have broken down, nothing is learned of the nature and development of the social controls themselves.' Thus researches into disorganization 'do need to be balanced

[15] E. Durkheim: *Les règles de la méthode sociologique*, p. 95.
[16] K. Mannheim: *Man in Society*, p. 178.

by the development of inquiries in other social situations than
the pathological'.[17] I do not think that the interests of social
scientists here have been limited in this way. One might expect, for instance, to find a concentration of interest on the
failures of our social system where the object of study and
teaching is to train students for careers devoted to helping
those in difficulty or distress. But I do not see any sign of
this in the department I have inherited from Mr Lloyd.[18]
His rare combination of wide practical knowledge with original and stimulating thought enabled him to guide the Social
Science Department triumphantly through a critical period
of rapid expansion, and the very names of his predecessors—
Tawney, Urwick, and Hobhouse—are guarantees that a narrow
utilitarian approach to social studies would be unthinkable.
The interest that has been developed in the department is not
pathological, but genuinely sociological.

Now let me add one final word. The need for co-operation
in the social sciences is generally recognized, and by no one
more than by the sociologist. Sociology in this country owes
much to men whose official allegiance was to other subjects.
In my own case the first urge towards the sociological view
of things came from studying the structure of medieval society—in the works of Seebohm, Vinogradoff, and especially
Maitland. Later I was deeply influenced by political scientists,
by meeting, talking to, and even bicycling along country roads
with Lowes Dickinson, and by the conversation and written
works of Graham Wallas and our Chairman[19] today. And
no one who teaches sociology in this School is likely to forget
his debt to Professor Tawney. These welcome visits from
neighbour sciences remind me of a story told in Calhoun's
Social History of the American Family, about the days of lav-
ish hospitality in the Old South. It is recounted that a man
and his wife who had been invited to dinner with some friends
'found that during the meal a boat had been sent to Darien

[17] *The Human Problem of an Industrial Civilization*, p. 141.
[18] C. M. Lloyd was Head of the Social Science Department of
the London School of Economics until 1944.
[19] Sir Ernest Barker.

fifteen miles distant for their luggage, and that so much pleased were host, hostess and guests with one another, that the stay was prolonged until two children had been born to the visiting couple'.[20] Now that is what I would call a fruitful sojourn, which might well have intellectual parallels. And so I hope that, as sociology studies the map at the crossroads, it will not imitate those passionate country lovers whose one desire is to find a path leading to some desolate spot where no other human being is likely to venture. The road sociology chooses should be one with busy traffic on it, and company and conversation with others of a kindred spirit.

[20] A. W. Calhoun: op. cit., Vol. II, p. 336.

CHAPTER II

SOCIOLOGY—THE ROAD AHEAD

When the Faculty of Economics and Politics invited me to give a public lecture[1] on sociology, I accepted at once, as in duty bound, but with some misgivings. The welcome given so far to this new arrival among the recognized subjects of instruction in this university has been a remarkably warm one. But I know very well that a rise in the stocks may be followed by a fall, that honeymoon periods do not last for ever, and that the primrose path may lead to the everlasting bonfire. Let us be quite frank about it—sociology in Cambridge is on trial. It has many friends, strong friends, who already believe in it. It may have enemies, too, who are sure that they at least will never believe in it. And there are certainly some who are of the opinion that, like the Duchess of Malfi's curse, sociology 'hath a long way to go' before it reaches the stars, that is to say, before it can be given full equality of status with the established disciplines of the academic firmament. So the invitation to lecture contained a challenge to stand sociology up in front of you and say to you: 'Here you are; this is the animal you have just bought. Take a good look at her.' In such circumstances the showman must walk delicately. A false step may have dire consequences. I must be careful not to do a Mark Antony in reverse and, having come to praise Caesar, end by burying him. In spite of this I welcome the invitation and the challenge and am grateful for them both.

[1] Delivered in Cambridge, 25 November 1960.

It has been suggested to me that this lecture is a sort of quasi-inaugural. Not, of course, to inaugurate me, since I am only an old lag who has returned to the scene of his juvenile delinquencies, but to inaugurate sociology as a Tripos subject. Be that as it may, I cannot help casting my mind back to the time when I did inaugurate myself in another place nearly fifteen years ago. My lecture on that occasion was entitled 'Sociology at the Crossroads' (see p. 3). It strikes me now that that particular chicken has come home to roost with a vengeance, for obviously you can challenge me to go back to those crossroads and tell you what I find there now. Is the poor creature still standing dithering there, like the travellers in the Randolph Caldecott picture book, baffled by the signpost whose four arms bore the words 'Flapley', 'Flepley', 'Flipley' and 'Flopley'? Or has she chosen a road and set out along it, confident in the rightness of her choice? And if so, is it the road that I recommended to her fifteen years ago, or a quite different one? And towards what destination is it leading her? I cannot complain of these questions, because in the circumstances they are quite fair. But at the same time they are misleading, because the metaphor of the crossroads should not be pressed to do more than serve as a title for a talk. No scientific discipline worthy of the name ever advances along one road only, and on no route followed by the inquiring human mind does one meet with crossroads only once. There is a constant interlacing of pathways and a perpetual probing of routes as the frontiers of knowledge move forward. But subject to these reservations I will do my best to answer the questions.

Before we return to the crossroads, however, equipped with field-glasses and a first-aid kit to find out what has happened, it would be as well to decide what we are talking about, or, if you like, who we are looking for. I am quite prepared to offer a definition of sociology, provided I'm allowed to follow one of my own favourite precepts, namely, when defining a class of objects or a concept, always aim at the bull's-eye. Don't bother about the outer edges. The frontier regions of any class or concept are always occupied by a hoard of oddities and eccentrics, belonging to no significant category of phenomena, but offering fascinating opportunities for interminable and quite fruitless argument. Among the worst of these are those discussions about social class in which somebody says: 'I knew a man whose father was a coal-miner who won a scholarship to the university and became a consulting engineer. He sent his son to Harrow and Oxford, but the son decided to become a small working farmer, and married the local barmaid. What will be the social class of their children?' You will not discover what sociology is by teasing sociologists in this way. A definition should focus on the centre, on the typical or normal, and then be pushed outwards to see how far it will reach and what modifications may be needed.

The central concern of sociology, then, is the analytical and explanatory study of social systems. The term 'social systems' must be interpreted as covering both large systems, such as the societies for which, oddly enough, we have no exact name but refer to as nations or states, and also smaller or more specialized systems which exist within these societies, or cut across their frontiers. It must also cover those abstractions designed to represent different types of social system, like feudalism, capitalism or communism. In using the question-begging word 'system' and giving it a central place in my definition, I am fully aware of the temerity of my action. There are those who question the propriety of assuming that there is any system at all in human affairs. To me on the contrary it seems obvious that if society were not systematic there could be no social science. And I would go further and add that if the fundamental elements of which social systems are made were not essentially the same in all societies (though differently combined), and if the possible ways of using these fundamental elements were not limited in number, the social sciences, so called, would be devoid of all general theory. And sociology, which depends more than any other discipline on comparative study, would be the hardest hit of all.

By a social system I mean a set of interrelated and reciprocal activities having the following characteristics. The activities are repetitive and predictable to the degree necessary, first, to permit of purposeful, peaceful and orderly behaviour among the members of the society, and secondly to enable the pattern of action to continue in being, that is to say to preserve its identity even while gradually changing its shape. Ideally a system of this kind, or the 'structure', as some would say, which is its conceptualization, could be represented as a model working outside the dimension of historical or chronological time, as a motor-car engine ticks over without regard to the movement of the hands of the clock from 2 p.m. to 2.30.[2] I believe that this concept of system can be used in the study of society, but only with great care.

But in saying this I do not imply either that all parts of the system are in direct dependence on each other, so that change in any one part must involve change in all the rest, or that everything we find in a society is integrated into the system. The central core consists of man-made constitutions and institutions, of written rules and unwritten customs known to all concerned, but the sum total of these is not the equivalent of the social system as a whole. There is more to it than that. There are uniformities and regularities of behaviour which are not prescribed by rule, and there are motives, attitudes, aspirations and value judgements which have meaning in relation to the system and exist within it. They flow through its interstices as the blood flows through the veins, giving it life and making it work. Sociology is not interested only in the perfectly institutionalized aspects of social structure, but peers through and behind them into a world which is being closely studied also by the social psychologist.

But that is not the end, because we can perceive in every society phenomena which seem to have little to do with the social system, as we have come to understand it, or which appear to be alien or actually antagonistic to it. In order to bring all these into the picture, I suggest that we may roughly divide social phenomena into the three classes of 'non-system', 'pro-system' and 'anti-system', which I would describe as fol-

[2] See for example Claude Lévi-Strauss: 'Social Structure', in *Anthropology Today*, ed. A. L. Kroeber, 1953.

lows. First, the 'non-system' category. This includes all those
things which happen in a society without being in any meaningful way relevant to the system as such. There are areas of
free choice, the results of which do not aid or hinder the
operation of the system, so that 'non-system' seems to be a
good way of describing them. Secondly, there are areas of
relatively free choice, within which activities are not strictly
repetitive but nevertheless have room made for them within
the system, and in fact help to make it work. It is to cover
these that Raymond Firth introduced the concept of 'social
organization' as distinct from 'social structure', which for him
denotes the bare bones of the system.[3] These are the 'pro-
system' variations and additions. Thirdly we have to introduce
the potentially 'anti-system' element of conflict and what
sociologists rather feebly call 'deviant behaviour', which may
cover anything from harmless eccentricity to capital murder.
I say 'potentially' because many forms of conflict and devia-
tion are not incompatible with the continuing operation of
the system; and some forms of conflict are actually an essential part of it. For instance, there are the contests which
are at the same time a mode of co-operation between the
rivals. An obvious example is a tennis match, where the conflict is enjoyed for its own sake, where each player needs
the other to make a game, but nevertheless tries to beat him.
A more important example is bargaining, a type of conflict
in which it is to the common interest of the parties to reach
a decision acceptable to both. And in some cultures the process of bargaining is just as enjoyable as a game of tennis, or
even more so. Then there are types of conflict in which it
can hardly be said that the parties are co-operating with each
other, but they are both contributing to the working of a
system, the authority of which they both recognize. A borderline case is the battle between counsel for the prosecution and
counsel for the defence in a British trial. The immediacy of
the common purpose, of arriving at the truth, and the precision and close observance by both of the rules of the game,

[3] *Elements of Social Organization*, pp. 35–40.

are such that we could almost say that the learned gentlemen are co-operating even in the heat of the conflict. But the fight between political parties in an election, and the competition between rivals in industry or trade have progressively less of the co-operative element in them. Nevertheless the political parties and the trade competitors, by waging battle with each other, are rendering a service which is essential to the working on the one hand of parliamentary democracy and on the other of a free market.

We now come to the area within which 'anti-system' conflict may appear. Bargaining, I said, is co-operative in character, and this is true both of individual and of collective bargaining. But in the latter, as we know, the element of conflict may grow in force until negotiations, as we say, 'break down' and there is a strike. This is a form of pure conflict, which imposes a strain on the social system and is regarded as painful. But it is tolerated, and even admitted as part of the system, because without it other parts of the system could not work. It is a necessary appendage to the bargaining process. But there have been strikes in which great bitterness was engendered because it was felt in some quarters that the connexion with the bargaining mechanism had almost disappeared. This was perhaps because the strikers believed they were demanding only what were their rights, and one should not have to bargain about one's rights. A point is then reached where the dispute is no longer about the terms and conditions under which the system should operate, but about the very acceptability of the system itself, or some essential part of it. Here 'anti-system' conflict begins, and it can be traced, often in less active forms, but sometimes also in more violent ones, running like a thread through the whole history of class relations.

I apologize for dwelling at some length on this question of the relations between systematic order and social conflict, but it is a subject crucial to my theme. Many years ago I wrote an article about it (see p. 180), which was republished in the little book *Citizenship and Social Class*, and a much more up-to-date treatment, in a quite different context, will be found in an article by David Lockwood in *The British Journal of Sociology* (1956). So the subject is not likely to be neglected in the teaching of sociology in Cambridge in the immediate future.

And now I have only one point to add, before I sum up my definition of sociology. It concerns social change. In spite of the fact that we can recognize social systems, social change is in some degree almost continuous. In part it is produced by mechanisms built into the system, like legislative bodies which have the power and even the duty to introduce systematic change. Sometimes it grows out of the non-systematic elements, the deviations and the conflicts I have been describing. And here one meets one of the most bothersome of the distinctions one has to make in this subject, because it obviously exists and yet is almost impossible to pin down; it is the distinction between evolution and revolution, between change that occurs smoothly within the system without breaking it or destroying its identity, and change which attacks it and swiftly transforms it into something different.

To sum up: sociology is devoted to the study of social systems, and, if the existence of social systems could not be postulated, sociology could not exist. Systems are sets of interrelated activities which are, to a high degree, predictable, repetitive and co-operative, either directly as between man and man, or indirectly by contributing to the operation of the common system. But there is much in society that is not systematic; there are important activities which are not exactly predictable; there are forms of conflict incorporated in the system itself; and there are other forms which attack the system and may even destroy it. Finally, systems are almost continuously changing; some change may be considered as growth of the system, or evolution, but there is also change which does violence to the system, and is revolution. The task of sociology is to explore the interplay of these elements and to find the clue to their relationships. And it undertakes this task by studying both social institutions and individual behaviour. There is nothing new in any of the items of interest I have listed. Comte's main purpose was to describe growth, or development, in terms of stages. Max Weber placed great emphasis on structure and its representation in 'ideal types'. Simmel was fascinated by the many shapes assumed by conflict. Durkheim, impressed by the phenomenon of consensus, and anxious to find an acceptable definition of the normal—the twin foundations of structure—recognized that *anomie*, or social dislocation, could exist and leave its mark on individual behaviour without a complete breakdown of the social system. And here is a relevant passage from a work of Herbert Spencer: 'To extend, as well as to make clearer, this conception of the Social Science, let me here set down a question which comes within its sphere. What is the relation in a society between structure and growth? Up to what point is structure necessary to growth? after what point does it retard growth? at what point does it arrest growth?'[4] Here, then, are the principal elements to be sorted out and fitted together in the study of social systems: consensus, the normal, and *anomie*; co-operation and conflict; structure and growth. The task is ambitious enough to satisfy anyone's aspirations.

I have taken an unconscionable time telling you who we are looking for, but now at last I can take you back to the crossroads to see what has happened to her. The choice with which sociology was confronted fifteen years ago seemed to me to be more a matter of means than of ends. As I have just said, all the elements which enter into a description of sociology's task today were then already represented in the literature. The question which pressed for an answer was: how much of all this can sociology properly undertake, and by advancing along which path or paths is she most likely to make decisive progress? And this is the question which occupied my attention in that official inaugural lecture.

When I looked at the various roads along which sociologists could then be seen tramping, shuffling or skipping, according to their nature, I singled out two which seemed to me to be both enticing and at the same time perilous. The first was

[4] *The Study of Sociology* (1883), p. 63.

the one which it was hoped would lead directly to a comprehensive system of sociological knowledge, or at least to a total explanation of social development. I christened it, not too happily, the way to the stars. I had in mind the attempts of the great founders of sociology, of Auguste Comte and Herbert Spencer, and also of Hobhouse, and I praised their noble attempts to achieve the impossible, and hoped that others from time to time might be equally ambitious, provided they were equally gifted. But I said that enterprises of this kind demand rare individual qualities of intellect and industry, and cannot be incorporated into the routine procedures of university graduate schools. The history of human society from its creation to the present day is not a good subject for a Ph.D. thesis. Branching off from this, but traversing very much the same country (and also bound for the stars), I found another path along which were advancing those whose aim was to elaborate a total apparatus of concepts in order to establish a total system of general theory. They didn't seem to me to be making very rapid progress, and I thought their path was leading them rather dangerously far from civilization (by which I mean the real world). Here again much may be learned from glorious failures, but the chance of getting substantial profit from excursions of this kind is smaller. For those who choose this path are almost inevitably led to substitute the elaboration of concepts, with the help of carefully selected factual examples, for the verification of propositions, with the help of genuine empirical research. And this is a most insidious disease which may easily develop into a form of creeping paralysis, which differs from its physical counterpart in that the victims become steadily more, instead of less, busily active as the sickness progresses.

It seemed to me that the travellers along both these paths were in danger of becoming airborne without realizing it, and that efforts should be made to get their feet back on to the ground.

At the other extreme I took note of the growing passion for the use of survey techniques and statistical apparatus to carry out inquiries, some of them vast and fabulously expensive, others minute and concerned with trifles of insignificant interest, a large proportion of which appeared to have no clear purpose and little hope of producing results of more lasting value than a few pages of print in a scientific journal, and possibly a Ph.D. for the author. I called this, rather more felicitously, the way into the sands—'the sands of whirling facts which blow into the eyes and ears until nothing can be clearly seen or heard' (I am quoting myself). Fifteen years ago there was considerable anxiety lest sociology be swamped in a flood of studies of this kind. This anxiety has diminished but has not entirely disappeared today.

Having looked at these two attractive but treacherous paths, I suggested that what sociology needed was something firm to tread on, somewhere between these two extremes of stars and sands, and I called this 'stepping-stones in the middle distance'. I was thinking of studies of the major social institutions, found in varying forms in all societies, and of the universal social processes and relationships which are manifested in and around those institutions, like co-operation, leadership, communication and the rest. And I cited as an example familiar to my audience at the London School of Economics the way in which Hobhouse's great work on social development and the evolution of morals was based on the careful and scientific comparison of institutions and processes of this kind.

Looking back now, I see no reason to alter the view I expressed then. It is true that somebody—I forget who—has recently rebuked me somewhere in print for having offered such pusillanimous advice. But there is nothing pusillanimous about an invitation to take the middle road, when, as in this case, the middle road does not represent a feeble compromise which misses the best of both worlds. Quite the opposite. It means the choice of tasks to which the greatest efforts can be devoted with the hope of maximum returns. And more than that, only a steady advance along the middle road can provide the base from which profitable excursions can be made in the other directions. It should be obvious, I think, that careful studies in depth of limited areas of selected social systems are the best and most trustworthy stepping-stones on which one may advance towards the fuller comprehension of social systems *in toto* and in general. Let me give an example taken from current trends in sociological research. The interest of sociologists in social development is unabated, and there are those who do, from time to time, review and amend the all-embracing visions of the early masters. But the line taken by contemporary research is rather different. In place of telescopes sweeping the horizons of human history we see microscopes, or at least magnifying glasses, beginning to be applied to the detailed study of so-called underdeveloped—or 'developing'—countries, their social systems, their evolution and their problems. In these studies use is being made, for purposes of comparison, of our historical knowledge of the corresponding phase of development of what are now the 'advanced' civilizations. Already interest in this area of research is strong enough to have led the International Sociological Association to choose the 'sociology of development'—to be treated in the way I have described—as the major theme of the Fifth World Congress of Sociology to be held in Washington, D.C., in 1962.

The most noticeable weakness of many of the sample surveys and quantitative studies of behaviour and attitudes is the absence of any guiding body of theory or supporting background of tested knowledge. They may seem to be very much on the ground, among the pedestrian affairs of everyday life, but in fact they are up in the air, without any cord to attach them to the meaning of things. It is probably true that the failure of such empirical studies is due less often to defective survey techniques than to the lack of a firm base of knowledge and theory, and the consequent lack of creative purpose. As C. A. Moser says: 'It must be stressed that fact-collecting is no substitute for thought and desk research, and that the comparative ease with which survey techniques can be mastered is all the more reason why their limitations as well as their capabilities should be understood.'[5] Their capabilities

[5] C. A. Moser: *Survey Methods in Social Investigation*, p. 3.

are greatest and their limitations least when they are used as instruments by those who are travelling on the middle road, or who are sent out by them to reconnoitre with pretty clear instructions in their pocket.

If I were asked where to look for good typical examples of the recent work of these middle-road travellers, my first reply would be: in the studies of social stratification and mobility; in the careful and cumulative investigation of the forms and working of bureaucracy, both public and private; in industrial sociology and its several branches; in the analysis (in collaboration with political scientists and psychologists) of voting behaviour and political affiliation; and in communication research—and I should recommend that an eye be kept on current developments in the sociology of religion and the sociology of law. This is a very inadequate reply, but clearly there is no time now to make a survey of recent sociological literature, nor should I be able to make such a survey, having spent the last four years as a busy civil servant.

I have now done my best to identify sociology for you, and to indicate the road along which she appears to me to be travelling. So the next problem, clearly, is transportation; what, in other words, are the resources of which sociology can dispose, in the shape of methods and techniques, and of data which can be assembled with their aid? If I can persuade you to consider that these may be respectable, I shall feel that I have done a good day's work.

The material used by sociologists can be roughly classed into two categories, documentary and live. By documentary material I mean the kind used by historians, the only material they have apart from physical objects surviving from the past. By live material I mean information collected directly and with a specific purpose, by interview, questionnaire and case study, or by direct observation of events in progress. It refers only to the present and the recent past, in so far as the picture of the past is reliably mirrored in the memory of people still alive. One of the main strategic problems of sociology is how to combine the use of these two types of material so as to produce something greater than the sum of the products of the two sources taken separately.

Nobody can be criticized for making use of documentary sources, provided he makes good use of them, and on this point I admit that the reputation of sociology is not entirely free from blemish. But then, whose reputation is? I am not concerned here with the faults committed by incompetent practitioners, but only with any special characteristics which may distinguish the use made of this kind of material by sociologists as such. For instance, sociologists must inevitably rely extensively on secondary authorities, without going back to the original sources. They do this partly because life is too short to do anything else when using the comparative method, and they need data assembled from a wide historical field; and partly because original sources are very tricky things to use, especially if the category is extended to cover documents which, though not 'original' in the strictest sense, are contemporary with the events concerned. Nothing is more unreliable than the first-hand account of an eye-witness, nor more liable to deceive than diaries and correspondence whose authors thoroughly enjoyed writing them. And even the accounts of treasurers cannot always be accepted as representing the final and absolute truth. It is the business of historians to sift this miscellaneous collection of dubious authorities and to give to others the results of their careful professional assessment. And surely they will not rebuke the sociologist for putting his faith in what historians write. But of course the use of secondary authorities demands skill and understanding, which cannot be acquired without some training and a fair amount of practice. This is a point on which the European sociological tradition is good, and the American is definitely improving.

Secondly, sociologists use documentary sources to study the present and the very recent past. They embark on the perilous waters of contemporary history. Historians used to say, and perhaps they still do, that events, like wine, need time to mature. It is certainly true that some time must pass before the documentation of the period is fully accessible. Is it also true that time must pass before you can see events in perspective? Or does this merely mean that, if you wish to assess them in terms of historical sequence and the chain of causation, it is better to wait until you can see clearly what their sequel and their effects actually were? The historian is fortunate in this respect. A social science, we are told, must be judged by its ability to predict; but it is the business of the historian to be wise after the event, and that is a most valuable and very satisfying kind of wisdom.

But the sociologist cannot wait to see what happens because, as I have said, he needs to combine historical data, whether past or contemporary, with the live data which can only refer to the present and the immediate past. So he must do his best without that kind of perspective. This is not too serious a disadvantage for him, because he is less concerned than the historian with the sequence of events in the unique setting of a particular time and place, and more with generalized knowledge of the social processes of which these events are an example. To a considerable extent he can substitute comparison, or horizontal perspective, as it were, for the temporal, or vertical, perspective of the historian.

And what of the sociologist's live data? Can their respectability be admitted? I shall not discuss the techniques of sampling and of statistical analysis, partly because I am not competent to do so, and partly because, although grave errors have been made in these departments of research techniques, the experts are constantly at work perfecting their instruments, and nobody seriously doubts their value and validity. So leaving these technical matters to the technicians, I shall confine myself to two points of a more general character.

The first is this. Material collected by the direct method of questionnaire, interview and case study has a standing in the scale of originality of source one step below genuinely original and authentic operational documents, like statutes, ordinances and official correspondence. But I would place it one step above records and writings contemporary with the events described but lacking this direct operational character, like the diaries and letters I mentioned just now. For these are uncontrolled and usually unsystematic accounts, liable to every kind of subjective distortion, whereas the sociologist creates, as it were, his own original sources by the careful employment of instruments designed for this very purpose, namely to elicit exactly the kind of information he needs, freed, as far as scientific procedures can free it, from the effects of bias, forgetfulness and malice. Of course these instruments are not yet perfect, and sometimes slovenly use is made of them, but experience steadily increases our understanding of the art of combining a series of questions using different methods of approach, so as to create a 'battery' (as the psychologists call it) far more effective and reliable than any number of isolated pieces of ordinance. I cannot express too strongly my belief that these methods of investigation have opened up for social scientists and social historians sources of information of inestimable value and of a kind that they never possessed before, and that it would be sheer lunacy to refuse to make the maximum use of them on the grounds that they must be handled with care and discrimination and that, even then, they are not infallible. The honest investigator should not be deterred by fear of making mistakes. The remedy for these mistakes is more research, not less, so that the errors of the pioneers may be corrected by their successors in the field.

My second point can be introduced by referring to a recent review article in which I was rash enough to comment on a sentence in a book by Barbara Wootton to the effect that 'no matter who has the first word, the last is always with the statistician'. I said this was a very dangerous doctrine, for two reasons. In the first place it matters very much who has the first word; nothing, in fact, is more important for the success of the enterprise than the initial definition of its nature and purpose. The statement, I believe, is true, but the comment, I admit, was unfair. The words 'no matter who has' are not equivalent to the words 'it doesn't matter who has'. I apologize. My second point was that 'it is not so much the last, as the penultimate word that belongs to the statistician, except when his verdict is clearly negative or relates to a proposition about the existence, rather than the significance, of a quantitative relationship'.[6] And that comment, I believe, is both fair and true. Sociological interpretation must go beyond statistical correlation, which merely points to a possibility worthy of further investigation by other means. When I say 'possibility', I refer, of course, not to the existence of a relationship, which can be established statistically as a fact, but to its explanation in terms of causation or interconnected processes. For this the sociologist must draw on his knowledge of how individuals and groups of individuals behave and of how social systems work. 'A fully developed social theory', says Sir Alexander Carr-Saunders, 'is a statement of what happens when typical human dispositions encounter typical situations'.[7] Perfectly true, and that is why the man who formulates or who uses social theory must have a profound knowledge both of dispositions and of situations. But when Carr-Saunders says, on the previous page of the same essay, 'it is in fact by analogy with our own minds that we make the actions of other men intelligible to ourselves', I think he is making this process of explanation or understanding of social phenomena appear more individual, irresponsible and limited than it really is.

A word often used in this context is 'insight'. But frequently the reference is to a process of communication rather than of discovery. The so-called 'insight' is a happy inspiration about a way of making a point intelligible to somebody else by relating it to what is already in his mind. It is a kind of translation into a language known to the hearer, and is therefore governed by the limited capacities of the individual. But, if 'insight' refers to that power to understand which the social scientist possesses and the natural scientist does not, namely, the power derived from the fact that he is part and parcel of the world he is studying, and can look at the objects in it from the inside, then it is a much less purely personal affair. It is not true that we can only understand

[6] 'Sociology and Social Pathology', in The British Journal of Sociology, March 1960, p. 85.
[7] Natural Science and Social Science, p. 9.

emotions, motives and situations which we have ourselves experienced. If it were true, not only would the social sciences be reduced to a fraction of their present stature, but young novelists would be forbidden to introduce old characters into their novels and men would be unable to write stories about women. The insight of the sociologist does not spring fully armed from his native and untutored brain. It is distilled from the accumulated experience and reflection of men of all times and places, as recorded in their studies of human societies and expressed in their actions. It must be the result of training and discipline and the careful cultivation of judgement. It is an acquired skill, capable of being developed into a professional expertise similar to those found in other academic disciplines.

So, however much emphasis may be placed on the role of insight and understanding in sociology—and it would be difficult to exaggerate its importance—it should not lead to the conclusion that sociology cannot be scientific. It can, but it must be scientific in the manner appropriate to itself, and not by imitation of false models. Science, I suggest, is knowledge acquired by the collection and analysis of information through the scrupulous use of procedures sufficiently systematic to enable the work done by one man to be repeated by another, and their results to be combined or compared, so that in this way the body of knowledge may grow. I believe that sociology can be scientific in this sense, even though sociological explanation does consist, in the last resort, of the application to the problem in question of the collective wisdom of the discipline, through the judgement of individual scholars. It is far better to recognize the true nature of the sociological method than to fall a victim to so-called 'scientism', 'this Moloch worship, sacrificing life to an idol of science', as Donald MacRae has called it, for which measurement is all, and everything that is measurable is worth measuring.[8]

[8] 'Between Science and the Arts', in *The Twentieth Century*, May 1960, p. 473.

This brings me to the concluding remarks I wish to make, which bear more directly on the position of sociology in a university curriculum. I hope that what I have said has made it clear that sociology is not an easy subject or a soft option. What makes it difficult, I think, is its relative shortage of apparatus. It possesses tools for the collection of data, quite elaborate and efficient ones. It also has an important equipment of concepts for use in the systematic classification of its data. The manufacture of these instruments is, in fact, one of the sociology's most valuable services to the social sciences, in the performance of which it has to rely very much on its own resources. But it is not very well provided with those other kinds of mechanical aid which sharpen the vision of the human eye, extend the range of perception far beyond the limits of the human senses, or provide schemes of analysis by which complicated problems are reduced to simple formulae. It is true that sociologists are making increasingly effective use of techniques of multivariate analysis to disentangle and identify the strands of interdependence and multiple causation in complex situations. But there is a limit to the degree of complexity with which such methods can cope, and the results must always stop short of the final explanation desired. In the handling of its major problems, related as they are to social systems treated as wholes, sociology cannot express the vital issues in neat algebraic formulae like those often used by economists when dealing with a vast problem such as the pattern of economic growth. Such technical devices would not have helped Max Weber in his study of the relations between the protestant ethic and the spirit of capitalism. There are too many variables involved, and the sociologist must feel his way through the maze without this kind of assistance.

Even when he descends to the micro-sociological level and tries to isolate chosen facets of individual behaviour in small groups he may fare no better. George Homans, inspired by Pareto, has tried to submit this kind of question to expression in propositions of a quasi-equational character, but the results are not encouraging.[9] No, the sociologist must not only learn to use instruments, he must learn to grow them on the tips of his fingers, and that takes time, as any violinist will tell you.

That is why it is so important not to allow sociology to be flooded by people who mistake elementary hunches for the painfully acquired wisdom and sensibility of the genuine scholar. Such people should not try to write sociology, but by all means let them come and read it. I am certain that sociology has a great deal to offer as an ingredient in a general education, especially in the general education of social scientists. And I am also convinced that its contribution to a course of undergraduate study can be made from the very beginning; it can be quickly appreciated and readily absorbed in its elementary form by anyone who is genuinely interested and is prepared to do some work and to discipline his mind and his emotions.

But when we turn from the beginning of the university course to the final stage of undergraduate study the position becomes more difficult. A really good subject should enable the student to feel that everything he learns marks a step upwards to a higher level of competence from which, and only from which, he can take the next step. I am sure that sociology can satisfy this requirement. Secondly it should teach him how to master a new mental process and to manipulate a body of theory and a battery of techniques; it should not merely enlarge the contents of his mind but add to its working machinery. Here sociology is a little less satisfactory than some other sciences because it is not so well supplied with exact and self-sufficient apparatus. It is therefore harder to see and measure the progress made in this direction. Thirdly, the perfect subject should lead to a closing situation which is well rounded off, in the sense that those who do not wish to go any further and become specialists can leave with a feeling that something has been accomplished, and that they have acquired something which they can carry away with

[9] *The Human Group, passim.*

them and use in after life with a fair measure of assurance. In sociology it is not easy to reach this point in three years; there is a risk that the intellectual parcel will not be safely wrapped up and ready to take away when the time comes to go.

There are, I think, two ways of overcoming this difficulty. One is to avoid like the plague all temptation to be encyclopaedic, and to include in the syllabus at least one subject of strictly limited extent and complexity, the study of which should give a clear picture of how sociology operates and what it can do. The other is to marry sociology, for some little time to come, with another discipline, such as economics, which is better equipped with precision tools and can get quicker results all along the line. But it is when you pass on to the post-graduate stage that sociology comes fully into its own as an independent discipline, self-reliant but co-operative. Here the select few can be trained to become the practitioners of the future, and when I say 'trained' I am thinking of real systematic training, and not merely the supervision of a thesis. But at this point I must come to an abrupt halt, because I see I am in danger of treating a public lecture as if it were a faculty meeting.

CHAPTER III

INTERNATIONAL COMPREHENSION IN AND THROUGH SOCIAL SCIENCE

When I received the invitation to deliver the Hobhouse Memorial Lecture this year,[1] I was torn by conflicting emotions —gratitude for the honour done me and for the opportunity it would give me to return for a moment, in an academic capacity, to these very familiar surroundings, and anxiety as to my ability to find a subject on which I could put together some thoughts that might be worthy of the occasion. After three years as an international civil servant, living in that hectic state of constant rush which seems to be characteristic of international organizations, I obviously cannot offer you a scholarly dissertation or the fruits of original research. So I decided to delve into the experience gained in the course of my work and see if I could unearth something which would be of sufficient interest for the purpose. And when I called to mind the picture of Hobhouse, as I remember him, and also some of his vigorous comments on current affairs, I ventured to believe that he himself would have regarded the work of the organization in which I am now serving, and the lessons to be learned from it about co-operation and communication between people of different cultures, as matters worthy of serious attention. Let me hasten to add that I am not about to deliver a talk on UNESCO and all its works; far from it. I mean only that my theme has been sug-

[1] 7 May 1959.

gested to me by my present occupation and can be illustrated from the same source.

This theme is divided into two parts which, although they represent different levels of approach to the subject, are closely linked. The first approach may be called the professional one, and can be explained as follows. Let us assume that the social sciences, in their various disciplines, are developing systems of concepts, theories and methods by means of which research carried out by different people in the same field can be objectively assessed, compared, and integrated into a collective body of knowledge. The question then arises whether, in this process, the frontiers between nations and cultures have any significance. If we boldly cry: 'Social Scientists of the world, unite', are we merely ignoring barriers which effectively keep them apart? Should we concentrate on our task of building systems, convinced that their fundamental universality will ultimately become apparent, or ought we to turn part of our attention to the barriers between nations and cultures and make these barriers themselves the object of scientific study, in order to discover exactly what is their nature and how best they can be overcome?

The second approach is that which the French elegantly term *vulgarisation*, a word which official translators have been known, in an off moment, to transcribe letter by letter into an English text, thereby putting their finger on the very crux of the matter. How can we have *vulgarisation* without vulgarization? It is evident to us all that the pictures which people of one culture form of the cultures of others are pathetically inadequate and often dangerously false. It is also clear that this lack of mutual understanding today breeds a sense of frustration, which degenerates easily into irritation, and that great efforts are being made from many directions to remedy it. Lack of understanding may be due to emotional forces which give rise to prejudice, or to a feeling of insecurity; it may be the result of the passive acceptance of traditional stereotypes, but it is always founded on ignorance. So the question is: can the social sciences, by the use of their own professional methods, increase mutual understanding between cultures? You may think that this is a foolish question, and that the answer is obviously, 'Yes'. For the whole purpose of the social sciences is to increase and deepen our knowledge of human society, in its various manifestations, and an increase of knowledge must necessarily increase understanding. But the matter is not so simple. I am speaking about the understanding that may be achieved, not by professional social scientists, but by peoples or, to use a crude but useful phrase, by educated publics. And understanding of this kind will always be built on foundations of ignorance. The educated public can never know all there is to know about a foreign culture. The task of those who set out to improve mutual understanding at this level is that of conveying the essential truth without teaching all the facts. There are, therefore, two processes involved—first, the accumulation of knowledge and the acquisition of understanding, and secondly, the communication of this understanding to others, who can never be expected to absorb all the knowledge. This second process requires special skills, which may not always be found in social scientists.

Now, nobody can work for long in an international organization today without noticing that the very intensity of the desire, all over the world, to explain one culture to the people of another has a certain tendency to self-frustration. The eagerness to make yourself known and understood to others may lead you to maintain that only somebody who is a product of your culture is qualified to understand and explain it. And this attitude is likely to be most unyielding when the others, by whom you wish to be understood, recently exercised over you a superior power which made them, so you think, contemptuous of your way of life. You begin to regard with suspicion the foreign scholars who specialize in the study of your civilization. But from the other side there then comes the claim that nobody who is not a product of *their* culture can communicate to their educated public knowledge and understanding of *your* culture. The two processes of acquiring knowledge and of communicating knowledge become separated by the very barrier they have set out to overcome. If the goal is to be reached, there must be mutual understanding, and mutual confidence, between social scientists of different cultures, in order that the two processes may be harmonized. And in this fact is to be found the link between the two parts of my theme.

If we look back at the events out of which modern sociology has grown (and here I am including social anthropology), we can see what a large part was played, both in the great surveys of human evolution attempted by the founders and in the empirical research that followed or accompanied them, by studies of the civilization of people who were not in a position to answer back, because they were either dead or illiterate. The situation has changed considerably. I do not know whether the Trobriand Islanders can now read the works of Malinowski. If they can, I expect they feel both flattered and instructed by them.

It is certainly true—and this is to be regretted—that historical material, information about people who have been silenced by death, is less widely and effectively used by sociologists than it used to be. But the most important fact is that anthropologists have increasingly turned their attention to the examination and interpretation of cultures which are both literate and highly sophisticated, while at the same time the methods and techniques of modern sociological research and analysis have been adopted by the scholars of these countries and are rapidly coming into ever more extensive and intensive use in their hands.

Before this happened, we had a situation in which societies differing widely in their culture and structure were being studied and compared by specialists who had all been trained in approximately the same school. The variety of the material was reduced to order by the unity of approach used by the observers. In the earlier anthropological descriptions, it has been said, 'cultures were described in terms of the traditional institutional categories of Western cultures'.[2] Gross misunderstandings resulted, which anthropologists, still acting

[2] Wayne Untereiner: *Cultural Analysis and Interpretation* (unpublished), p. 2.

fundamentally in concert, strove to remedy by the application to the problem of new techniques. Professor Lévi-Strauss
has stated that the French sociological school of Durkheim
and Mauss, has 'always taken care to substitute, as a starting-
point for the survey of native categories of thought, the conscious representations prevailing among the natives themselves for those grown out of the anthropologist's own
culture'. But, he continues, though this was an important advance, it was not enough, 'because these authors were not
sufficiently aware that native conscious representations, important as they are, may be just as remote from the unconscious reality as any other'.[3] So the observer, who is still a
foreign visitor, must impose on the material he collects, not
the concepts appropriate to his own culture, but the 'model'
which in his opinion (and not necessarily in that of the people he is studying) is appropriate to his material. I am not
questioning the truth of this assertion, but only pointing out
that it becomes difficult to put it into practice when the people you are studying are able to answer back—both as qualified social scientists, and as political equals. They are quite
likely to deny the superiority of the foreigner's model over
their own conscious representations. And they construct models of their own which, I am quite certain, deserve to be
treated with the greatest respect.

The civilizations of Asia and the Middle East cannot be
treated as the passive objects of comparative study by 'Western' scientists. They contain active practitioners of a sociology
which they direct mainly, though not exclusively, at themselves. But, while the methods of scientific sociology are
spreading outwards from the 'Western' culture in which they
originated, we have not yet achieved what Arvid Brodersen
calls the 'substantive policy objective of internationalizing
the social sciences'[4] to the same extent that we have internationalized the natural sciences. The so-called 'traditional'

[3] C. Lévi-Strauss: 'Social Structure', *Anthropology Today*, ed.
A. L. Kroeber, 1953, p. 527.
[4] 'Soviet Social Science and Our Own', *Social Research*, Vol.
XXIV, No. 3, 1957, p. 284.

societies have broken through the crust of their traditional attitudes towards the means by which human society should be studied and by which a deeper understanding of it should be sought, and have begun to apply the methods of modern science to the study of mankind. But tradition is not only a matter of conscious beliefs or intellectual practices which can be changed by an act of will. It is much more deeply rooted than that. And, for some time, the co-existence of a disturbed traditionalism with a still slightly exotic scientism may produce a combination unlike anything to be found in the countries in which the scientific method had its birth. This combination may have its defects. But it can also deepen our understanding of traditional cultures in ways which were not possible before.

Traditionalism is associated with a qualitative analysis, dominated by a religious philosophy, reinforced in varying ways and degrees by history. The mixture is, of course, not by any means the same wherever tradition has ruled. For example, a professor of Indian civilization has stated that, while Christian and Moslem scholars are both deeply interested in historical dates and facts, 'in India, on the other hand, the pundits have never attached any importance to these matters. In the everlasting cycle of time and in the endless succession of reincarnations, it is quite meaningless to know when something occurred; only the fact itself and its moral implications are important.'[5]

Obviously there is a great gulf fixed between a mode of thought in which a kind of timeless history is combined with a religious philosophy and, at the opposite extreme, the attitude of mind that prizes accuracy in the recording of facts and dates in history, on the one hand, and the use of questionnaires, punched cards, and I.B.M. machines to produce, as a contribution to sociological research, a sort of X-ray snapshot of a society's vitals, on the other. And yet there is a likelihood that, in many cases, it is precisely this opposite extreme that will be embraced by those who are shaking off

[5] *Humanism and Education in East and West* (UNESCO 1953), p. 1.

what they feel to be the restrictive bonds of tradition. A glance, for example, at bibliographies of recent literature and current research in India makes it clear that this is so. While it is equally clear that the injudicious and indiscriminate use of Western sample survey methods provokes, among other Indian sociologists, a reaction and a resistance which could, in certain circumstances, lead to the rejection of Western influences altogether and the assertion of a sociological isolationism. At a recent congress of Indian sociologists reference was made to 'the use of modern "scientific" techniques imported from outside as part of technical aid and "knowhow"' to which Indian scholars are inclined to succumb. And it was further argued that problems of cultural change 'cannot be analysed and understood from a value-neutral or positivistic and empirical standpoint to which, however, modern social scientists show a superstitious attachment'.

It is clear to me that, if we are to internationalize social science, we must concentrate on achieving mutual understanding in that intermediate area which lies between general theory and philosophical (or ideological) explanation on the one hand, and data-collecting on the other. It is here that one finds most misunderstanding, and when I use the word, I do not mean disagreement. Maximum disagreement will be found at the ideological level, but I believe that this matters less than one might imagine. But by 'misunderstanding' I mean the situation in which one man does not realize what the other is trying to do.

To illustrate this, let me turn to what I regard as the third group of social scientists in the contemporary world. The first two are the group of those who belong to the originating European civilization, wherever they may now be located, and the group of those who belong to the traditional cultures of Asia, the Middle East and Africa. The third group consists of those who live and work in societies whose ideology is dominated by the teaching of Marx and his disciples. There are no peoples more continuously preoccupied with a conception of their society than these, but this conception is based on a social science which is radically different from those of the other two groups. We must have all three groups in view to complete the picture of the divided world in which we are trying to internationalize the social sciences.

During the past year and a half I have been concerned with the planning of a number of conferences of social scientists coming from the area of which the geographical, and perhaps also the ideological, extremes are represented by the United States and the Soviet Union. Each meeting was confined to one social science discipline, and the general aim was to promote international understanding in and through the social sciences. The political science meeting was organized in too great a hurry, made a poor start, and never really settled into its stride. The barriers to understanding were least in evidence among the lawyers, who found that on most points they all spoke much the same language. The economists also found common ground to meet on, but there were some interesting episodes from which certain tentative conclusions can be drawn. The main subject under discussion was the factors that determine the level and structure of national production, and this led to a comparison of notes on the methods used by economists, and by governments, to collect the information and make the estimates on which their plans or policies must be based. At a very early stage a conflict arose over the question whether the relations within the productive process should be regarded as one of the factors of production. The Westerner said 'no' and the Easterner with equal emphasis said 'yes'. The 'Westerners' said they fully realized the importance of these relations, but that they did not belong to the same category of concepts as the factors of production as presented in their analytical system. The 'Easterners' said, or implied, that in that case their analytical system was at fault and that, if they did not include these relations among the factors of production then, whatever they might say to the contrary, they would not in fact give them the importance they deserved. If one casts an eye back over the history of economics in the West, one may well feel that there were some grounds for this suspicion. But the point of the story is that neither side yielded an inch:

the deadlock was complete. This cannot be wondered at, since the role of the relations of production in the body of Marxist theory is absolutely crucial. Nevertheless, the subject was dropped and, as the debate moved on, it appeared that the failure to resolve this theoretical issue had no effect whatever on the mutual understanding achieved when the economists began to discuss more practical matters.

There was a second episode which, if I remember right, arose from the discussion of a theoretical paper which had described, in simplified terms, the 'ideal type' of a free market economy in which a satisfactory distribution of resources is obtained because the operation of the price system automatically corrects maldistribution. Often it over-corrects a little, so that the economic system advances by a process of oscillation about a moving point of equilibrium. This concept of progress by feed-back was quite alien to the minds of the 'Easterners'. It appeared to them to be wasteful—a system composed of a series of errors. If maldistribution occurs, it means that planning is inefficient, and steps should be taken to see that it does not occur again. Here, too, there was a deadlock. Nevertheless the failure to agree on this point did not seem to create any serious obstacle to understanding in the discussion that followed. This is not altogether surprising. Once you get down to an examination of the methods used to estimate the demand for capital and labour, and of the maldistributions which have occurred in the past, it is easy to forget the difference of opinion as to whether maldistribution is a natural feature of economic progress or the regrettable result of defective planning. In either case the practical objective is to reduce maldistribution to the minimum. And the need to set limits to the impact of theory on practice arises also from the fact that differences of opinion with regard to theory are bound to develop within a single school of thought, as well as between different schools. The view I have just quoted, that socialist planning should, in principle, be perfect, sounds dangerously like the 'voluntarist' heresy which, according to Oskar Lange, 'denied that economic laws operated under socialism and put forward the assumption that in a socialist State the controllers of economic policy can do whatever they wish'.[6]

The sociologists, who met in Moscow, knew very well that they could not expect to make much progress towards mutual understanding in a week. There are too many fundamentally different conceptions in the world as to what sociology is, and it is not only a question of differences between Marxists and others. Here again, as with the economists, it was found that one cannot expect to achieve greater mutual understanding by making a direct attack on differences in basic theory. Attention should be directed rather to matters of fact and of method. The most helpful questions are: what do you know about your social conditions, and by what means do you gather this knowledge?

I have time to give only one example. In comparing inequalities of income in different societies the sociologists inevitably touched on the theory of class structure. An argument developed as to what is really meant by the statement that class structure is based on ownership of the instruments of production. It eventually appeared that the crucial difference between capitalist and socialist societies, in the eyes of the Soviet sociologists, was the existence in the former of a small group of big industrial tycoons, of millionaires, who exercise enormous power over the economic life of the society without being responsible to any public authority. The fact that there are thousands of persons having a share in the ownership of the instruments of production, without exercising any power, and the possibility that the power of the millionaires may be only to a limited extent based on ownership might be admitted, and the discussion could then concentrate on the question whether the Marxist estimate of the power of these industrial magnates was or was not exaggerated. The theoretical controversy remained unresolved, but faded somewhat into the background.

It is more difficult to proceed towards a better mutual understanding by concentrating on facts in sociology than

[6] 'The Political Economy of Socialism', *Science and Society*, Vol. XXIII, No. 1, 1959, pp. 2–3.

in economics, because sociological facts contain a larger element of subjective interpretation, which cannot be detached from them. Even, let us suppose, if it were established that the actual scale of income inequality were much the same in two countries with different ideologies, it could still be argued that the effects of this inequality were quite different. When social studies are dominated by an all-embracing and all-sufficient theory, which is married to a political ideology, this subjectivity of factual data has to be protected. Objectivity in any discussion of the nature of society is a menace. But operationally, in a planned society, scientific objectivity is necessary. The natural sciences, at least, must be scientifically used, and their acceptance may be cautiously extended to the social sciences, in their more practical aspects. The story can be followed in the reactions of Christianity to the first challenge of, say, astronomy or Darwinism, and in its gradual accommodation to and eventual acceptance of the new world of ideas that they created. It can also be illustrated by the way in which orthodox Communism handled the problem of statistics. In 1950, at a specially convened conference of statisticians in Moscow, the leading spokesman said that the main obstacle to the proper development of statistical method was 'the formal mathematics school of thought (which) considers statistics (to be) a universal science for the study of nature and society based ultimately on the mathematical law of large numbers and not on Marxist-Leninist theory'. When one speaker objected that it might be dangerous 'to exclude nature and its laws as a subject to be studied by statistics', he was told that he 'was guilty of objectivism in his defence of the bourgeois position on statistics'. But four years later a new pronouncement was made to the effect that there are two kinds of statistics, 'one called "mathematical statistics", which applies to nature, and another called simply "statistics" which applies to society'.[7] The latter was still to be subject to ideological control. This view met with strong opposition from those who wished to

[7] Arvid Brodersen: 'New Trends in Soviet Social Theory', *American Slavic and East European Review*, Vol. XVII, No. 3, pp. 283–5.

free statistics from such restraints, an opposition which could not be silenced. In 1956, at the Twentieth Congress of the Communist Party of the Soviet Union, Mr Mikoyan said: 'Without a most careful examination of all the statistical data, . . . without systematizing these data, without analyzing and drawing general conclusions from them, no scientific economic work is possible.'[8] And without scientific economic work of some kind, a planned society cannot long survive.

Let me make one final comment on this theme. At the Moscow meeting of sociologists a hot debate developed, as it obviously must, on the role of theory in sociology. Those who maintained that only one theory was needed, because it was true and universal, namely the theory of historical materialism, accused the sociologists in capitalist countries of collecting facts on the basis of no theory at all. The accused hotly denied this charge and explained that inability to accept any one theory as containing the whole truth and final truth did not imply indifference to theory as such; quite the contrary in fact. Obviously there was a definite misunderstanding here about the nature of 'Western' sociology, and it was one which could be substantially reduced by discussion. Was there any misunderstanding in the opposite direction? In a sense there was. A Soviet sociologist spoke with feeling, drawing, it seemed, on his own personal experience, about the needs of a people who have overturned the edifice of social tradition and, after passing through chaos, begun to create a new society extending over vast expanses of territory, a society in which they must play a more active part than was ever played by their fathers under the old régime. The first necessity, he said, is to help these people to see and understand the society they are creating, to grasp the essential meaning of its nature and to appreciate its position in the history of mankind and in the contemporary world. Compared with this, the refinement of hypotheses about the ranking of occupations, or sociological research into the factors which cause miners to keep pigeons (one of the exam-

[8] A. I. Mikoyan: Speech to the Twentieth Congress of the Communist Party, *Soviet News Booklet*, No. 8, 1956, p. 21.

ples cited during the debate), seemed to him to be of little importance. The point was well made. Whatever might be the final judgement on it, obviously one could not understand the situation without taking it into account.

I have cited this incident here, because it may act as a bridge from the first to the second aspect of my theme, from understanding *in* to understanding *through* social science. In what follows I shall draw on the report of another UNESCO Conference[9] (with which I was not personally concerned) designed to explore ways of deepening understanding between the Americas and Europe. The participants included philosophers, historians and social scientists.

Let us take a glance to see what happens when a group of highly intelligent, well-educated and widely read scholars meet together with the express object of arriving at a better understanding of their respective cultures, and come prepared to contribute towards this end. How near do they get to concensus on these issues, and how quickly does misunderstanding evaporate under the warm sun of knowledge? The result of this brief inspection is, I fear, rather discouraging. The subject was the cultural and moral relations between the Old and the New World. This was discussed at two meetings, the first of which was held in Brazil. At the very outset the spokesman of the host country complained bitterly that only one of the contributions submitted to the meeting had paid the slightest attention to the existence, in the New World, of Latin America. They all concentrated their attention on the United States. This was an unfortunate opening to the proceedings, and it gradually became clear that deep anxiety was felt by the Latin Americans present about the invasion of their countries by certain elements of the culture of the United States, an anxiety so clearly expressed that Robert Frost was prompted to exclaim, 'Do you regard us as monsters?'[10] And, according to one speaker, the position as regards North America and Europe was no better. 'Relations

9 *The Old and the New World—Their Cultural and Moral Relations* (UNESCO 1956).
10 ibid.

between these two continents, the Old and the New, are bad,'
he said, 'so bad, indeed, that they are a cause for serious
anxiety.' (ibid., p. 221.)

It was also clear that the speakers believed that profound
misunderstanding as to the true nature of European, Latin-
American and United States cultures underlay the suspicion
obviously felt by members of each about the others. To drive
home this point they sketched the mistaken views which,
they said, were prevalent in some places. Let me give two
examples. Latin America was referred to as 'that part of the
continent which many politicians, and indeed men of culture, especially in Europe, tend to regard as the abode of
savages, Negroes, half-castes and illiterates', and Roger Bas-
tide said that 'South America seems to the European to be a
second primeval chaos, a new creation, while North America
seems an apocalypse' (pp. 20–1). Secondly, George Shuster
said that the false picture Europe held of American culture
'was jazz blared out from dawn till midnight, was a certain
type of motion picture, was anti-intellectualism, was an infantile purely quantitative sex mania given to festooning a
sequence of temporarily cherished squaws with bracelets and
beads' (p. 56).

One might think that, if these learned men started by drawing such an alarming picture of current misunderstanding,
they should find it easy to demonstrate that great progress
could be made towards a better understanding by that sober
contemplation of reality of which they themselves were capable. But the discussions did not turn out quite like that. Expression was given to the familiar idea that North America
is a new society, and still somewhat crude in many respects.
But one speaker doubted this. Referring to the years of economic crisis in the 1930's, he said: 'I wonder whether they
did not mark the beginning of a process of ageing, or at any
rate maturing in America, which is deeply graven in the mental attitude.' It is clear that he must have used the word
'sclerosis', because his remarks were followed by an explosion
from Lucien Fèbvre, who exclaimed, 'Sclerosis—No! Sclerosis
of what? Sclerosis of a world bursting with life and youthful

vitality as America is? We cannot begin to speak of this world without the word "young" springing to our minds' (pp. 170–2). Yet a third point of view was expressed by André Maurois, who said: 'Those who do not like America are much inclined to criticize it as infantile. The term is exceedingly ill-chosen. America is adolescent' (p. 318). So you see, you can take your choice. America may be infantile, young, adolescent or senile. For each opinion you can quote high authority.

Let me mention another case, which is amusing rather than disturbing. Speaking of Americanization, one representative of Europe said: 'The threat hanging over us, the threat we feel to be hanging over us, is not something evil, it is a vacuum, such as is produced by rapid movement.' But another, considering the same phenomenon, called it 'a flood of American products poured into the ideological vacuum of the Old World' (p. 224). So we are presented with the illuminating spectacle of one vacuum invading another.

The speakers I have quoted were not professional social scientists, giving us the fruits of their studies and research, although they may be said to represent very closely related disciplines. Were the professional social scientists, of whom a few were present, more successful? In one respect yes, but in another, no. For instance, Paul Rivet put at the disposal of the conference his great knowledge of Latin America, but by doing so he did not merely chase from the room the false and facile generalizations of the intelligent amateurs. He shattered all possibility of generalization of any kind, at least on a level that would be intelligible to the educated public of another continent. He said that, 'in the case of Spanish and Portuguese America, similarity of languages is a mere screen for the profound divergences which exist between the different parts of that vast territory'. And this similarity itself was an illusion, because of the great variety of dialects. The same was true of religion. Christianity had undergone considerable modifications, and the former native religion had left its mark on the ceremonies of many churches. Nevertheless, language and religion together provided a foundation for cultural unity which was firm compared with the numerous differences in all other aspects of life (pp. 39–40). And yet Rivet was all too ready to offer generalizations about the United States, on whose cultures he was not to the same extent a specialist.

Time will not allow me to pursue this subject in any detail. It is not necessary for me to give you examples of the attempts that have been made to render one culture intelligible to the representatives of another. You are all familiar with many of them. It is obvious that any account which aims at the enlightenment of the educated public must make use of simplification and generalization. We know that works of this kind, written by professional social scientists, have had a great public success. But often, at the same time, they have been sharply criticized by the experts. And they may also be rejected by the lay reader belonging to the culture that is being described. Ruth Benedict's careful analysis of Japanese society,[11] and Geoffrey Gorer's vivid picture of life in the United States[12] have been attacked on both fronts.

From this we see that there are two pertinent questions to ask about the communication of understanding of foreign cultures. First: is this best done by a native of the culture described, or by a native of the culture to whom the communication is addressed? And secondly: is it best done by a sociologist or by somebody else?

I feel certain that, generally speaking, communication is best made by a member of the society to whom it is addressed. For understanding of the unfamiliar is most effectively conveyed by explicit, or even more by implicit, comparison or contrast with what is familiar.

More difficult to answer is the question whether the sociologist is the best agent for communication of this kind. I am inclined to believe that he usually is not. The very fact that the sociologist is trained to see social systems as wholes, and to use the results of analysis to arrive at a synthesis, constitutes a temptation to him, if he is asked to simplify down

[11] *The Chrysanthemum and the Sword.*
[12] *The American People, a Study in National Character* (1948).

to the level of the educated public, to try to do too much with too little. 'The study of national character', says Professor Ginsberg, 'is to be approached not through an investigation of individual differences in behaviour, but of the qualities manifested in the collective life of nations, their traditions and public policy.'[13] One reason why many attempts by sociologists (or anthropologists) to convey an understanding of national character have met with strong criticism is that they have not followed this advice. But even if they do, their troubles are not over. The 'collective life of nations, their traditions and public policy' are matters in which sociologists should feel completely at home, but when you begin to explain 'the qualities manifested' in them to the lay reader and the general public, then you must watch your step. It is all too easy to pick on one or two striking traits, and to make them explain everything. It is very probable that the historian, being by nature more modest in his attempts to explain (in the above sense), is better at communication. Perhaps the educated public can get a clearer understanding of traditional Chinese society from a Tawney[14] than from a Talcott Parsons.[15]

In fact it may be the case that a statement asserting that a particular attitude, mode of thought, or pattern of action is characteristic of a people may be most useful if no attempt is made to apply it. It may give a sudden insight into a strange and unfamiliar world, and thus open the mind to a true understanding of information about that world as it is gradually accumulated. The interpretation is not applied until, so to speak, the information clamours for it. The response is of the 'of course! now I remember!' kind, rather than the 'yes, I suppose I see what you mean' of the weary student who has had his nose well rubbed in a pet theory, or the 'how fascinating it all is!' of the credulous romantic.

Here are two examples of statements about the time-sense

[13] M. Ginsberg: 'National Character', *Reason and Unreason in Society* (1947), p. 154.

[14] R. H. Tawney: *Land and Labour in China* (1932).

[15] See *The Social System* (1952), Chapter 5, Sec. 3.

which happen to have come my way while I was preparing this lecture. A recent study of the adaptation of the Egyptian villager to urban life and industrial employment revealed that the first things he buys with his savings are a watch and a mirror. He becomes aware of time and anxious about his personal appearance. Discussion of this report led, however, to the tentative conclusion that what he had discovered about time was that you could identify fixed points within it at which certain things must be done. He knew what it meant to be on time, to be punctual. But he did not yet know what it meant to waste time. That involved an effort of abstraction which he could not yet make. Such was the hypothesis put forward.[16]

An anthropologist, in a report on a field study of a nomadic people in Persia, says, 'a breakdown of the migratory cycle in the two main dimensions of place and time is meaningless in the normal contexts of nomadic life; "March", as generally conceptualized by the nomadic herder, is a place, just as much as a season.' When he tried to get them to distinguish between the time of the year and the locality as possible causes of a luxuriant crop of truffles, he failed. 'My two alternatives were to them two ways of expressing the same experience.'[17] These are essentially sociological insights, and they are valuable, provided you do not try to make them explain too much.

But my answer to this question remains inconclusive. I am suggesting that the essential task of the sociologist is to provide the material for mutual understanding, and that he is not necessarily the best person to communicate this material to others. And that brings me back, in conclusion, to my first theme—international comprehension *in* the social sciences—the professional aspect of the subject. Because I am convinced that the proper execution of this task of collecting and arranging the material demands, in the contemporary world, close collaboration between the social scientists at the two ends of

[16] Hassan el Saaty: *Some Aspects of the Social Implications of Technological Change* (unpublished), p. 6.
[17] Frederik Barth: *Report on a Study of the Nomads in Iran* (unpublished).

the communication process. And from this follows, in turn, the need to internationalize the social sciences.

When I reflect on this situation, I find again and again that the difficulty with which we have to contend is that of persuading people that the best course is one that lies between two extremes. Such advice smacks of compromise, and compromise has won for itself a bad name in a world of conflicting ideals, a name which, perhaps on account of some defect in my nature, I cannot believe that it deserves.

One middle course which is relevant here is that between the extreme which denies all value to subjective insight, or intuition, and the other extreme which asserts that a sociologist cannot understand anything that he has not himself experienced. Subjective insight is sociology's great compensation for the disadvantage of dealing with a universe not composed of elements which, when isolated, are always found to have identical properties. But subjective insight is not in itself a sufficient source of information. It is an indispensable aid to scientific research. It needs to be harnessed to a discipline. So it would be madness for Western sociologists to deny the importance of the contribution that trained Asian sociologists can make, with the help of their insight, to the study of their own culture. On the other hand, it is equally inadmissible for Asian sociologists to deny the contribution that can be made to that same study by the objective scrutiny of the foreigner.

I would call this the middle path between introspection and positivism. My second example also relates, but in a different way, to the problem of sociological ethnocentrism. We might call it the middle path between universalism and regionalism. I have deliberately chosen to say 'regionalism' and not 'nationalism', because this is an outstanding phenomenon of today. As seen through the eyes of the European or North American, the world falls into a number of cultural regions, defined, not so much in terms of actual cultural homogeneity, but rather by reference to an overt assertion of cultural unity, which is operational and even institutional in character. And in some cases it continues to be so even though the cultural region may be split by acute political rivalries. The important regions are Latin America, Asia (but not quite the whole of it), the Arab States and Africa (essentially tropical Africa). Eastern Europe is not a region in this sense, since its dominating ideology claims to be universal.

In a region in which sociology is weak or relatively new, or in which it has not yet been intensively or extensively developed, but is now beginning to grow and spread, it is likely to be assumed that programmes of teaching and research should be focussed on the regional society itself, almost to the exclusion of everything else. This is natural and, up to a point, acceptable. But it can go too far. It may, as we have seen, encourage the idea that, because the regional society is 'different', therefore the regional sociology must be 'different' too. And that is dangerous. But it should be noted that, in many respects, the allegedly universal sociology practised in the more advanced countries strikes our regional friends as being in fact very parochial; and this is admitted by many of its practitioners, as they become conscious of their relative ignorance of the remoter areas of the world. That, no doubt, is why there is so much evidence today of a desire on the part of American and European sociologists to enrich their store of knowledge and understanding by turning their attention more seriously to such regions as Asia and Latin America.

The middle path, in this case, is the one which runs between an extreme regionalism, which holds that regional cultures must have their own regional sociologies, on the one side, and a rather blind universalism on the other, which imagines, with Tennyson, that a complete grasp of the nature of the flower in the crannied wall is sufficient to reveal what God and man is, or, in other words, that universal truth about the whole is to be found in any one of its parts.

At the moment I believe the chief need in sociology is for the deeper study of the differences which distinguish one culture from another. Such a development may be obstructed both by the search for universal concepts and laws (which in any case are liable, when found, to be somewhat jejune), and by the parochialism which rivets attention on the immediate neighbourhood. I want to see comparative studies, for example, of Europe and Asia in which both European and Asian sociologists collaborate, but not by each studying exclusively in his own culture, but by each studying both cultures. And if collaboration of this kind is to take place, there must be agreement as to what a sociological investigation really is; to this extent sociology must be internationalized.

My experience suggests that this kind of agreement cannot be reached by attacking the points at which the major conflicts of ideology exist. These, and the political conflicts associated with them, are the most stubborn aspects you can find. Basic theory, which is linked with ideology, may prove equally intractable. The most hopeful way of starting is by exchanging experience gained in the gathering of information needed for practical purposes, whether in relation to official social programmes or to the education of the citizen. The questions to be asked are: how do you find out the things that you need to know about your society? how do you explain its nature to your growing children and young people? and how do you deal with this or that social problem, and why? A similar conclusion was reached by those who were set the task of defining a body of universally acceptable human rights. Professor McKeon has noted that the search for 'eventual principles' led merely to the elaboration and to the strengthening of contradictory philosophies. 'On the other hand, no difficulty arose in the way of an agreement on a list of rights and on a plan designed to co-ordinate them.'[18]

But this method of procedure is only a means to an end. It does not solve the problem; it only prepares the ground for a solution, by increasing mutual understanding at a very practical level. The crucial point at which a real advance can be made towards an internationalized social science is the point at which data of this limited kind are fitted into a framework of concept and theory at the appropriate level of generalization. It is here that misunderstanding is most likely to yield to the forces of argument and to the free exchange of ideas, even in the present state of ideological division from which

[18] R. McKeon: *Human Rights—Comments and Interpretations* (1949), pp. 31–2.

the world is suffering. It is easy to see why many of those who devote themselves to the cause of peace and international co-operation should regard the social sciences as trouble-makers. For it would hardly be an exaggeration to say that the wars of religion have been succeeded by the wars of social doctrine. And social doctrines, everywhere today, are expounded and defended by what is believed to be social science. But this is no reason for denouncing social science as a source of discord. On the contrary. It is precisely because it is so deeply involved in the conflicts which are born 'in the minds of men' that it should have the power, if not quickly to resolve them, at least gradually to eat away the misconceptions and the misunderstandings from which so much of their strength is drawn.

It is the business of social science to investigate things in order to achieve true knowledge. Let us hope that the results of its efforts may be such as were described by Confucius, when he said:

> The achieving of true knowledge depends upon the investigation of things. When things are investigated, then true knowledge is achieved; when true knowledge is achieved, then the will becomes sincere; when the will is sincere, then the heart is set right (for then the mind sees right); when the heart is set right, then the personal life is cultivated; when the personal life is cultivated, then the family life is regulated; when the family life is regulated, then the national life is orderly; and when the national life is orderly, then there is peace in this world.[19]

[19] F. S. C. Northrop: *The Meeting of East and West* (1947).

PART TWO

SOCIAL CLASS

CHAPTER IV

CITIZENSHIP AND SOCIAL CLASS

The invitation to deliver these lectures[1] gave me both personal and professional pleasure. But, whereas my personal response was a sincere and modest appreciation of an honour I had no right to expect, my professional reaction was not modest at all. Sociology, it seemed to me, had every right to claim a share in this annual commemoration of Alfred Marshall, and I considered it a sign of grace that a University which has not yet accepted sociology as an inmate should nevertheless be prepared to welcome her as a visitor. It may be—and the thought is a disturbing one—that sociology is on trial here in my person. If so, I am sure I can rely on you to be scrupulously fair in your judgement, and to regard any merit you may find in my lectures as evidence of the academic value of the subject I profess, while treating everything in them that appears to you paltry, common or ill-conceived as the product of qualities peculiar to myself and not to be found in any of my colleagues.

I will not defend the relevance of my subject to the occasion by claiming Marshall as a sociologist. For, once he had deserted his first loves of metaphysics, ethics and psychology, he devoted his life to the development of economics as an independent science and to the perfection of its own special methods of investigation and analysis. He deliberately chose a path markedly different from that followed by Adam Smith and John Stuart Mill, and the mood in which he made this

[1] The Marshall Lectures, Cambridge 1949.

choice is indicated in the inaugural lecture which he delivered here in Cambridge in 1885. Speaking of Comte's belief in a unified social science, he said: 'No doubt if that
existed economics would gladly find shelter under its wing.
But it does not exist; it shows no signs of coming into existence. There is no use in waiting idly for it; we must do what
we can with our present resources.'[2] He therefore defended
the autonomy and the superiority of the economic method, a
superiority due mainly to its use of the measuring rod of
money, which 'is so much the best measure of motives that no
other can compete with it'.[3]

Marshall was, as you know, an idealist; so much so that
Keynes has said of him that he 'was too anxious to do good'.[4]
The last thing I wish to do is to claim him for sociology on
that account. It is true that some sociologists have suffered
from a similar affliction of benevolence, often to the detriment
of their intellectual performance, but I should hate to distinguish the economist from the sociologist by saying that
the one should be ruled by his head while the other may
be swayed by his heart. For every honest sociologist, like
every honest economist, knows that the choice of ends or
ideals lies outside the field of social science and within the
field of social philosophy. But idealism made Marshall passionately eager to put the science of economics at the service
of policy by using it—as a science may legitimately be used—
to lay bare the full nature and content of the problems with
which policy has to deal and to assess the relative efficacy of
alternative means for the achievement of given ends. And
he realized that, even in the case of what would naturally be
regarded as economic problems, the science of economics was
not of itself able fully to render these two services. For they
involved the consideration of social forces which are as im-
mune to attack by the economist's tape-measure as was the
croquet ball to the blows which Alice tried in vain to strike
with the head of her flamingo. It was, perhaps, on this ac-

[2] *Memorials of Alfred Marshall*, ed. A. C. Pigou, p. 164.
[3] ibid., p. 158.
[4] ibid., p. 37.

count that, in certain moods, Marshall felt a quite unwarranted disappointment at his achievements, and even expressed regret that he had preferred economics to psychology, a science which might have brought him nearer to the pulse and life-blood of society and given him a deeper understanding of human aspirations.

It would be easy to cite many passages in which Marshall was drawn to speak of these elusive factors of whose importance he was so firmly convinced, but I prefer to confine my attention to one essay whose theme comes very near to that which I have chosen for these lectures. It is a paper he read to the Cambridge Reform Club in 1873 on *The Future of the Working Classes,* and it has been republished in the memorial volume edited by Professor Pigou. There are some textual differences between the two editions which, I understand, are to be attributed to corrections made by Marshall himself after the original version had appeared in print as a pamphlet.[5] I was reminded of this essay by my colleague, Professor Phelps Brown, who made use of it in his inaugural lecture last November.[6] It is equally well suited to my purpose today, because in it Marshall, while examining one facet of the problem of social equality from the point of view of economic cost, came right up to the frontier beyond which lies the territory of sociology, crossed it, and made a brief excursion on the other side. His action could be interpreted as a challenge to sociology to send an emissary to meet him at the frontier, and to join with him in the task of converting no-man's-land into common ground. I have been presumptuous enough to answer the challenge by setting out to travel, as historian and sociologist, towards a point on the economic frontier of that same general theme, the problem of social equality.

In his Cambridge paper Marshall posed the question 'whether there be valid ground for the opinion that the

5 Privately printed by Thomas Tofts. The page references are to this edition.

6 Published under the title 'Prospects of Labour' in *Economica,* February, 1949.

amelioration of the working classes has limits beyond which it cannot pass'. 'The question', he said, 'is not whether all men will ultimately be equal—that they certainly will not— but whether progress may not go on steadily, if slowly, till, by occupation at least, every man is a gentleman. I hold that it may, and that it will.'[7] His faith was based on the belief that the distinguishing feature of the working classes was heavy and excessive labour, and that the volume of such labour could be greatly reduced. Looking round he found evidence that the skilled artisans, whose labour was not deadening and soul-destroying, were already rising towards the condition which he foresaw as the ultimate achievement of all. They are learning, he said, to value education and leisure more than 'mere increase of wages and material comforts'. They are 'steadily developing independence and a manly respect for themselves and, therefore, a courteous respect for others; they are steadily accepting the private and public duties of a citizen; steadily increasing their grasp of the truth that they are men, and not producing machines. They are steadily becoming gentlemen.'[8] When technical advance has reduced heavy labour to a minimum, and that minimum is divided in small amounts among all, then, 'in so far as the working classes are men who have such excessive work to do, in so far will the working classes have been abolished.'[9]

Marshall realized that he might be accused of adopting the ideas of the socialists, whose works, as he has himself told us, he had, during this period of his life, been studying with great hopes and with greater disappointment. For, he said: 'The picture to be drawn will resemble in some respects those which have been shown to us by the Socialists, that noble set of untutored enthusiasts who attributed to all men an unlimited capacity for those self-forgetting virtues that they found in their own breasts.'[10] His reply was that

[7] op. cit., pp. 3 and 4.
[8] *The Future of the Working Classes*, p. 6.
[9] ibid., p. 16.
[10] ibid., p. 9. The revised version of this passage is significantly different. It runs: 'The picture to be drawn will resemble in many

his system differed fundamentally from socialism in that it would preserve the essentials of a free market. He held, however, that the State would have to make some use of its power of compulsion, if his ideals were to be realized. It must compel children to go to school, because the uneducated cannot appreciate, and therefore freely choose, the good things which distinguish the life of gentlemen from that of the working classes. 'It is bound to compel them and to help them to take the first step upwards; and it is bound to help them, if they will, to make many steps upwards.'[11] Notice that only the first step is compulsory. Free choice takes over as soon as the capacity to choose has been created.

Marshall's paper was built round a sociological hypothesis and an economic calculation. The calculation provided the answer to his initial question, by showing that world resources and productivity might be expected to prove sufficient to provide the material bases needed to enable every man to be a gentleman. In other words, the cost of providing education for all and of eliminating heavy and excessive labour could be met. There was no impassable limit to the amelioration of the working classes—at least on this side of the point that Marshall described as the goal. In working out these sums Marshall was using the ordinary techniques of the economist, though admittedly he was applying them to a problem which involved a high degree of speculation.

The sociological hypothesis does not lie so completely on the surface. A little excavation is needed to uncover its total shape. The essence of it is contained in the passages I have quoted, but Marshall gives us an additional clue by suggesting that, when we say a man belongs to the working classes, 'we are thinking of the effect that his work produces on him rather than the effect that he produces on his work'.[12] This

---

respects those which have been shown to us by some socialists, who attributed to all men . . .' etc. The condemnation is less sweeping and Marshall no longer speaks of the Socialists, *en masse* and with a capital 'S', in the past tense. *Memorials*, p. 109.

[11] ibid., p. 15.

[12] ibid., p. 5.

is certainly not the sort of definition we should expect from an economist, and, in fact, it would hardly be fair to treat it as a definition at all or to subject it to close and critical examination. The phrase was intended to catch the imagination, and to point to the general direction in which Marshall's thoughts were moving. And that direction was away from a quantitative assessment of standards of living in terms of goods consumed and services enjoyed towards a qualitative assessment of life as a whole in terms of the essential elements in civilization or culture. He accepted as right and proper a wide range of quantitative or economic inequality, but condemned the qualitative inequality or difference between the man who was, 'by occupation at least, a gentleman' and the man who was not. We can, I think, without doing violence to Marshall's meaning, replace the word 'gentleman' by the word 'civilized'. For it is clear that he was taking as the standard of civilized life the conditions regarded by his generation as appropriate to a gentleman. We can go on to say that the claim of all to enjoy these conditions is a claim to be admitted to a share in the social heritage, which in turn means a claim to be accepted as full members of the society, that is, as citizens.

Such, I think, is the sociological hypothesis latent in Marshall's essay. It postulates that there is a kind of basic human equality associated with the concept of full membership of a community—or, as I should say, of citizenship—which is not inconsistent with the inequalities which distinguish the various economic levels in the society. In other words, the inequality of the social class system may be acceptable provided the equality of citizenship is recognized. Marshall did not identify the life of a gentleman with the status of citizenship. To do so would have been to express his ideal in terms of legal rights to which all men were entitled. That, in turn, would have put the responsibility for granting those rights fair and square on the shoulders of the State, and so led, step by step, to acts of State interference which he would have deplored. When he mentioned citizenship as something which skilled artisans learned to appreciate in the course of developing into gentlemen, he mentioned only its duties and not its rights. He thought of it as a way of life growing within a man, not presented to him from without. He recognized only one definite right, the right of children to be educated, and in this case alone did he approve the use of compulsory powers by the State to achieve his object. He could hardly go further without imperilling his own criterion for distinguishing his system from socialism in any form—the preservation of the freedom of the competitive market.

Nevertheless, his sociological hypothesis lies as near to the heart of our problem today as it did three-quarters of a century ago—in fact nearer. The basic human equality of membership, at which I maintain that he hinted, has been enriched with new substance and invested with a formidable array of rights. It has developed far beyond what he foresaw, or would have wished. It has been clearly identified with the status of citizenship. And it is time we examined his hypothesis and posed his questions afresh, to see if the answers are still the same. Is it still true that basic equality, when enriched in substance and embodied in the formal rights of citizenship, is consistent with the inequalities of social class? I shall suggest that our society today assumes that the two are still compatible, so much so that citizenship has itself become, in certain respects, the architect of legitimate social inequality. Is it still true that the basic equality can be created and preserved without invading the freedom of the competitive market? Obviously it is not true. Our modern system is frankly a Socialist system, not one whose authors are, as Marshall was, eager to distinguish it from socialism. But it is equally obvious that the market still functions—within limits. Here is another possible conflict of principles which demands examination. And thirdly, what is the effect of the marked shift of emphasis from duties to rights? Is this an inevitable feature of modern citizenship—inevitable and irreversible? Finally, I want to put Marshall's initial question again in a new form. He asked if there were limits beyond which the amelioration of the working classes could not pass, and he was thinking of limits set by natural resources and

productivity. I shall ask whether there appear to be limits
beyond which the modern drive towards social equality cannot, or is unlikely to, pass, and I shall be thinking, not of the
economic cost (I leave that vital question to the economists),
but of the limits inherent in the principles that inspire the
drive. But the modern drive towards social equality is, I believe, the latest phase of an evolution of citizenship which
has been in continuous progress for some 250 years. My first
task, therefore, must be to prepare the ground for an attack
on the problems of today by digging for a while in the sub-
soil of past history.

The Development of Citizenship to the End of the Nineteenth Century

I shall be running true to type as a sociologist if I begin by
saying that I propose to divide citizenship into three parts.
But the analysis is, in this case, dictated by history even more
clearly than by logic. I shall call these three parts, or elements,
civil, political and social. The civil element is composed of
the rights necessary for individual freedom—liberty of the person, freedom of speech, thought and faith, the right to own
property and to conclude valid contracts, and the right to
justice. The last is of a different order from the others, because it is the right to defend and assert all one's rights on
terms of equality with others and by due process of law. This
shows us that the institutions most directly associated with
civil rights are the courts of justice. By the political element
I mean the right to participate in the exercise of political
power, as a member of a body invested with political authority or as an elector of the members of such a body. The corresponding institutions are parliament and councils of local
government. By the social element I mean the whole range
from the right to a modicum of economic welfare and security
to the right to share to the full in the social heritage and to
live the life of a civilized being according to the standards
prevailing in the society. The institutions most closely con-

nected with it are the educational system and the social services.[13]

In early times these three strands were wound into a single thread. The rights were blended because the institutions were amalgamated. As Maitland said: 'The further back we trace our history the more impossible it is for us to draw strict lines of demarcation between the various functions of the State: the same institution is a legislative assembly, a governmental council and a court of law . . . Everywhere, as we pass from the ancient to the modern, we see what the fashionable philosophy calls differentiation.'[14] Maitland is speaking here of the fusion of political and civil institutions and rights. But a man's social rights, too, were part of the same amalgam, and derived from the status which also determined the kind of justice he could get and where he could get it, and the way in which he could take part in the administration of the affairs of the community of which he was a member. But this status was not one of citizenship in our modern sense. In feudal society status was the hall-mark of class and the measure of inequality. There was no uniform collection of rights and duties with which all men—noble and common, free and serf —were endowed by virtue of their membership of the society. There was, in this sense, no principle of the equality of citizens to set against the principle of the inequality of classes. In the medieval towns, on the other hand, examples of genuine and equal citizenship can be found. But its specific rights and duties were strictly local, whereas the citizenship whose history I wish to trace is, by definition, national.

Its evolution involved a double process, of fusion and of separation. The fusion was geographical, the separation functional. The first important step dates from the twelfth century, when royal justice was established with effective power to define and defend the civil rights of the individual—such

[13] By this terminology, what economists sometimes call 'income from civil rights' would be called 'income from social rights'. Cf. H. Dalton: *Some Aspects of the Inequality of Incomes in Modern Communities*, Part 3, Chapters 3 and 4.
[14] F. Maitland: *Constitutional History of England*, p. 105.

as they then were—on the basis, not of local custom, but of the common law of the land. As institutions the courts were national, but specialized. Parliament followed, concentrating in itself the political powers of national government and shedding all but a small residue of the judicial functions which formerly belonged to the Curia Regis, that 'sort of constitutional protoplasm out of which will in time be evolved the various councils of the crown, the houses of parliament, and the courts of law'.[15] Finally, the social rights which had been rooted in membership of the village community, the town and the gild, were gradually dissolved by economic change until nothing remained but the Poor Law, again a specialized institution which acquired a national foundation, although it continued to be locally administered.

Two important consequences followed. First, when the institutions on which the three elements of citizenship depended parted company, it became possible for each to go its separate way, travelling at its own speed under the direction of its own peculiar principles. Before long they were spread far out along the course, and it is only in the present century, in fact I might say only within the last few months, that the three runners have come abreast of one another.

Secondly, institutions that were national and specialized could not belong so intimately to the life of the social groups they served as those that were local and of a general character. The remoteness of parliament was due to the mere size of its constituency; the remoteness of the courts, to the technicalities of their law and their procedure, which made it necessary for the citizen to employ legal experts to advise him as to the nature of his rights and to help him to obtain them. It has been pointed out again and again that, in the Middle Ages, participation in public affairs was more a duty than a right. Men owed suit and service to the court appropriate to their class and neighbourhood. The court belonged to them and they to it, and they had access to it because it needed them and because they had knowledge of its affairs. But the result of the twin process of fusion and separation was that the

[15] A. F. Pollard: *Evolution of Parliament*, p. 25.

machinery giving access to the institutions on which the rights of citizenship depended had to be shaped afresh. In the case of political rights the story is the familiar one of the franchise and the qualifications for membership of parliament. In the case of civil rights the issue hangs on the jurisdiction of the various courts, the privileges of the legal profession, and above all on the liability to meet the costs of litigation. In the case of social rights the centre of the stage is occupied by the Law of Settlement and Removal and the various forms of means test. All this apparatus combined to decide, not merely what rights were recognized in principle, but also to what extent rights recognized in principle could be enjoyed in practice.

When the three elements of citizenship parted company, they were soon barely on speaking terms. So complete was the divorce between them that it is possible, without doing too much violence to historical accuracy, to assign the formative period in the life of each to a different century—civil rights to the eighteenth, political to the nineteenth and social to the twentieth. These periods must, of course, be treated with reasonable elasticity, and there is some evident overlap, especially between the last two.

To make the eighteenth century cover the formative period of civil rights it must be stretched backwards to include Habeas Corpus, the Toleration Act, and the abolition of the censorship of the press; and it must be extended forwards to include Catholic Emancipation, the repeal of the Combination Acts, and the successful end of the battle for the freedom of the press associated with the names of Cobbett and Richard Carlile. It could then be more accurately, but less briefly, described as the period between the Revolution and the first Reform Act. By the end of that period, when political rights made their first infantile attempt to walk in 1832, civil rights had come to man's estate and bore, in most essentials, the appearance that they have today.[16] 'The specific work of

16 The most important exception is the right to strike, but the conditions which made this right vital for the workman and acceptable to political opinion had not yet fully come into being.

the earlier Hanoverian epoch', writes Trevelyan, 'was the establishment of the rule of law; and that law, with all its grave faults, was at least a law of freedom. On that solid foundation all our subsequent reforms were built.'[17] This eighteenth-century achievement, interrupted by the French Revolution and completed after it, was in large measure the work of the courts, both in their daily practice and also in a series of famous cases in some of which they were fighting against parliament in defence of individual liberty. The most celebrated actor in this drama was, I suppose, John Wilkes, and, although we may deplore the absence in him of those noble and saintly qualities which we should like to find in our national heroes, we cannot complain if the cause of liberty is sometimes championed by a libertine.

In the economic field the basic civil right is the right to work, that is to say the right to follow the occupation of one's choice in the place of one's choice, subject only to legitimate demands for preliminary technical training. This right had been denied by both statute and custom; on the one hand by the Elizabethan Statute of Artificers, which confined certain occupations to certain social classes, and on the other by local regulations reserving employment in a town to its own members and by the use of apprenticeship as an instrument of exclusion rather than of recruitment. The recognition of the right involved the formal acceptance of a fundamental change of attitude. The old assumption that local and group monopolies were in the public interest, because 'trade and traffic cannot be maintained or increased without order and government',[18] was replaced by the new assumption that such restrictions were an offence against the liberty of the subject and a menace to the prosperity of the nation. As in the case of the other civil rights, the courts of law played a decisive part in promoting and registering the advance of the new principle. The Common Law was elastic enough for the

[17] G. M. Trevelyan: *English Social History*, p. 351.
[18] City of London Case, 1610. See E. F. Heckscher: *Mercantilism*, Vol. I, pp. 269–325, where the whole story is told in considerable detail.

judges to apply it in a manner which, almost imperceptibly, took account of gradual changes in circumstances and opinion and eventually installed the heresy of the past as the orthodoxy of the present. The Common Law is largely a matter of common sense, as witness the judgement given by Chief Justice Holt in the case of Mayor of Winton v. Wilks (1705): 'All people are at liberty to live in Winchester, and how can they be restrained from using the lawful means of living there? Such a custom is an injury to the party and a prejudice to the public.'[19] Custom was one of the two great obstacles to the change. But, when ancient custom in the technical sense was clearly at variance with contemporary custom in the sense of the generally accepted way of life, its defences began to crumble fairly rapidly before the attacks of a Common Law which had, as early as 1614, expressed its abhorrence of 'all monopolies which prohibit any from working in any lawful trade'.[20] The other obstacle was statute law, and the judges struck some shrewd blows even against this doughty opponent. In 1756 Lord Mansfield described the Elizabethan Statute of Artificers as a penal law, in restraint of natural right and contrary to the Common Law of the kingdom. He added that 'the policy upon which the Act was made is, from experience, become doubtful'.[21]

By the beginning of the nineteenth century this principle of individual economic freedom was accepted as axiomatic. You are probably familiar with the passage quoted by the Webbs from the report of the Select Committee of 1811, which states that:

no interference of the legislature with the freedom of trade, or with the perfect liberty of every individual to dispose of his time and of his labour in the way and on the terms which he may judge most conducive to his own interest, can take place without violating general princi-

[19] *King's Bench Reports* (Holt), p. 1002.
[20] Heckscher, op. cit., Vol. I, p. 283.
[21] ibid., p. 316.

ples of the first importance to the prosperity and happiness of the community.[22]

The repeal of the Elizabethan statutes followed quickly, as the belated recognition of a revolution which had already taken place.

The story of civil rights in their formative period is one of the gradual addition of new rights to a status that already existed and was held to appertain to all adult members of the community—or perhaps one should say to all male members, since the status of women, or at least of married women, was in some important respects peculiar. This democratic, or universal, character of the status arose naturally from the fact that it was essentially the status of freedom, and in seventeenth-century England all men were free. Servile status, or villeinage by blood, had lingered on as a patent anachronism in the days of Elizabeth, but vanished soon afterwards. This change from servile to free labour has been described by Professor Tawney as 'a high landmark in the development both of economic and political society', and as 'the final triumph of the common law' in regions from which it had been excluded for four centuries. Henceforth the English peasant 'is a member of a society in which there is, nominally at least, one law for all men'.[23] The liberty which his predecessors had won by fleeing into the free towns had become his by right. In the towns the terms 'freedom' and 'citizenship' were interchangeable. When freedom became universal, citizenship grew from a local into a national institution.

The story of political rights is different both in time and in character. The formative period began, as I have said, in the early nineteenth century, when the civil rights attached to the status of freedom had already acquired sufficient substance to justify us in speaking of a general status of citizenship. And, when it began, it consisted, not in the creation of

[22] Sidney and Beatrice Webb: *History of Trade Unionism* (1920), p. 60.
[23] R. H. Tawney: *Agrarian Problem in the Sixteenth Century* (1916), pp. 43–4.

new rights to enrich a status already enjoyed by all, but in the granting of old rights to new sections of the population. In the eighteenth century political rights were defective, not in content, but in distribution—defective, that is to say, by the standards of democratic citizenship. The Act of 1832 did little, in a purely quantitative sense, to remedy that defect. After it was passed the voters still amounted to less than one-fifth of the adult male population. The franchise was still a group monopoly, but it had taken the first step towards becoming a monopoly of a kind acceptable to the ideas of nineteenth-century capitalism—a monopoly which could, with some degree of plausibility, be described as open and not closed. A closed group monopoly is one into which no man can force his way by his own efforts; admission is at the pleasure of the existing members of the group. The description fits a considerable part of the borough franchise before 1832; and it is not too wide of the mark when applied to the franchise based on freehold ownership of land. Freeholds are not always to be had for the asking, even if one has the money to buy them, especially in an age in which families look on their lands as the social, as well as the economic, foundation of their existence. Therefore the Act of 1832, by abolishing rotten boroughs and by extending the franchise to leaseholders and occupying tenants of sufficient economic substance, opened the monopoly by recognizing the political claims of those who could produce the normal evidence of success in the economic struggle.

It is clear that, if we maintain that in the nineteenth century citizenship in the form of civil rights was universal, the political franchise was not one of the rights of citizenship. It was the privilege of a limited economic class, whose limits were extended by each successive Reform Act. It can nevertheless be argued that citizenship in this period was not politically meaningless. It did not confer a right, but it recognized a capacity. No sane and law-abiding citizen was debarred by personal status from acquiring and recording a vote. He was free to earn, to save, to buy property or to rent a house, and to enjoy whatever political rights were attached to these economic achievements. His civil rights entitled him, and electoral reform increasingly enabled him, to do this.

It was, as we shall see, appropriate that nineteenth-century capitalist society should treat political rights as a secondary product of civil rights. It was equally appropriate that the twentieth century should abandon this position and attach political rights directly and independently to citizenship as such. This vital change of principle was put into effect when the Act of 1918, by adopting manhood suffrage, shifted the basis of political rights from economic substance to personal status. I say 'manhood' deliberately in order to emphasize the great significance of this reform quite apart from the second, and no less important, reform introduced at the same time—namely the enfranchisement of women. But the Act of 1918 did not fully establish the political equality of all in terms of the rights of citizenship. Remnants of an inequality based on differences of economic substance lingered on until, only last year, plural voting (which had already been reduced to dual voting) was finally abolished.

When I assigned the formative periods of the three elements of citizenship each to a separate century—civil rights to the eighteenth, political to the nineteenth and social to the twentieth—I said that there was a considerable overlap between the last two. I propose to confine what I have to say now about social rights to this overlap, in order that I may complete my historical survey to the end of the nineteenth century, and draw my conclusions from it, before turning my attention to the second half of my subject, a study of our present experiences and their immediate antecedents. In this second act of the drama social rights will occupy the centre of the stage.

The original source of social rights was membership of local communities and functional associations. This source was supplemented and progressively replaced by a Poor Law and a system of wage regulation which were nationally conceived and locally administered. The latter—the system of wage regulation—was rapidly decaying in the eighteenth century, not only because industrial change made it administratively impossible, but also because it was incompatible with the new conception of civil rights in the economic sphere, with its emphasis on the right to work where and at what you pleased under a contract of your own making. Wage regulation infringed this individualist principle of the free contract of employment.

The Poor Law was in a somewhat ambiguous position. Elizabethan legislation had made of it something more than a means for relieving destitution and suppressing vagrancy, and its constructive aims suggested an interpretation of social welfare reminiscent of the more primitive, but more genuine, social rights which it had largely superseded. The Elizabethan Poor Law was, after all, one item in a broad programme of economic planning whose general object was, not to create a new social order, but to preserve the existing one with the minimum of essential change. As the pattern of the old order dissolved under the blows of a competitive economy, and the plan disintegrated, the Poor Law was left high and dry as an isolated survival from which the idea of social rights was gradually drained away. But at the very end of the eighteenth century there occurred a final struggle between the old and the new, between the planned (or patterned) society and the competitive economy. And in this battle citizenship was divided against itself; social rights sided with the old and civil with the new.

In his book *Origins of Our Time*, Karl Polanyi attributes to the Speenhamland system of poor relief an importance which some readers may find surprising. To him it seems to mark and symbolize the end of an epoch. Through it the old order rallied its retreating forces and delivered a spirited attack into the enemy's country. That, at least, is how I should describe its significance in the history of citizenship. The Speenhamland system offered, in effect, a guaranteed minimum wage and family allowances, combined with the right to work or maintenance. That, even by modern standards, is a substantial body of social rights, going far beyond what one might regard as the proper province of the Poor Law. And it was fully realized by the originators of the scheme that the Poor Law was being invoked to do what wage regulation was no longer able to accomplish. For the Poor Law was the last remains of a system which tried to adjust real income to the social needs and status of the citizen and not solely to the market value of his labour. But this attempt to inject an element of social security into the very structure of the wage system through the instrumentality of the Poor Law was doomed to failure, not only because of its disastrous practical consequences, but also because it was utterly obnoxious to the prevailing spirit of the times.

In this brief episode of our history we see the Poor Law as the aggressive champion of the social rights of citizenship. In the succeeding phase we find the attacker driven back far behind his original position. By the Act of 1834 the Poor Law renounced all claim to trespass on the territory of the wages system, or to interfere with the forces of the free market. It offered relief only to those who, through age or sickness, were incapable of continuing the battle, and to those other weaklings who gave up the struggle, admitted defeat, and cried for mercy. The tentative move towards the concept of social security was reversed. But more than that, the minimal social rights that remained were detached from the status of citizenship. The Poor Law treated the claims of the poor, not as an integral part of the rights of the citizen, but as an alternative to them—as claims which could be met only if the claimants ceased to be citizens in any true sense of the word. For paupers forfeited in practice the civil right of personal liberty, by internment in the workhouse, and they forfeited by law any political rights they might possess. This disability of defranchisement remained in being until 1918, and the significance of its final removal has, perhaps, not been fully appreciated. The stigma which clung to poor relief expressed the deep feelings of a people who understood that those who accepted relief must cross the road that separated the community of citizens from the outcast company of the destitute.

The Poor Law is not an isolated example of this divorce of social rights from the status of citizenship. The early Factory Acts show the same tendency. Although in fact they led to an improvement of working conditions and a reduction of working hours to the benefit of all employed in the industries to which they applied, they meticulously refrained from giving this protection directly to the adult male—the citizen *par excellence*. And they did so out of respect for his status as a citizen, on the grounds that enforced protective measures curtailed the civil right to conclude a free contract of employment. Protection was confined to women and children, and champions of women's rights were quick to detect the implied insult. Women were protected because they were not citizens. If they wished to enjoy full and responsible citizenship, they must forgo protection. By the end of the nineteenth century such arguments had become obsolete, and the factory code had become one of the pillars in the edifice of social rights.

The history of education shows superficial resemblances to that of factory legislation. In both cases the nineteenth century was, for the most part, a period in which the foundations of social rights were laid, but the principle of social rights as an integral part of the status of citizenship was either expressly denied or not definitely admitted. But there are significant differences. Education, as Marshall recognized when he singled it out as a fit object of State action, is a service of a unique kind. It is easy to say that the recognition of the right of children to be educated does not affect the status of citizenship any more than does the recognition of the right of children to be protected from overwork and dangerous machinery, simply because children, by definition, cannot be citizens. But such a statement is misleading. The education of children has a direct bearing on citizenship, and, when the State guarantees that all children shall be educated, it has the requirements and the nature of citizenship definitely in mind. It is trying to stimulate the growth of citizens in the making. The right to education is a genuine social right of citizenship, because the aim of education during childhood is to shape the future adult. Fundamentally it should be regarded, not as the right of the child to go to school, but as the right of the adult citizen to have been educated. And there is here no conflict with civil rights as interpreted in an age of individualism. For civil rights are designed for use by reasonable and intelligent persons, who have learned to read and write. Education is a necessary prerequisite of civil freedom.

But, by the end of the nineteenth century, elementary education was not only free, it was compulsory. This signal departure from *laissez faire* could, of course, be justified on the grounds that free choice is a right only for mature minds, that children are naturally subject to discipline, and that parents cannot be trusted to do what is in the best interests of their children. But the principle goes deeper than that. We have here a personal right combined with a public duty to exercise the right. Is the public duty imposed merely for the benefit of the individual—because children cannot fully appreciate their own interests and parents may be unfit to enlighten them? I hardly think that this can be an adequate explanation. It was increasingly recognized, as the nineteenth century wore on, that political democracy needed an educated electorate, and that scientific manufacture needed educated workers and technicians. The duty to improve and civilize oneself is therefore a social duty, and not merely a personal one, because the social health of a society depends upon the civilization of its members. And a community that enforces this duty has begun to realize that its culture is an organic unity and its civilization a national heritage. It follows that the growth of public elementary education during the nineteenth century was the first decisive step on the road to the re-establishment of the social rights of citizenship in the twentieth.

When Marshall read his paper to the Cambridge Reform Club, the State was just preparing to shoulder the responsibility he attributed to it when he said that it was 'bound to compel them (the children) and help them to take the first step upwards'. But this would not go far towards realizing his ideal of making every man a gentleman, nor was that in the least the intention. And as yet there was little sign of any desire 'to help them, if they will, to make many steps upwards'. The idea was in the air, but it was not a cardinal point of policy. In the early nineties the L.C.C., through its Technical Education Board, instituted a scholarship system which Beatrice Webb obviously regarded as epoch-making. For she wrote of it:

> In its popular aspect this was an educational ladder of unprecedented dimensions. It was, indeed, among educational ladders the most gigantic in extent, the most elaborate in its organization of 'intakes' and promotions, and the most diversified in kinds of excellence selected and in types of training provided that existed anywhere in the world.[24]

The enthusiasm of these words enables us to see how far we have advanced our standards since those days.

The Early Impact of Citizenship on Social Class

So far my aim has been to trace in outline the development of citizenship in England to the end of the nineteenth century. For this purpose I have divided citizenship into three elements, civil, political and social. I have tried to show that civil rights came first, and were established in something like their modern form before the first Reform Act was passed in 1832. Political rights came next, and their extension was one of the main features of the nineteenth century, although the principle of universal political citizenship was not recognized until 1918. Social rights, on the other hand, sank to vanishing point in the eighteenth and early nineteenth centuries. Their revival began with the development of public elementary education, but it was not until the twentieth century that they attained to equal partnership with the other two elements in citizenship.

I have as yet said nothing about social class, and I should explain here that social class occupies a secondary position in my theme. I do not propose to embark on the long and diffi-

[24] *Our Partnership*, p. 79.

cult task of examining its nature and analysing its components. Time would not allow me to do justice to so formidable a subject. My primary concern is with citizenship, and my special interest is in its impact on social inequality. I shall discuss the nature of social class only so far as is necessary for the pursuit of this special interest. I have paused in the narrative at the end of the nineteenth century because I believe that the impact of citizenship on social inequality after that date was fundamentally different from what it had been before it. That statement is not likely to be disputed. It is the exact nature of the difference that is worth exploring. Before going any further, therefore, I shall try to draw some general conclusions about the impact of citizenship on social inequality in the earlier of the two periods.

Citizenship is a status bestowed on those who are full members of a community. All who possess the status are equal with respect to the rights and duties with which the status is endowed. There is no universal principle that determines what those rights and duties shall be, but societies in which citizenship is a developing institution create an image of an ideal citizenship against which achievement can be measured and towards which aspiration can be directed. The urge forward along the path thus plotted is an urge towards a fuller measure of equality, an enrichment of the stuff of which the status is made and an increase in the number of those on whom the status is bestowed. Social class, on the other hand, is a system of inequality. And it too, like citizenship, can be based on a set of ideals, beliefs and values. It is therefore reasonable to expect that the impact of citizenship on social class should take the form of a conflict between opposing principles. If I am right in my contention that citizenship has been a developing institution in England at least since the latter part of the seventeenth century, then it is clear that its growth coincides with the rise of capitalism, which is a system, not of equality, but of inequality. Here is something that needs explaining. How is it that these two opposing principles could grow and flourish side by side in the same soil? What made it possible for them to be reconciled with one another and to become, for a time at least, allies instead of antagonists? The question is a pertinent one, for it is clear that, in the twentieth century, citizenship and the capitalist class system have been at war.

It is at this point that a closer scrutiny of social class becomes necessary. I cannot attempt to examine all its many and varied forms, but there is one broad distinction between two different types of class which is particularly relevant to my argument. In the first of these class is based on a hierarchy of status, and the difference between one class and another is expressed in terms of legal rights and of established customs which have the essential binding character of law. In its extreme form such a system divides a society into a number of distinct, hereditary human species—patricians, plebeians, serfs, slaves and so forth. Class is, as it were, an institution in its own right, and the whole structure has the quality of a plan, in the sense that it is endowed with meaning and purpose and accepted as a natural order. The civilization at each level is an expression of this meaning and of this natural order, and differences between social levels are not differences in standard of living, because there is no common standard by which they can be measured. Nor are there any rights— at least none of any significance—which all share in common.[25] The impact of citizenship on such a system was bound to be profoundly disturbing, and even destructive. The rights with which the general status of citizenship was invested were extracted from the hierarchical status system of social class, robbing it of its essential substance. The equality implicit in the concept of citizenship, even though limited in content, undermined the inequality of the class system, which was in principle a total inequality. National justice and a law common to all must inevitably weaken and eventually destroy class justice, and personal freedom, as a universal birthright, must drive out serfdom. No subtle argument is needed to show that citizenship is incompatible with medieval feudalism.

[25] See the admirable characterization given by R. H. Tawney in *Equality*, pp. 121–2.

Social class of the second type is not so much an institution in its own right as a by-product of other institutions. Although we may still refer to 'social status', we are stretching the term beyond its strict technical meaning when we do so. Class differences are not established and defined by the laws and customs of the society (in the medieval sense of that phrase), but emerge from the interplay of a variety of factors related to the institutions of property and education and the structure of the national economy. Class cultures dwindle to a minimum, so that it becomes possible, though admittedly not wholly satisfactory, to measure the different levels of economic welfare by reference to a common standard of living. The working classes, instead of inheriting a distinctive though simple culture, are provided with a cheap and shoddy imitation of a civilization that has become national.

It is true that class still functions. Social inequality is regarded as necessary and purposeful. It provides the incentive to effort and designs the distribution of power. But there is no over-all pattern of inequality, in which an appropriate value is attached, *a priori*, to each social level. Inequality therefore, though necessary, may become excessive. As Patrick Colquhoun said, in a much-quoted passage: 'Without a large proportion of poverty there could be no riches, since riches are the offspring of labour, while labour can result only from a state of poverty. . . . Poverty therefore is a most necessary and indispensable ingredient in society, without which nations and communities could not exist in a state of civilization.'[26] But Colquhoun, while accepting poverty, deplored 'indigence', or, as we should say, destitution. By 'poverty' he meant the situation of a man who, owing to lack of any economic reserves, is obliged to work, and to work hard, in order to live. By 'indigence' he meant the situation of a family which lacks the minimum necessary for decent living. The system of inequality which allowed the former to exist as a driving force inevitably produced a certain amount of the latter as well. Colquhoun, and other humanitarians, regretted

[26] A *Treatise on Indigence* (1806), pp. 7–8.

this and sought means to alleviate the suffering it caused. But they did not question the justice of the system of inequality as a whole. It could be argued, in defence of its justice, that, although poverty might be necessary, it was not necessary that any particular family should remain poor, or quite as poor as it was. The more you look on wealth as conclusive proof of merit, the more you incline to regard poverty as evidence of failure—but the penalty for failure may seem to be greater than the offence warrants. In such circumstances it is natural that the more unpleasant features of inequality should be treated, rather irresponsibly, as a nuisance, like the black smoke that used to pour unchecked from our factory chimneys. And so in time, as the social conscience stirs to life, class-abatement, like smoke-abatement, becomes a desirable aim to be pursued as far as is compatible with the continued efficiency of the social machine.

But class-abatement in this form was not an attack on the class system. On the contrary it aimed, often quite consciously, at making the class system less vulnerable to attack by alleviating its less defensible consequences. It raised the floor-level in the basement of the social edifice, and perhaps made it rather more hygienic than it was before. But it remained a basement, and the upper stories of the building were unaffected. And the benefits received by the unfortunate did not flow from an enrichment of the status of citizenship. Where they were given officially by the State, this was done by measures which, as I have said, offered alternatives to the rights of citizenship, rather than additions to them. But the major part of the task was left to private charity, and it was the general, though not universal, view of charitable bodies that those who received their help had no personal right to claim it.

Nevertheless it is true that citizenship, even in its early forms, was a principle of equality, and that during this period it was a developing institution. Starting at the point where all men were free and, in theory, capable of enjoying rights, it grew by enriching the body of rights which they were capable of enjoying. But these rights did not conflict with the inequalities of capitalist society; they were, on the contrary, necessary to the maintenance of that particular form of inequality. The explanation lies in the fact that the core of citizenship at this stage was composed of civil rights. And civil rights were indispensable to a competitive market economy. They gave to each man, as part of his individual status, the power to engage as an independent unit in the economic struggle and made it possible to deny to him social protection on the ground that he was equipped with the means to protect himself. Maine's famous dictum that 'the movement of the progressive societies has hitherto been a movement from Status to Contract'[27] expresses a profound truth which has been elaborated, with varying terminology, by many sociologists, but it requires qualification. For both status and contract are present in all but the most primitive societies. Maine himself admitted this when, later in the same book, he wrote that the earliest feudal communities, as contrasted with their archaic predecessors, 'were neither bound together by mere sentiment nor recruited by a fiction. The tie which united them was Contract.'[28] But the contractual element in feudalism co-existed with a class system based on status and, as contract hardened into custom, it helped to perpetuate class status. Custom retained the form of mutual undertakings, but not the reality of a free agreement. Modern contract did not grow out of feudal contract; it marks a new development to whose progress feudalism was an obstacle that had to be swept aside. For modern contract is essentially an agreement between men who are free and equal in status, though not necessarily in power. Status was not eliminated from the social system. Differential status, associated with class, function and family, was replaced by the single uniform status of citizenship, which provided the foundation of equality on which the structure of inequality could be built.

When Maine wrote, this status was clearly an aid, and not a menace, to capitalism and the free-market economy, because it was dominated by civil rights, which confer the legal

[27] H. S. Maine: *Ancient Law* (1878), p. 170.
[28] ibid., p. 365.

capacity to strive for the things one would like to possess but do not guarantee the possession of any of them. A property right is not a right to possess property, but a right to acquire it, if you can, and to protect it, if you can get it. But, if you use these arguments to explain to a pauper that his property rights are the same as those of a millionaire, he will probably accuse you of quibbling. Similarly, the right to freedom of speech has little real substance if, from lack of education, you have nothing to say that is worth saying, and no means of making yourself heard if you say it. But these blatant inequalities are not due to defects in civil rights, but to lack of social rights, and social rights in the mid-nineteenth century were in the doldrums. The Poor Law was an aid, not a menace, to capitalism, because it relieved industry of all social responsibility outside the contract of employment, while sharpening the edge of competition in the labour market. Elementary schooling was also an aid, because it increased the value of the worker without educating him above his station.

But it would be absurd to contend that the civil rights enjoyed in the eighteenth and nineteenth centuries were free from defects, or that they were as egalitarian in practice as they professed to be in principle. Equality before the law did not exist. The right was there, but the remedy might frequently prove to be out of reach. The barriers between rights and remedies were of two kinds: the first arose from class prejudice and partiality, the second from the automatic effects of the unequal distribution of wealth, working through the price system. Class prejudice, which undoubtedly coloured the whole administration of justice in the eighteenth century, cannot be eliminated by law, but only by social education and the building of a tradition of impartiality. This is a slow and difficult process, which presupposes a change in the climate of thought throughout the upper ranks of society. But it is a process which I think it is fair to say has been successfully accomplished, in the sense that the tradition of impartiality as between social classes is firmly established in our civil justice. And it is interesting that this should have

happened without any fundamental change in the class structure of the legal profession. We have no exact knowledge on
this point, but I doubt whether the picture has radically altered since Professor Ginsberg found that the proportion of
those admitted to Lincoln's Inn whose fathers were wage-
earners had risen from 0.4 per cent. in 1904–8 to 1.8 per cent.
in 1923–7, and that at this latter date nearly 72 per cent.
were sons of professional men, high-ranking business men and
gentlemen.[29] The decline of class prejudice as a barrier to
the full enjoyment of rights is, therefore, due less to the dilu-
tion of class monopoly in the legal profession than to the
spread in all classes of a more humane and realistic sense of
social equality.

It is interesting to compare with this the corresponding development in the field of political rights. Here too class prejudice, expressed through the intimidation of the lower classes
by the upper, prevented the free exercise of the right to vote
by the newly enfranchised. In this case a practical remedy
was available, in the secret ballot. But that was not enough.
Social education, and a change of mental climate, were
needed as well. And, even when voters felt free from undue
influence, it still took some time to break down the idea,
prevalent in the working as well as other classes, that the
representatives of the people, and still more the members of
the government, should be drawn from among the *élites* who
were born, bred and educated for leadership. Class monopoly
in politics, unlike class monopoly in law, has definitely been
overthrown. Thus, in these two fields, the same goal has been
reached by rather different paths.

The removal of the second obstacle, the effects of the unequal distribution of wealth, was technically a simple matter
in the case of political rights, because it costs little or nothing
to register a vote. Nevertheless, wealth can be used to influence an election, and a series of measures was adopted to
reduce this influence. The earlier ones, which go back to the
seventeenth century, were directed against bribery and cor-

[29] M. Ginsberg: *Studies in Sociology*, p. 171.

ruption, but the later ones, especially from 1883 onwards, had the wider aim of limiting election expenses in general, in order that candidates of unequal wealth might fight on more or less equal terms. The need for such equalizing measures has now greatly diminished, since working-class candidates can get financial support from party and other funds. Restrictions which prevent competitive extravagance are, therefore, probably welcomed by all. It remained to open the House of Commons to men of all classes, regardless of wealth, first by abolishing the property qualification for members, and then by introducing payment of members in 1911.

It has proved far more difficult to achieve similar results in the field of civil rights, because litigation, unlike voting, is very expensive. Court fees are not high, but counsel's fees and solicitor's charges may mount up to very large sums indeed. Since a legal action takes the form of a contest, each party feels that his chances of winning will be improved if he secures the services of better champions than those employed on the other side. There is, of course, some truth in this, but not as much as is popularly believed. But the effect in litigation, as in elections, is to introduce an element of competitive extravagance which makes it difficult to estimate in advance what the costs of an action will amount to. In addition, our system by which costs are normally awarded to the winner increases the risk and the uncertainty. A man of limited means, knowing that, if he loses, he will have to pay his opponent's costs (after they have been pruned by the Taxing Master) as well as his own, may easily be frightened into accepting an unsatisfactory settlement, especially if his opponent is wealthy enough not to be bothered by any such considerations. And even if he wins, the taxed costs he recovers will usually be less than his actual expenditure, and often considerably less. So that, if he has been induced to fight his case expensively, the victory may not be worth the price paid.

What, then, has been done to remove these barriers to the full and equal exercise of civil rights? Only one thing of real substance, the establishment in 1846 of the County Courts to provide cheap justice for the common people. This important innovation has had a profound and beneficial effect on our legal system, and done much to develop a proper sense of the importance of the case brought by the small man—which is often a very big case by his standards. But County Court costs are not negligible, and the jurisdiction of the County Courts is limited. The second major step taken was the development of a poor person's procedure, under which a small fraction of the poorer members of the community could sue *in forma pauperis*, practically free of all cost, being assisted by the gratuitous and voluntary services of the legal profession. But, as the income limit was extremely low (£2 a week since 1919), and the procedure did not apply in the County Courts, it has had little effect except in matrimonial causes. The supplementary service of free legal advice was, until recently, provided by the unaided efforts of voluntary bodies. But the problem has not been overlooked, nor the reality of the defects in our system denied. It has attracted increasing attention during the last hundred years. The machinery of the Royal Commission and the Committee has been used repeatedly, and some reforms of procedure have resulted. Two such Committees are at work now, but it would be most improper for me to make any reference to their deliberations.[30] A third, which started earlier, issued a report on which is based the Legal Aid and Advice Bill laid before parliament just three months ago.[31] This is a bold measure, going far beyond anything previously attempted for the assistance of the poorer litigants, and I shall have more to say about it later on.

It is apparent from the events I have briefly narrated that there developed, in the latter part of the nineteenth century, a growing interest in equality as a principle of social justice

[30] The Austin Jones Committee on County Court Procedure and the Evershed Committee on Supreme Court Practice and Procedure. The report of the former and an interim report of the latter have since been published.

[31] The Rushcliffe Committee on Legal Aid and Legal Advice in England and Wales.

and an appreciation of the fact that the formal recognition of an equal capacity for rights was not enough. In theory even the complete removal of all the barriers that separated civil rights from their remedies would not have interfered with the principles or the class structure of the capitalist system. It would, in fact, have created a situation which many supporters of the competitive market economy falsely assumed to be already in existence. But in practice the attitude of mind which inspired the efforts to remove these barriers grew out of a conception of equality which overstepped these narrow limits, the conception of equal social worth, not merely of equal natural rights. Thus although citizenship, even by the end of the nineteenth century, had done little to reduce social inequality, it had helped to guide progress into the path which led directly to the egalitarian policies of the twentieth century.

It also had an integrating effect, or, at least, was an important ingredient in an integrating process. In a passage I quoted just now Maine spoke of pre-feudal societies as bound together by a sentiment and recruited by a fiction. He was referring to kinship, or the fiction of common descent. Citizenship requires a bond of a different kind, a direct sense of community membership based on loyalty to a civilization which is a common possession. It is a loyalty of free men endowed with rights and protected by a common law. Its growth is stimulated both by the struggle to win those rights and by their enjoyment when won. We see this clearly in the eighteenth century, which saw the birth, not only of modern civil rights, but also of modern national consciousness. The familiar instruments of modern democracy were fashioned by the upper classes and then handed down, step by step, to the lower: political journalism for the intelligentsia was followed by newspapers for all who could read, public meetings, propaganda campaigns and associations for the furtherance of public causes. Repressive measures and taxes were quite unable to stop the flood. And with it came a patriotic nationalism, expressing the unity underlying these controversial outbursts. How deep or widespread this was it is difficult to say, but

there can be no doubt about the vigour of its outward manifestation. We still use those typically eighteenth-century
songs, 'God Save the King' and 'Rule Britannia', but we omit
the passages which would offend our modern, and more modest, sensibilities. This jingo patriotism, and the 'popular and
parliamentary agitation' which Temperley found to be 'the
main factor in causing the war' of Jenkins's era,[32] were new
phenomena in which can be recognized the first small trickle
which grew into the broad stream of the national war efforts
of the twentieth century.

This growing national consciousness, this awakening public
opinion, and these first stirrings of a sense of community
membership and common heritage did not have any material
effect on class structure and social inequality for the simple
and obvious reason that, even at the end of the nineteenth
century, the mass of the working people did not wield effective political power. By that time the franchise was fairly
wide, but those who had recently received the vote had not
yet learned how to use it. The political rights of citizenship,
unlike the civil rights, were full of potential danger to the
capitalist system, although those who were cautiously extending them down the social scale probably did not realize quite
how great the danger was. They could hardly be expected to
foresee what vast changes could be brought about by the
peaceful use of political power, without a violent and bloody
revolution. The Planned Society and the Welfare State had
not yet risen over the horizon or come within the view of the
practical politician. The foundations of the market economy
and the contractual system seemed strong enough to stand
against any probable assault. In fact, there were some grounds
for expecting that the working classes, as they became educated, would accept the basic principles of the system and be
content to rely for their protection and progress on the civil
rights of citizenship, which contained no obvious menace to
competitive capitalism. Such a view was encouraged by the
fact that one of the main achievements of political power in

[32] C. Grant Robertson: *England under the Hanoverians*, p. 491.

the later nineteenth century was the recognition of the right of collective bargaining. This meant that social progress was being sought by strengthening civil rights, not by creating social rights; through the use of contract in the open market, not through a minimum wage and social security.

But this interpretation underrates the significance of this extension of civil rights in the economic sphere. For civil rights were in origin intensely individual, and that is why they harmonized with the individualistic phase of capitalism. By the device of incorporation groups were enabled to act legally as individuals. This important development did not go unchallenged, and limited liability was widely denounced as an infringement of individual responsibility. But the position of trade unions was even more anomalous, because they did not seek or obtain incorporation. They can, therefore, exercise vital civil rights collectively on behalf of their members without formal collective responsibility, while the individual responsibility of the workers in relation to contract is largely unenforceable. These civil rights became, for the workers, an instrument for raising their social and economic status, that is to say, for establishing the claim that they, as citizens, were entitled to certain social rights. But the normal method of establishing social rights is by the exercise of political power, for social rights imply an absolute right to a certain standard of civilization which is conditional only on the discharge of the general duties of citizenship. Their content does not depend on the economic value of the individual claimant. There is therefore a significant difference between a genuine collective bargain through which economic forces in a free market seek to achieve equilibrium and the use of collective civil rights to assert basic claims to the elements of social justice. Thus the acceptance of collective bargaining was not simply a natural extension of civil rights; it represented the transfer of an important process from the political to the civil sphere of citizenship. But 'transfer' is, perhaps, a misleading term, for at the time when this happened the workers either did not possess, or had not yet learned to use, the political right of the franchise. Since then they have obtained and made full use of that right. Trade unionism has, therefore, created a secondary system of industrial citizenship parallel with and supplementary to the system of political citizenship.

It is interesting to compare this development with the history of parliamentary representation. In the early parliaments, says Pollard, 'representation was nowise regarded as a means of expressing individual right or forwarding individual interests. It was communities, not individuals, who were represented.'[33] And, looking at the position on the eve of the Reform Act of 1918, he added: 'Parliament, instead of representing communities or families, is coming to represent nothing but individuals.'[34] A system of manhood and womanhood suffrage treats the vote as the voice of the individual. Political parties organize these voices for group action, but they do so nationally and not on the basis of function, locality or interest. In the case of civil rights the movement has been in the opposite direction, not from the representation of communities to that of individuals, but from the representation of individuals to that of communities. And Pollard makes another point. It was a characteristic of the early parliamentary system, he says, that the representatives were those who had the time, the means and the inclination to do the job. Election by a majority of votes and strict accountability to the electors was not essential. Constituencies did not instruct their members, and election promises were unknown. Members 'were elected to bind their constituents, and not to be bound by them'.[35] It is not too fanciful to suggest that some of these features are reproduced in modern trade unions, though, of course, with many profound differences. One of these is that trade union officials do not undertake an onerous unpaid job, but enter on a remunerative career. This remark is not meant to be offensive, and, indeed, it would hardly be seemly for a university professor to criticize a public institution on the ground that its affairs are managed largely by its salaried employees.

[33] R. W. Pollard: *The Evolution of Parliament*, p. 155.
[34] ibid., p. 165.
[35] ibid., p. 152.

All that I have said so far has been by way of introduction to my main task. I have not tried to put before you new facts culled by laborious research. The limit of my ambition has been to regroup familiar facts in a pattern which may make them appear to some of you in a new light. I thought it necessary to do this in order to prepare the ground for the more difficult, speculative and controversial study of the contemporary scene, in which the leading role is played by the social rights of citizenship. It is to the impact of these on social class that I must now turn my attention.

Social Rights in the Twentieth Century

The period of which I have hitherto been speaking was one during which the growth of citizenship, substantial and impressive though it was, had little direct effect on social inequality. Civil rights gave legal powers whose use was drastically curtailed by class prejudice and lack of economic opportunity. Political rights gave potential power whose exercise demanded experience, organization and a change of ideas as to the proper functions of government. All these took time to develop. Social rights were at a minimum and were not woven into the fabric of citizenship. The common purpose of statutory and voluntary effort was to abate the nuisance of poverty without disturbing the pattern of inequality of which poverty was the most obviously unpleasant consequence.

A new period opened at the end of the nineteenth century, conveniently marked by Booth's survey of Life and Labour of the People in London and the Royal Commission on the Aged Poor. It saw the first big advance in social rights, and this involved significant changes in the egalitarian principle as expressed in citizenship. But there were other forces at work as well. A rise of money incomes unevenly distributed over the social classes altered the economic distance which separated these classes from one another, diminishing the gap between skilled and unskilled labour and between skilled labour and non-manual workers, while the steady increase in small savings blurred the class distinction between the capitalist and the propertyless proletarian. Secondly, a system of direct taxation, ever more steeply graduated, compressed the whole scale of disposable incomes. Thirdly, mass production for the home market and a growing interest on the part of industry in the needs and tastes of the common people enabled the less well-to-do to enjoy a material civilization which differed less markedly in quality from that of the rich than it had ever done before. All this profoundly altered the setting in which the progress of citizenship took place. Social integration spread from the sphere of sentiment and patriotism into that of material enjoyment. The components of a civilized and cultured life, formerly the monopoly of the few, were brought progressively within reach of the many, who were encouraged thereby to stretch out their hands towards those that still eluded their grasp. The diminution of inequality strengthened the demand for its abolition, at least with regard to the essentials of social welfare.

These aspirations have in part been met by incorporating social rights in the status of citizenship and thus creating a universal right to real income which is not proportionate to the market value of the claimant. Class-abatement is still the aim of social rights, but it has acquired a new meaning. It is no longer merely an attempt to abate the obvious nuisance of destitution in the lowest ranks of society. It has assumed the guise of action modifying the whole pattern of social inequality. It is no longer content to raise the floor-level in the basement of the social edifice, leaving the superstructure as it was. It has begun to remodel the whole building, and it might even end by converting a skyscraper into a bungalow. It is therefore important to consider whether any such ultimate aim is implicit in the nature of this development, or whether, as I put it at the outset, there are natural limits to the contemporary drive towards greater social and economic equality. To answer this question I must survey and analyse the social services of the twentieth century.

I said earlier that the attempts made to remove the barriers between civil rights and their remedies gave evidence of a new attitude towards the problem of equality. I can therefore conveniently begin my survey by looking at the latest example of such an attempt, the Legal Aid and Advice Bill, which offers a social service designed to strengthen the civil right of the citizen to settle his disputes in a court of law. It also brings us face to face at once with one of the major issues of our problem, the possibility of combining in one system the two principles of social justice and market price. The State is not prepared to make the administration of justice free for all. One reason for this—though not, of course, the only one— is that costs perform a useful function by discouraging frivolous litigation and encouraging the acceptance of reasonable settlements. If all actions which are started went to trial, the machinery of justice would break down. Also, the amount that it is appropriate to spend on a case depends largely on what it is worth to the parties, and of this, it is argued, they themselves are the only judges. It is very different in a health service, where the seriousness of the disease and the nature of the treatment required can be objectively assessed with very little reference to the importance the patient attaches to it. Nevertheless, though some payment is demanded, it must not take a form which deprives the litigant of his right to justice or puts him at a disadvantage *vis-à-vis* his opponent.

The main provisions of the scheme are as follows. The service will be confined to an economic class—those whose disposable income and capital do not exceed £420 and £500 respectively.[36] 'Disposable' means the balance after considerable deductions have been allowed for dependants, rent, ownership of house and tools, and so forth. The maximum contributable by the litigant towards his own costs is limited to half the excess of his disposable income over £156 plus the excess of his disposable capital above £75. His liability towards the costs of the other side, if he loses, is entirely in the discretion of the court. He will have the professional assistance of solicitor and counsel drawn from a panel of volun-

[36] Where disposable capital exceeds £500, legal aid may still be granted, at the discretion of the local committee, if disposable income does not exceed £420.

teers, and they will be remunerated for their services, in the High Court (and above) at rates 15 per cent. below what the Taxing Master would regard as reasonable in the free market, and in the County Court according to uniform scales not yet fixed.

The scheme, it will be seen, makes use of the principles of the income limit and the means test, which have just been abandoned in the other major social services. And the means test will be applied, or the maximum contribution assessed, by the National Assistance Board, whose officers, in addition to making the allowances prescribed in the regulations, 'will have general discretionary powers to enable them to deduct from income any sums which they normally disregard in dealing with an application for assistance under the National Assistance Act, 1948'.[37] It will be interesting to see whether this link with the old Poor Law will make Legal Aid unsavoury to many of those entitled to avail themselves of it, who will include persons with gross incomes up to £600 or £700 a year. But, quite apart from the agents employed to enforce it, the reason for introducing a means test is clear. The price payable for the service of the court and of the legal profession plays a useful part by testing the urgency of the demand. It is, therefore, to be retained. But the impact of price on demand is to be made less unequal by adjusting the bill to the income out of which it must be met. The method of adjustment resembles the operation of a progressive tax. If we consider income only, and ignore capital, we see that a man with a disposable income of £200 would be liable to contribute £22, or 11 per cent. of that income, and a man with a disposable income of £420 would have a maximum contribution of £132, or over 31 per cent. of that income.

A system of this kind may work quite well (assuming the scale of adjustment to be satisfactory) provided the market price of the service is a reasonable one for the smallest income that does not qualify for assistance. Then the price scale can taper down from this pivotal point until it vanishes where

[37] Cmd. 7563: Summary of the Proposed New Service, p. 7, para. 17.

the income is too small to pay anything. No awkward gap will appear at the top between the assisted and the unassisted. The method is in use for State scholarships to universities. The cost to be met in this case is the standardized figure for maintenance plus fees. Deductions are made from the gross income of the parents on lines similar to those proposed for Legal Aid, except that income tax is not deducted. The resulting figure is known as the 'scale income'. This is applied to a table which shows the parental contribution at each point on the scale. Scale incomes up to £600 pay nothing, and the ceiling above which parents must pay the full costs, without subsidy, is £1,500. A Working Party has recently recommended that the ceiling should be raised 'to at least £2,000' (before tax),[38] which is a fairly generous poverty line for a social service. It is not unreasonable to assume that, at that income level, the market cost of a university education can be met by the family without undue hardship.

The Legal Aid Scheme will probably work in much the same way for County Court cases, where costs are moderate. Those with incomes at the top of the scale will not normally receive any subsidy towards their own costs, even if they lose their case. The contribution they can be called on to make out of their own funds will usually be enough to cover them. They will thus be in the same position as those just outside the scheme, and no awkward gap will appear. Litigants coming within the scheme will, however, get professional legal assistance at a controlled and reduced price, and that is in itself a valuable privilege. But in a heavy High Court case the maximum contribution of the man at the top of the scale would be far from sufficient to meet his own costs if he was defeated. His liability under the scheme could, therefore, be many times less than that of a man, just outside the scheme, who fought and lost an identical action. In such cases the gap may be very noticeable, and this is particularly serious in litigation, which takes the form of a contest. The contest may

[38] Ministry of Education: *Report of the Working Party on University Awards*, 1948, para. 60. The general account of the present system is taken from the same source.

be between an assisted litigant and an unassisted one, and they will be fighting under different rules. One will be protected by the principle of social justice, while the other is left to the mercy of the market and the ordinary obligations imposed by contract and the rules of the court. A measure of class-abatement may, in some cases, create a form of class privilege. Whether this will happen depends largely on the content of regulations which have not yet been issued, and on the way in which the court uses its discretion in awarding costs against assisted litigants who lose their actions.

This particular difficulty could be overcome if the system were made universal, or nearly so, by carrying the scale of maximum contributions up to much higher income levels. In other words, the means test could be preserved, but the income limit dropped. But this would mean bringing all, or practically all, legal practitioners into the scheme, and subjecting them to controlled prices for their services. It would amount almost to the nationalization of the profession, so far as litigation is concerned, or so it would probably appear to the barristers, whose profession is inspired by a strong spirit of individualism. And the disappearance of private practice would deprive the Taxing Masters of a standard by which to fix the controlled price.

I have chosen this example to illustrate some of the difficulties that arise when one tries to combine the principles of social equality and the price system. Differential price adjustment by scale to different incomes is one method of doing this. It was widely used by doctors and hospitals until the National Health Service made this unnecessary. It frees real income, in certain forms, from its dependence on money income. If the principle were universally applied, differences in money income would become meaningless. The same result could be achieved by making all gross incomes equal, or by reducing unequal gross incomes to equal net incomes by taxation. Both processes have been going on, up to a point. Both are checked by the need to preserve differential incomes as a source of economic incentive. But, when different methods of doing much the same thing are combined, it may be possible to carry the process much further without upsetting the economic machine, because their various consequences are not easily added together, and the total effect may escape notice in the general confusion. And we must remember that gross money incomes provide the measuring-rod by which we traditionally assess social and economic achievement and prestige. Even if they lost all meaning in terms of real income, they might still function, like orders and decorations, as spurs to effort and badges of success.

But I must return to my survey of the social services. The most familiar principle in use is not, of course, the scaled price (which I have just been discussing), but the guaranteed minimum. The State guarantees a minimum supply of certain essential goods and services (such as medical attention and supplies, shelter and education) or a minimum money income available to be spent on essentials—as in the case of Old Age Pensions, insurance benefits and family allowances. Anyone able to exceed the guaranteed minimum out of his own resources is at liberty to do so. Such a system looks, on the face of it, like a more generous version of class-abatement in its original form. It raises the floor-level at the bottom, but does not automatically flatten the superstructure. But its effects need closer examination.

The degree of equalization achieved depends on four things —whether the benefit is offered to all or to a limited class; whether it takes the form of money payment or service rendered; whether the minimum is high or low; and how the money to pay for the benefit is raised. Cash benefits subject to income limit and means test had a simple and obvious equalizing effect. They achieved class-abatement in the early and limited sense of the term. The aim was to ensure that all citizens should attain at least to the prescribed minimum, either by their own resources or with assistance if they could not do it without. The benefit was given only to those who needed it, and thus inequalities at the bottom of the scale were ironed out. The system operated in its simplest and most unadulterated form in the case of the Poor Law and Old Age Pensions. But economic equalization might be accom-

panied by psychological class discrimination. The stigma
which attached to the Poor Law made 'pauper' a derogatory
term defining a class. 'Old Age Pensioner' may have had a
little of the same flavour, but without the taint of shame.

The general effect of social insurance, when confined to an
income group, was similar. It differed in that there was no
means test. Contribution gave a right to benefit. But, broadly
speaking, the income of the group was raised by the excess
of benefits over total expenditure by the group in contributions and additional taxes, and the income gap between this
group and those above it was thereby reduced. The exact effect is hard to estimate, because of the wide range of incomes
within the group and the varying incidence of the risks covered. When the scheme was extended to all, this gap was
reopened, though again we have to take account of the combined effects of the regressive flat-rate levy and the, in part,
progressive taxation which contributed to the financing of the
scheme. Nothing will induce me to embark on a discussion
of this problem. But a total scheme is less specifically class-
abating in a purely economic sense than a limited one, and
social insurance is less so than a means-test service. Flat-rate
benefits do not reduce the gaps between different incomes.
Their equalizing effect depends on the fact that they make
a bigger percentage addition to small incomes than to large.
And, even though the concept of diminishing marginal utility
(if one may still refer to it) can strictly be applied only to
the rising income of one unchanging individual, that remains
a matter of some significance. When a free service, as in the
case of health, is extended from a limited income group to
the whole population, the direct effect is in part to increase
the inequality of disposable incomes, again subject to modifi-
cation by the incidence of taxes. For members of the middle
classes, who used to pay their doctors, find this part of their
income released for expenditure on other things.

I have been skating gingerly over this very thin ice in order
to make one point. The extension of the social services is not
primarily a means of equalizing incomes. In some cases it
may, in others it may not. The question is relatively unim-

portant; it belongs to a different department of social policy. What matters is that there is a general enrichment of the concrete substance of civilized life, a general reduction of risk and insecurity, an equalization between the more and the less fortunate at all levels—between the healthy and the sick, the employed and the unemployed, the old and the active, the bachelor and the father of a large family. Equalization is not so much between classes as between individuals within a population which is now treated for this purpose as though it were one class. Equality of status is more important than equality of income.

Even when benefits are paid in cash, this class fusion is outwardly expressed in the form of a new common experience. All learn what it means to have an insurance card that must be regularly stamped (by somebody), or to collect children's allowances or pensions from the post office. But where the benefit takes the form of a service, the qualitative element enters into the benefit itself, and not only into the process by which it is obtained. The extension of such services can therefore have a profound effect on the qualitative aspects of social differentiation. The old elementary schools, though open to all, were used by a social class (admittedly a very large and varied one) for which no other kind of education was available. Its members were brought up in segregation from the higher classes and under influences which set their stamp on the children subjected to them. 'Ex-elementary schoolboy' became a label which a man might carry through life, and it pointed to a distinction which was real, and not merely conventional, in character. For a divided educational system, by promoting both intra-class similarity and inter-class difference, gave emphasis and precision to a criterion of social distance. As Professor Tawney has said, translating the views of educationalists into his own inimitable prose: 'The intrusion into educational organization of the vulgarities of the class system is an irrelevance as mischievous in effect as it is odious in conception.'[39] The limited service was class-

[39] R. H. Tawney: *Secondary Education for All*, p. 64.

making at the same time as it was class-abating. Today the segregation still takes place, but subsequent education, available to all, makes it possible for a re-sorting to take place. I shall have to consider in a moment whether class intrudes in a different way into this re-sorting.

Similarly the early health service added 'panel patient' to our vocabulary of social class, and many members of the middle classes are now learning exactly what the term signifies. But the extension of the service has reduced the social importance of the distinction. The common experience offered by a general health service embraces all but a small minority at the top and spreads across the important class barriers in the middle ranks of the hierarchy. At the same time the guaranteed minimum has been raised to such a height that the term 'minimum' becomes a misnomer. The intention, at least, is to make it approximate so nearly to the reasonable maximum that the extras which the rich are still able to buy will be no more than frills and luxuries. The provided service, not the purchased service, becomes the norm of social welfare. Some people think that, in such circumstances, the independent sector cannot survive for long. If it disappears, the skyscraper will have been converted into a bungalow. If the present system continues and attains its ideals, the result might be described as a bungalow surmounted by an architecturally insignificant turret.

Benefits in the form of a service have this further characteristic that the rights of the citizen cannot be precisely defined. The qualitative element is too great. A modicum of legally enforceable rights may be granted, but what matters to the citizen is the superstructure of legitimate expectations. It may be fairly easy to enable every child below a certain age to spend the required number of hours in school. It is much harder to satisfy the legitimate expectation that the education should be given by trained teachers in classes of moderate size. It may be possible for every citizen who wishes it to be registered with a doctor. It is much harder to ensure that his ailments will be properly cared for. And so we find that legislation, instead of being the decisive step that puts policy into immediate effect, acquires more and more the character of a declaration of policy that it is hoped to put into effect some day. We think at once of County Colleges and Health Centres. The rate of progress depends on the magnitude of the national resources and their distribution between competing claims. Nor can the State easily foresee what it will cost to fulfill its obligations, for, as the standard expected of the service rises—as it inevitably must in a progressive society —the obligations automatically get heavier. The target is perpetually moving forward, and the State may never be able to get quite within range of it. It follows that individual rights must be subordinated to national plans.

Expectations officially recognized as legitimate are not claims that must be met in each case when presented. They become, as it were, details in a design for community living. The obligation of the State is towards society as a whole, whose remedy in case of default lies in parliament or a local council, instead of to individual citizens, whose remedy lies in a court of law, or at least in a quasi-judicial tribunal. The maintenance of a fair balance between these collective and individual elements in social rights is a matter of vital importance to the democratic socialist State.

The point I have just made is clearest in the case of housing. Here the tenure of existing dwellings has been protected by firm legal rights, enforceable in a court of law. The system has become very complicated, because it has grown piecemeal, and it cannot be maintained that the benefits are equally distributed in proportion to real need. But the basic right of the individual citizen to have a dwelling at all is minimal. He can claim no more than a roof over his head, and his claim can be met, as we have seen in recent years, by a shake-down in a disused cinema converted into a rest centre. Nevertheless, the general obligation of the State towards society collectively with regard to housing is one of the heaviest it has to bear. Public policy has unequivocally given the citizen a legitimate expectation of a home fit for a family to live in, and the promise is not now confined to heroes. It is true that, in dealing with individual claims, authorities work as far as possible on a priority scale of needs. But, when a slum is being cleared, an old city remodelled, or a new town planned, individual claims must be subordinated to the general programme of social advance. An element of chance, and therefore of inequality, enters. One family may be moved ahead of its turn into a model dwelling, because it is part of a community due for early treatment. A second will have to wait, although its physical conditions may be worse than those of the first. As the work goes on, though in many places inequalities vanish, in others they become more apparent. Let me give you one small example of this. In the town of Middlesbrough, part of the population of a blighted area had been moved to a new housing estate. It was found that, among the children living on this estate, one in eight of those who competed for places in secondary schools were successful. Among the section of the same original population that had been left behind the proportion was one in one hundred and fifty-four.[40] The contrast is so staggering that one hesitates to offer any precise explanation of it, but it remains a striking example of inequality between individuals appearing as the interim result of the progressive satisfaction of collective social rights. Eventually, when the housing programme has been completed, such inequalities should disappear.

There is another aspect of housing policy which, I believe, implies the intrusion of a new element into the rights of citizenship. It comes into play when the design for living, to which I have said individual rights must be subordinated, is not limited to one section at the bottom of the social scale nor to one particular type of need, but covers the general aspects of the life of a whole community. Town planning is total planning in this sense. Not only does it treat the community as a whole, but it affects and must take account of all social activities, customs and interests. It aims at creating new physical environments which will actively foster the growth of new human societies. It must decide what these societies are to be like, and try to provide for all the major

[40] Ruth Glass: *The Social Background of a Plan*, p. 129.

diversities which they ought to contain. Town planners are fond of talking about a 'balanced community' as their objective. This means a society that contains a proper mixture of all social classes, as well as of age and sex groups, occupations and so forth. They do not want to build working-class neighbourhoods and middle-class neighbourhoods, but they do propose to build working-class houses and middle-class houses. Their aim is not a classless society, but a society in which class differences are legitimate in terms of social justice, and in which, therefore, the classes co-operate more closely than at present to the common benefit of all. When a planning authority decides that it needs a larger middle-class element in its town (as it very often does) and makes designs to meet its needs and fit its standards, it is not, like a speculative builder, merely responding to a commercial demand. It must re-interpret the demand in harmony with its total plan and then give it the sanction of its authority as the responsible organ of a community of citizens. The middle-class man can then say, not 'I will come if you pay the price I feel strong enough to demand', but 'If you want me as a citizen, you must give me the status which is due as of right to the kind of citizen I am'. This is one example of the way in which citizenship is itself becoming the architect of social inequality.

The second, and more important, example is in the field of education, which also illustrates my earlier point about the balance between individual and collective social rights. In the first phase of our public education, rights were minimal and equal. But, as we have observed, a duty was attached to the right, not merely because the citizen has a duty to himself, as well as a right, to develop all that is in him—a duty which neither the child nor the parent may fully appreciate—but because society recognized that it needed an educated population. In fact the nineteenth century has been accused of regarding elementary education solely as a means of providing capitalist employers with more valuable workers, and higher education merely as an instrument to increase the power of the nation to compete with its industrial rivals. And you may have noticed that recent studies of educational opportunity in the pre-war years have been concerned to reveal the magnitude of social waste quite as much as to protest against the frustration of natural human rights.

In the second phase of our educational history, which began in 1902, the educational ladder was officially accepted as an important, though still small, part of the system. But the balance between collective and individual rights remained much the same. The State decided what it could afford to spend on free secondary and higher education, and the children competed for the limited number of places provided. There was no pretence that all who could benefit from more advanced education would get it, and there was no recognition of any absolute natural right to be educated according to one's capacities. But in the third phase, which started in 1944, individual rights have ostensibly been given priority. Competition for scarce places is to be replaced by selection and distribution into appropriate places, sufficient in number to accommodate all, at least at the secondary school level. In the Act of 1944 there is a passage which says that the supply of secondary schools will not be considered adequate unless they 'afford for all pupils opportunities for education offering such variety of instruction and training as may be desirable in view of their different ages, abilities and aptitudes'. Respect for individual rights could hardly be more strongly expressed. Yet I wonder whether it will work out like that in practice.

If it were possible for the school system to treat the pupil entirely as an end in himself, and to regard education as giving him something whose value he could enjoy to the full whatever his station in after-life, then it might be possible to mould the educational plan to the shape demanded by individual needs, regardless of any other considerations. But, as we all know, education today is closely linked with occupation, and one, at least, of the values the pupil expects to get from it is a qualification for employment at an appropriate level. Unless great changes take place, it seems likely that the educational plan will be adjusted to occupational demand. The proportion between Grammar, Technical and Modern

Secondary Schools cannot well be fixed without reference to the proportion between jobs of corresponding grades. And a balance between the two systems may have to be sought in justice to the pupil himself. For if a boy who is given a Grammar School education can then get nothing but a Modern School job, he will cherish a grievance and feel that he has been cheated. It is highly desirable that this attitude should change, so that a boy in such circumstances will be grateful for his education and not resentful at his job. But to accomplish such a change is no easy task.

I see no signs of any relaxation of the bonds that tie education to occupation. On the contrary, they appear to be growing stronger. Great and increasing respect is paid to certificates, matriculation, degrees and diplomas as qualifications for employment, and their freshness does not fade with the passage of the years. A man of forty may be judged by his performance in an examination taken at the age of fifteen. The ticket obtained on leaving school or college is for a life journey. The man with a third-class ticket who later feels entitled to claim a seat in a first-class carriage will not be admitted, even if he is prepared to pay the difference. That would not be fair to the others. He must go back to the start and rebook, by passing the prescribed examination. And it is unlikely that the State will offer to pay his return fare. This is not, of course, true of the whole field of employment, but it is a fair description of a large and significant part of it, whose extension is being constantly advocated. I have, for instance, recently read an article in which it is urged that every aspirant to an administrative or managerial post in business should be required to qualify 'by passing the matriculation or equivalent examination'.[41] This development is partly the result of the systematization of techniques in more and more professional, semi-professional and skilled occupations, though I must confess that some of the claims of so-called professional bodies to exclusive possession of esoteric skill and knowledge appear to me to be rather thin. But it is also fos-

[41] J. A. Bowie, in *Industry* (January 1949), p. 17.

tered by the refinement of the selective process within the educational system itself. The more confident the claim of education to be able to sift human material during the early years of life, the more is mobility concentrated within those years, and consequently limited thereafter.

The right of the citizen in this process of selection and mobility is the right to equality of opportunity. Its aim is to eliminate hereditary privilege. In essence it is the equal right to display and develop differences, or inequalities; the equal right to be recognized as unequal. In the early stages of the establishment of such a system the major effect is, of course, to reveal hidden equalities—to enable the poor boy to show that he is as good as the rich boy. But the final outcome is a structure of unequal status fairly apportioned to unequal abilities. The process is sometimes associated with ideas of *laissez faire* individualism, but within the educational system it is a matter, not of *laissez faire*, but of planning. The process through which abilities are revealed, the influences to which they are subjected, the tests by which they are measured, and the rights given as a result of the tests are all planned. Equality of opportunity is offered to all children entering the primary schools, but at an early age they are usually divided into three streams—the best, the average and the backward. Already opportunity is becoming unequal, and the children's range of chances limited. About the age of eleven they are tested again, probably by a team of teachers, examiners and psychologists. None of these is infallible, but perhaps sometimes three wrongs may make a right. Classification follows for distribution into the three types of secondary school. Opportunity becomes still more unequal, and the chances of further education has already been limited to a select few. Some of these, after being tested again, will go on to receive it. In the end the jumble of mixed seed originally put into the machine emerges in neatly labelled packets ready to be sown in the appropriate gardens.

I have deliberately couched this description in the language of cynicism in order to bring out the point that, however genuine may be the desire of the educational authorities to offer enough variety to satisfy all individual needs, they must, in a mass service of this kind, proceed by repeated classification into groups, and this is followed at each stage by assimilation within each group and differentiation between groups. That is precisely the way in which social classes in a fluid society have always taken shape. Differences within each class are ignored as irrelevant; differences between classes are given exaggerated significance. Thus qualities which are in reality strung out along a continuous scale are made to create a hierarchy of groups, each with its special character and status. The main features of the system are inevitable, and its advantages, in particular the elimination of inherited privilege, far outweigh its incidental defects. The latter can be attacked and kept within bounds by giving as much opportunity as possible for second thoughts about classification, both on the educational system itself and in after-life.

The conclusion of importance to my argument is that, through education in its relations with occupational structure, citizenship operates as an instrument of social stratification. There is no reason to deplore this, but we should be aware of its consequences. The status acquired by education is carried out into the world bearing the stamp of legitimacy, because it has been conferred by an institution designed to give the citizen his just rights. That which the market offers can be measured against that which the status claims. If a large discrepancy appears, the ensuing attempts to eliminate it will take the form, not of a bargain about economic value, but of a debate about social rights. And it may be that there is already a serious discrepancy between the expectations of those who reach the middle grades in education and the status of the non-manual jobs for which they are normally destined.

I said earlier that in the twentieth century citizenship and the capitalist class system have been at war. Perhaps the phrase is rather too strong, but it is quite clear that the former has imposed modifications on the latter. But we should not be justified in assuming that, although status is a principle that conflicts with contract, the stratified status system which is creeping into citizenship is an alien element in the economic world outside. Social rights in their modern form imply an invasion of contract by status, the subordination of market price to social justice, the replacement of the free bargain by the declaration of rights. But are these principles quite foreign to the practice of the market today, or are they there already, entrenched within the contract system itself? I think it is clear that they are.

As I have already pointed out, one of the main achievements of political power in the nineteenth century was to clear the way for the growth of trade unionism by enabling the workers to use their civil rights collectively. This was an anomaly, because hitherto it was political rights that were used for collective action, through parliament and local councils, whereas civil rights were intensely individual, and had therefore harmonized with the individualism of early capitalism. Trade unionism created a sort of secondary industrial citizenship, which naturally became imbued with the spirit appropriate to an institution of citizenship. Collective civil rights could be used, not merely for bargaining in the true sense of the term, but for the assertion of basic rights. The position was an impossible one and could only be transitional. Rights are not a proper matter for bargaining. To have to bargain for a living wage in a society which accepts the living wage as a social right is as absurd as to have to haggle for a vote in a society which accepts the vote as a political right. Yet the early twentieth century attempted to make sense of this absurdity. It fully endorsed collective bargaining as a normal and peaceful market operation, while recognizing in principle the right of the citizen to a minimum standard of civilized living, which was precisely what the trade unions believed, and with good reason, that they were trying to win for their members with the weapon of the bargain.

In the outburst of big strikes immediately before the First World War this note of a concerted demand for social rights was clearly audible. The government was forced to intervene. It professed to do so entirely for the protection of the public, and pretended not to be concerned with the issues in dispute. In 1912 Mr Askwith, the chief negotiator, told Mr Asquith, the Prime Minister, that intervention had failed and government prestige had suffered. To which the Prime Minister replied: 'Every word you have spoken endorses the opinion I have formed. It is a degradation of government.'[42] History soon showed that such a view was a complete anachronism. The government can no longer stand aloof from industrial disputes, as though the level of wages and the standard of living of the workers were matters with which it need not concern itself. And government intervention in industrial disputes has been met from the other side by trade union intervention in the work of government. This is both a significant and a welcome development, provided its implications are fully realized. In the past trade unionism had to assert social rights by attacks delivered from outside the system in which power resided. Today it defends them from inside, in cooperation with government. On major issues crude economic bargaining is converted into something more like a joint discussion of policy.

The implication is that decisions reached in this way must command respect. If citizenship is invoked in the defence of rights, the corresponding duties of citizenship cannot be ignored. These do not require a man to sacrifice his individual liberty or to submit without question to every demand made by government. But they do require that his acts should be inspired by a lively sense of responsibility towards the welfare of the community. Trade union leaders in general accept this implication, but this is not true of all members of the rank and file. The traditions built up at a time when trade unions were fighting for their existence, and when conditions of employment depended wholly on the outcome of unequal bargaining, make its acceptance very difficult. Unofficial strikes have become very frequent, and it is clear that one important element in industrial disputes is discord between trade union leaders and certain sections of trade union members. Now duties can derive either from status or from contract. Leaders of unofficial strikes are liable to reject both. The

[42] Lord Askwith: *Industrial Problems and Disputes*, p. 228.

strikes usually involve breach of contract or the repudiation of agreements. Appeal is made to some allegedly higher principle—in reality, though this may not be expressly asserted, to the status rights of industrial citizenship. There are many precedents today for the subordination of contract to status. Perhaps the most familiar are to be found in our handling of the housing problem. Rents are controlled and the rights of occupants protected after their contracts have expired, houses are requisitioned, agreements freely entered into are set aside or modified by tribunals applying the principles of social equity and the just price. The sanctity of contract gives way to the requirements of public policy, and I am not suggesting for a moment that this ought not to be so. But if the obligations of contract are brushed aside by an appeal to the rights of citizenship, then the duties of citizenship must be accepted as well. In some recent unofficial strikes an attempt has, I think, been made to claim the rights both of status and of contract while repudiating the duties under both these heads.

But my main concern is not with the nature of strikes, but rather with the current conception of what constitutes a fair wage. I think it is clear that this conception includes the notion of status. It enters into every discussion of wage rates and professional salaries. What *ought* a medical specialist or a dentist to earn, we ask? Would twice the salary of a university professor be about right, or is that not enough? And, of course, the system envisaged is one of stratified, not uniform, status. The claim is not merely for a basic living wage with such variations above that level as can be extracted by each grade from the conditions in the market at the moment. The claims of status are to a hierarchical wage structure, each level of which represents a social right and not merely a market value. Collective bargaining must involve, even in its elementary forms, the classification of workers into groups, or grades, within which minor occupational differences are ignored. As in mass schooling, so in mass employment, questions of rights, standards, opportunities and so forth can be intelligibly discussed and handled only in terms of a limited number of categories and by cutting up a continuous chain of differences into a series of classes whose names instantly ring the appropriate bell in the mind of the busy official. As the area of negotiation spreads, the assimilation of groups necessarily follows on the assimilation of individuals, until the stratification of the whole population of workers is, as far as possible, standardized. Only then can general principles of social justice be formulated. There must be uniformity within each grade, and difference between grades. These principles dominate the minds of those discussing wage claims, even though rationalization produces other arguments, such as that profits are excessive and the industry can afford to pay higher wages, or that higher wages are necessary to maintain the supply of suitable labour or to prevent its decline.

The White Paper on Personal Incomes[43] flashed a beam of light into these dark places of the mind, but the end result has been only to make the process of rationalization more intricate and laborious. The basic conflict between social rights and market value has not been resolved. One labour spokesman said: 'An equitable relationship must be established between industry and industry.'[44] An equitable relationship is a social, not an economic, concept. The General Council of the T.U.C. approved the principles of the White Paper to the extent that 'they recognize the need to safeguard those wage differentials which are essential elements in the wages structure of many important industries, and are required to sustain those standards of craftsmanship, training and experience that contribute directly to industrial efficiency and higher productivity'.[45] Here market value and economic incentive find a place in an argument which is fundamentally concerned with status. The White Paper itself took a rather different, and possibly a truer, view of differentials. 'The last hundred years have seen the growth of certain traditional or customary relationships between personal incomes—including wages and

[43] Cmd. 7321, 1948.
[44] As reported in *The Times*.
[45] Recommendations of the Special Committee on the Economic Situation as accepted by the General Council at their Special Meeting on 18 February 1948.

salaries—in different occupations. . . . These have no necessary relevance to modern conditions.' Tradition and custom
are social, not economic, principles, and they are old names
for the modern structure of status rights.

The White Paper stated frankly that differentials based on
these social concepts could not satisfy current economic requirements. They did not provide the incentives needed to
secure the best distribution of labour. 'Relative income levels
must be such as to encourage the movement of labour to those
industries where it is most needed, and should not, as in some
cases they still do, tempt it in a contrary direction.' Notice
that it says *still* do'. Once again the modern conception of
social rights is treated as a survival from the dark past. As we
go on, the confusion thickens. 'Each claim for an increase in
wages or salaries must be considered on its national merits',
that is, in terms of national policy. But this policy cannot be
directly enforced by the exercise of the political rights of citizenship through government, because that would involve 'an
incursion by the Government into what has hitherto been
regarded as a field of free contract between individuals and organizations', that is, an invasion of the civil rights of the citizen. Civil rights are therefore to assume political responsibility, and free contract is to act as the instrument of national
policy. And there is yet another paradox. The incentive that
operates in the free contract system of the open market is the
incentive of personal gain. The incentive that corresponds to
social rights is that of public duty. To which is the appeal
being made? The answer is, to both. The citizen is urged to
respond to the call of duty by allowing some scope to the motive of individual self-interest. But these paradoxes are not the
invention of muddled brains; they are inherent in our contemporary social system. And they need not cause us undue
anxiety, for a little common sense can often move a mountain
of paradox in the world of action, though logic may be unable to surmount it in the world of thought.

Conclusions

I have tried to show how citizenship, and other forces outside it, have been altering the pattern of social inequality. To complete the picture I ought now to survey the results as a whole on the structure of social class. They have undoubtedly been profound, and it may be that the inequalities permitted, and even moulded, by citizenship do not any longer constitute class distinctions in the sense in which that term is used for past societies. But to examine this question I should require another lecture, and it would probably consist of a mixture of dry statistics of uncertain meaning and meaningful judgements of doubtful validity. For our ignorance of this matter is profound. It is therefore perhaps fortunate for the reputation of sociology that I should be obliged to confine myself to a few tentative observations, made in an attempt to answer the four questions which I posed at the end of my introduction to my theme.

We have to look for the combined effects of three factors. First, the compression, at both ends, of the scale of income distribution. Second, the great extension of the area of common culture and common experience. And third, the enrichment of the universal status of citizenship, combined with the recognition and stabilization of certain status differences chiefly through the linked systems of education and occupation. The first two have made the third possible. Status differences can receive the stamp of legitimacy in terms of democratic citizenship provided they do not cut too deep, but occur within a population united in a single civilization; and provided they are not an expression of hereditary privilege. This means that inequalities can be tolerated within a fundamentally egalitarian society provided they are not dynamic, that is to say that they do not create incentives which spring from dissatisfaction and the feeling that 'this kind of life is not good enough for me', or 'I am determined that my son shall be spared what I had to put up with'. But the kind of inequality pleaded for in the White Paper can be justified only if it *is* dynamic, and if it *does* provide an incentive to change and betterment. It may prove, therefore, that the inequalities permitted, and even moulded, by citizenship will not function in an economic sense as forces influencing the free distribution of manpower. Or that social stratification persists, but social ambition ceases to be a normal phenomenon, and becomes a deviant behaviour pattern—to use some of the jargon of sociology.

Should things develop to such lengths, we might find that the only remaining drive with a consistent distributive effect—distributive, that is, of manpower through the hierarchy of economic levels—was the ambition of the schoolboy to do well in his lessons, to pass his examinations, and to win promotion up the educational ladder. And if the official aim of securing 'parity of esteem' between the three types of secondary school were realized, we might lose the greater part even of that. Such would be the extreme result of establishing social conditions in which every man was content with the station of life to which it had pleased citizenship to call him.

In saying this I have answered two of my four questions, the first and the last. I asked whether the sociological hypothesis latent in Marshall's essay is valid today, the hypothesis, namely, that there is a kind of basic human equality, associated with full community membership, which is not inconsistent with a superstructure of economic inequality. I asked, too, whether there was any limit to the present drive towards social equality inherent in the principles governing the movement. My answer is that the preservation of economic inequalities has been made more difficult by the enrichment of the status of citizenship. There is less room for them, and there is more and more likelihood of their being challenged. But we are certainly proceeding at present on the assumption that the hypothesis is valid. And this assumption provides the answer to the second question. We are not aiming at absolute equality. There are limits inherent in the egalitarian movement. But the movement is a double one. It operates partly through citizenship and partly through the economic system. In both cases the aim is to remove inequalities which cannot be regarded as legitimate, but the standard of legitimacy is different. In the former it is the standard of social justice, in the latter it is social justice combined with economic necessity. It is possible, therefore, that the inequalities permitted by the two halves of the movement will not coincide. Class distinctions may survive which have no appropriate economic function, and economic differences which do not correspond with accepted class distinctions.

My third question referred to the changing balance between rights and duties. Rights have been multiplied, and they are precise. Each individual knows just what he is entitled to claim. The duty whose discharge is most obviously and immediately necessary for the fulfilment of the right is the duty to pay taxes and insurance contributions. Since these are compulsory, no act of will is involved, and no keen sentiment of loyalty. Education and military service are also compulsory. The other duties are vague, and are included in the general obligation to live the life of a good citizen, giving such service as one can to promote the welfare of the community. But the community is so large that the obligation appears remote and unreal. Of paramount importance is the duty to work, but the effect of one man's labour on the well-being of the whole society is so infinitely small that it is hard for him to believe that he can do much harm by withholding or curtailing it.

When social relations were dominated by contract, the duty to work was not recognized. It was a man's own affair whether he worked or not. If he chose to live idly in poverty, he was at liberty to do so, provided he did not become a nuisance. If he was able to live idly in comfort, he was regarded, not as a drone, but as an aristocrat—to be envied and admired. When the economy of this country was in process of transformation into a system of this kind, great anxiety was felt whether the necessary labour would be forthcoming. The driving forces of group custom and regulation had to be replaced by the incentive of personal gain, and grave doubts were expressed whether this incentive could be relied upon. This explains Colquhoun's views on poverty, and the pithy remark of

Mandeville, that labourers 'have nothing to stir them up to be serviceable but their wants, which it is prudence to relieve but folly to cure'.[46] And in the eighteenth century their wants were very simple. They were governed by established class habits of living, and no continuous scale of rising standards of consumption existed to entice the labourers to earn more in order to spend more on desirable things hitherto just beyond their reach—like radio sets, bicycles, cinemas or holidays by the sea. The following comment by a writer in 1728, which is but one example from many in the same sense, may well have been based on sound observation. 'People in low life', he said, 'who work only for their daily bread, if they can get it by three days work in the week, will many of them make holiday the other three, or set their own price on their labour.'[47] And, if they adopted the latter course, it was generally assumed that they would spend the extra money on drink, the only easily available luxury. The general rise in the standard of living has caused this phenomenon, or something like it, to reappear in contemporary society, though cigarettes now play a more important role than drink.

It is no easy matter to revive the sense of the personal obligation to work in a new form in which it is attached to the status of citizenship. It is not made any easier by the fact that the essential duty is not to have a job and hold it, since that is relatively simple in conditions of full employment, but to put one's heart into one's job and work hard. For the standard by which to measure hard work is immensely elastic. A successful appeal to the duties of citizenship can be made in times of emergency, but the Dunkirk spirit cannot be a permanent feature of any civilization. Nevertheless, an attempt is being made by trade union leaders to inculcate a sense of this general duty. At a conference on November 18 of last year Mr Tanner referred to 'the imperative obligation on both sides of industry to make their full contribution to the rehabilitation

[46] B. Mandeville: *The Fable of the Bees*, 6th ed. (1732), p. 213.
[47] E. S. Furniss: *The Position of the Laborer in a System of Nationalism*, p. 125.

of the national economy and world recovery'.[48] But the national community is too large and remote to command this kind of loyalty and to make of it a continual driving force. That is why many people think that the solution of our problem lies in the development of more limited loyalties, to the local community and especially to the working group. In this latter form industrial citizenship, devolving its obligations down to the basic units of production, might supply some of the vigour that citizenship in general appears to lack.

I come finally to the second of my original four questions, which was not, however, so much a question as a statement. I pointed out that Marshall stipulated that measures designed to raise the general level of civilization of the workers must not interfere with the freedom of the market. If they did, they might become indistinguishable from socialism. And I said that obviously this limitation on policy had since been abandoned. Socialist measures in Marshall's sense have been accepted by all political parties. This led me to the platitude that the conflict between egalitarian measures and the free market must be examined in the course of any attempt to carry Marshall's sociological hypothesis over into the modern age.

I have touched on this vast subject at several points, and in the concluding summary I will confine myself to one aspect of the problem. The unified civilization which makes social inequalities acceptable, and threatens to make them economically functionless, is achieved by a progressive divorce between real and money incomes. This is, of course, explicit in the major social services, such as health and education, which give benefits in kind without any *ad hoc* payment. In scholarships and legal aid, prices scaled to money incomes keep real income relatively constant, in so far as it is affected by these particular needs. Rent restriction, combined with security of tenure, achieves a similar result by different means. So, in varying degrees, do rationing, food subsidies, utility goods and price controls. The advantages obtained by having a

[48] *The Times*, 19 November 1948.

larger money income do not disappear, but they are confined to a limited area of consumption.

I spoke just now of the conventional hierarchy of the wage structure. Here importance is attached to differences in money income and the higher earnings are expected to yield real and substantial advantages—as, of course, they still do in spite of the trend towards the equalization of real incomes. But the importance of wage differentials is, I am sure, partly symbolic. They operate as labels attached to industrial status, not only as instruments of genuine economic stratification. And we also see signs that the acceptance of this system of economic inequality by the workers themselves—especially those fairly low down in the scale—is sometimes counteracted by claims to greater equality with respect to those forms of real enjoyment which are not paid for out of wages. Manual workers may accept it as right and proper that they should earn less money than certain clerical grades, but at the same time wage-earners may press for the same general amenities as are enjoyed by salaried employees, because these should reflect the fundamental equality of all citizens and not the inequalities of earnings or occupational grades. If the manager can get a day off for a football match, why not the workman? Common enjoyment is a common right.

Recent studies of adult and child opinion have found that, when the question is posed in general terms, there is a declining interest in the earning of big money. This is not due, I think, only to the heavy burden of progressive taxation, but to an implicit belief that society should, and will, guarantee all the essentials of a decent and secure life at every level, irrespective of the amount of money earned. In a population of secondary schoolboys examined by the Bristol Institute of Education, 86 per cent. wanted an interesting job at a reasonable wage and only 9 per cent. a job in which they could make a lot of money. And the average intelligence quotient of the second group was 16 points lower than that of the first.[49] In a poll conducted by the British Institute of Public Opin-

[49] *Research Bulletin*, No. 11, p. 23.

ion, 23 per cent. wanted as high wages as possible, and 73 per cent. preferred security at lower wages.[50] But at any given moment, and in response to a particular question about their present circumstances, most people, one would imagine, would confess to a desire for more money than they are actually getting. Another poll, taken in November 1947, suggests that even this expectation is exaggerated. For 51 per cent. said their earnings were at or above a level adequate to cover family needs, and only 45 per cent. that they were inadequate. The attitude is bound to vary at different social levels. The classes which have gained most from the social services, and in which real income in general has been rising, might be expected to be less preoccupied with differences in money income. But we should be prepared to find other reactions in that section of the middle classes in which the pattern of money incomes is at the moment most markedly incoherent, while the elements of civilized living traditionally most highly prized are becoming unattainable with the money incomes available—or by any other means.

The general point is one to which Professor Robbins referred when he lectured here two years ago. 'We are following', he said, 'a policy which is self-contradictory and self-frustrating. We are relaxing taxation and seeking, wherever possible, to introduce systems of payments which fluctuate with output. And, at the same time, our price fixing and the consequential rationing system are inspired by egalitarian principles. The result is that we get the worst of both worlds.'[51] And again: 'The belief that, in normal times, it is particularly sensible to try to mix the principles and run an egalitarian real income system side by side with an inegalitarian money income system seems to me somewhat *simpliste*.'[52] Yes, to the economist perhaps, if he tries to judge the situation according to the logic of a market economy. But not necessarily to the sociologist, who remembers that social behaviour is not governed by logic, and that a human society

[50] January 1946.
[51] L. Robbins: *The Economic Problem in Peace and War*, p. 9.
[52] ibid., p. 16.

can make a square meal out of a stew of paradox without getting indigestion—at least for quite a long time. The policy, in fact, may not be *simpliste* at all, but subtle; a newfangled application of the old maxim *divide et impera*—play one off against the other to keep the peace. But, more seriously, the word *simpliste* suggests that the antinomy is merely the result of the muddled thinking of our rulers and that, once they see the light, there is nothing to prevent them altering their line of action. I believe, on the contrary, that this conflict of principles springs from the very roots of our social order in the present phase of the development of democratic citizenship. Apparent inconsistencies are in fact a source of stability, achieved through a compromise which is not dictated by logic. This phase will not continue indefinitely. It may be that some of the conflicts within our social system are becoming too sharp for the compromise to achieve its purpose much longer. But, if we wish to assist in their resolution, we must try to understand their deeper nature and to realize the profound and disturbing effects which would be produced by any hasty attempt to reverse present and recent trends. It has been my aim in these lectures to throw a little light on one element which I believe to be of fundamental importance, namely the impact of a rapidly developing concept of the rights of citizenship on the structure of social inequality.

CHAPTER V

CHANGES IN SOCIAL STRATIFICATION
IN THE TWENTIETH CENTURY

The task assigned to the sub-section for which I speak[1] is to examine the changes that have been taking place in social stratification during the twentieth century. The material submitted is mostly in the form of papers on change in a particular country written by a representative sociologist of that country; this material is supplemented by one or two papers of a more general character (e.g. those by Professors Jessie Bernard, Ossowski and Eisenstadt). The emphasis is placed on changes in the structure of social systems rather than on the movement of individuals and groups within the systems; the latter topic belongs to sub-section 2. The approach is, in the main, historical, but it would be wrong to say that its function is to provide an historical background for the sociological analysis undertaken by Professor Gurvitch and his colleagues of sub-section 3. Social stratification is a subject about which it is impossible to write 'straight' history; every statement must be based on a careful analysis of social structure and a clear definition of concepts. And, as the account moves forward through time, the subject-matter changes and the concepts need to be re-examined and refurbished, and perhaps supplemented, to fit the new situation. This is a task for so-

[1] This paper was presented to the Third World Congress of Sociology in 1956. The general theme of the Congress was 'Social Change'. It was divided into Sections, and the sub-sections referred to here are the subdivisions of the Section on 'Class Structure'. See *Transactions*, Vol. III.

ciologists; nevertheless one may say that my colleagues and I are concerned primarily with the 'what', the 'when' and the 'where' of social change, and Professor Gurvitch and his colleagues with the 'why' and the 'how'. It should further be noticed that the theme allotted to my sub-section is 'stratification', not 'class'. There has been a good deal of discussion of the question whether classes are necessarily associated with strata (see the opening sentences of Professor Ossowski's paper), but the wording of our theme does not assume that they are; it means only that, in our discussion, the focus is on the phenomenon of stratification, whatever its basis.

The choice of 'social change' as the subject for this Congress was a bold one, since there is some truth in the assertion that modern sociologists have been prone to neglect this branch of sociology. In no field of study is this neglect more evident than in that of 'social class'. This is not altogether surprising. If change is to be fully understood, it should be possible to examine the beginning and the end of the process with the help of the same instruments. Where the phenomena studied are highly institutionalized and documented, this can be done with considerable completeness; where they are neither, it can hardly be done at all. It is therefore easier to study change in economic structure than in class structure. For many of the facts relevant to the latter lie concealed in the minds and in the unrecorded informal actions of men, and the refined modern methods used to disclose and assemble them by direct observation of a living society cannot now be applied to societies that have passed away. Concentration on the present is natural, but it is not simply on this account that some recent studies have been criticized.[2] Even an instantaneous picture of social stratification can throw light on structural change if it pays attention to the dynamic forces at work at the moment of study—the tensions and adjustments, the expressed regrets and hopes of the older and younger generations, which reflect the processes which have turned the past into the present and foreshadow those which will turn

[2] See Kurt Mayer: 'The Theory of Social Classes', in *Transactions of the Second World Congress of Sociology*, Vol. II, Part 6.

the present into the future. But the authors of these instantaneous pictures often deliberately eliminate these dynamic forces in an endeavour to discover the essence of the present system, viewed in its own right as a system. They sometimes go even further and take little account of the interaction processes within the system as a whole, and still less of those between it and the world outside. They describe what it looks like, or perhaps what it feels like, rather than how it works. It is to studies of this kind that Professor Mayer refers in his paper when he speaks of 'the essentially static approach which has characterized the many studies concerned with the delineation of status hierarchies in various local communities that have long dominated the field of stratification research in the United States'.

Material of this nature, whatever its intrinsic quality, is not easy to use for the purpose we have in hand. And when we try to piece together a number of 'static' individual studies in order to draw conclusions of a comparative or developmental kind, we are faced with a further difficulty. Terminology is not standardized; authors employ different concepts, and sometimes refer to different things when using the same word—or to the same thing when using different words. This is particularly confusing to the student of change, for he cannot always be sure whether the difference between pictures drawn at two dates is due to change in the phenomenon described at the start of the period, or to a shift of interest on the part of the investigators to a new phenomenon which is still being called by the old name. The way in which these troubles have bedevilled the study of the 'middle classes' and the *bourgeoisie* is familiar to all.[3]

However, it may be possible to make a virtue of necessity and to turn to advantage the apparent defects of the material —the shifts of interest, the multiplicity and ambiguity of concepts, and the vagaries of terminology. These studies are empirical, and we must assume that the aim of the authors is to describe what they find. The confusion in the literature,

[3] See, for instance, Georges Lavau: 'Les Classes moyennes', in M. Duverger: *Partis politiques et classes sociales en France.*

therefore, may reflect the complexities of the subject-matter. If we can disentangle the first, we may make progress towards understanding the second. It may be that changes in the focus of attention reflect changes in the structure of society, and not merely in the fashions current among sociologists—though one cannot be sure of this. This, at least, is a possible line of attack on the subject and the one which I propose to adopt in this paper, namely to search among the tangles of concepts and controversy for clues as to the nature of social change. My aim will be, in the first instance, to try to identify the crucial questions that must be asked about each modern society. The advantage of this apparently rather timid procedure is that one can fruitfully ask the same questions about a fairly wide variety of types of society, whereas any attempt to summarize answers to questions would have to be much more narrowly limited. Even so, what I have to say will refer mainly to what are loosely called 'western' societies, but will, I think, be in some measure applicable also to established Communist societies and to the more recent developments in the more 'westernized' societies of the East. To put it another way, if one accepts the familiar classification of types of stratification into 'caste', 'estate' and 'class', my analysis should apply, with minor modifications, to societies in which the institutions of caste and estate do not enter into the story of recent social change.

The omission of these two terms still leaves us with quite a number to consider. Those in most general use are 'class', 'social class', 'status', 'social status' and 'prestige'. The structure to which these contribute may be described as 'stratification', 'hierarchy' or 'rank order'. No such battery of concepts is found in studies of social systems dominated by caste and estate. So our first question asks whether this multiplication of terms indicates the growth of a multiplicity of stratified systems in each society. In an address delivered something over two years ago, Professor Milton Gordon spoke of the growing 'recognition that social class phenomena are multi-dimensional in nature. This point of view—briefly adumbrated by Max Weber and developed more systematically by recent writers—recognizes that, under the rubric of stratification, an economic dimension, a social status dimension and a political power dimension may be distinguished, and that other variables, such as cultural way of life, group separation, class consciousness, social mobility, and ethnic and group identification, are a part of the total picture.'[4] Notice that he said there has been a growing 'recognition' that the phenomena 'are' multidimensional. He did not say that the phenomena have in fact been becoming multidimensional, or increasingly so. But this is precisely the question we must put and the hypothesis we must examine.

It is both remarkable and slightly ludicrous that it should prove necessary to carry out the most elaborate research in order to discover what the shape of stratification is in modern societies. To past generations it constituted the 'social order' by which their lives were, and should be, governed, and they had no doubts about its nature. It is reasonable to suppose that our modern difficulties arise from the gradual replacement of a simple, clear and institutionalized structure by a complex, nebulous and largely informal one. But the term 'multidimensional' is not enough by itself to describe the new order. Its use may, and sometimes does, obscure the distinction between three significantly different phenomena. The first, to which Professor Gordon was referring, is multidimensional stratification proper, that is the coexistence in one society of two or more systems of stratification, based on different principles or interests. Now in any advanced society in which economic, political, social and cultural activities are well developed, it is almost certain that several dimensions of stratification will operate. The really important question is not whether they exist—they are bound to—but whether, and to what extent, their products converge. These dimensions may be more or less autonomous in their action, and the hierarchy of groups based upon them may coincide to a greater or lesser degree in size, shape and membership.

[4] Milton M. Gordon: 'Social Class and American Intellectuals', in *Bulletin of the American Association of University Professors*, Vol. 40, No. 44, pp. 519–20.

Where the groupings created by different dimensions co-incide, the result is a structure composed of what Professor Sorokin calls 'multibonded' groups. He defines such a group as 'the totality of interacting persons linked by two or more unibonded ties (values, meanings, or norms)'.[5] With these as units we should have, not several distinct systems of strati-fication, but one system based on the combined effect of several criteria. The two concepts—'multidimensional' and 'multi-bonded'—are related but different. In fact we may say that we become most acutely aware that stratification is multi-dimensional when it fails to produce strata that are multi-bonded. I am inclined to go further and suggest that the im-pression that stratification in modern societies has been becoming more multidimensional may be due to the fact that it has been becoming less multibonded.

But there is a quite different set of conditions which can produce two or more distinct systems of stratification in one society. And that is when the society as a whole is not a true unit for stratification in terms of a particular dimension, but must be divided into two or more sections or regional areas each with its own stratification structure. The most familiar example is a society fairly equally divided into agricultural and industrial—or rural and urban—sectors. The social status dimension can be applied to both, but the results cannot be combined into a single scale; the question whether a farmer stands higher or lower than a works manager may be quite meaningless. It is to such discrete social areas that Paul Hatt proposed to give the name of 'situs'.[6]

This brief glance at some recent arguments about terms and concepts leads us to a set of questions about the effects of social change. What has been its effect on (1) the number and nature of the dimensions relevant to stratification; (2) the extent to which these dimensions combine to produce multibonded groups; (3) the extent to which stratification within the various major functional and regional sectors of

[5] P. Sorokin: *Society, Culture and Personality*, p. 236.

[6] 'Occupation and Social Stratification', in *American Journal of Sociology* LV, May 1950.

the society fuses together to produce, with respect to any dimension or all of them, a single system for the whole society?

On the first question we can start with Max Weber's trilogy of the economic, social and political dimensions, or of Class, Status and Party. Of the first he says that 'the factor that creates "class" is unambiguously economic interest' and that 'with some oversimplification, one might thus say that "classes" are stratified according to their relations to the production and acquisition of goods; whereas "status groups" are stratified according to the principles of their consumption of goods as represented by special "styles of life" '.[7] His second dimension I prefer to call 'social status', simply because the term 'status' already has two useful meanings and can hardly be expected to carry a third. It is used by lawyers to denote membership of a group carrying distinctive rights or duties, capacities or incapacities, determined and upheld by public law. And it is used, more broadly, by sociologists and social psychologists, following Linton, to denote any position in a social structure associated with a distinctive role. Neither of these usages necessarily involves the concept of stratification at all, but 'social status' does. The comparative, or invidious, element is essentially implied.[8] Social status, then, is membership of a multibonded group whose various criteria (or dimensions) are valued, weighted and combined so as to produce a single assessment. But each assessment scale may be valid only within a limited area of the society. Of the political dimension it should be noted that, in modern democracies, there can be no stratification of individuals on the basis of voting power, since it is equally distributed. But there may be stratification of political groups or parties in terms of their size and strength, and there must be stratification within parties and within governmental structure (or sphere of political action) as expressed in such a scale as 'leaders, officials, active members, voters', or in the bureaucratic hierarchy of the civil service and so forth.

[7] Quoted from H. H. Gerth and C. Wright Mills: *From Max Weber*, pp. 183, 193.
[8] See Chapter IX.

We can now ask whether these three dimensions still figure in current analysis of stratification, whether there has been any change in the relative importance attached to them, and whether any new dimensions have forced themselves into the picture. It is clear, I think, that the second, social status, has made a strong bid to steal the stage from the other two. At the same time there have been protests that the first, class, must not be overlooked, since it exerts a greater influence than the second on the ways in which social systems work and change. Nevertheless, it is curiously elusive. If class is linked with production, then occupation must be its chief index. But we find that, in study after study, occupation is used only as an index of social status. Or again, if we turn to studies of the influence of social and economic position (including position in the production system) on political attitudes and behaviour—an aspect crucial to the Marxist and Weberian concepts of class—we find that class does not emerge as a substantive social group, but is little more than a middle term in the chain that links position to opinion. Richard Centers, for example, writes: 'Just as people who differ in socio-economic position differ in class affiliation, so people who differ in class affiliation differ in turn in politico-economic orientation.'[9] But, when one looks closer, it seems that this 'class affiliation' can hardly be said to have any independent existence, and that no concrete social group can be pointed to which is the 'class' towards which this 'affiliation' is felt. To find out what is known about the dynamics of class (in the restricted Weberian sense) one must turn to researches in the field of industrial relations, trade unionism, and the bases of power in the economic world. These are often microcosmic, and are not, as a rule, conceived of primarily as contributions to the study of stratification. The same might be said of the third dimension, the political. When politics and stratification are thought of together, the focus of interest is more often the effect of social stratification on political life than the effect of the political factor on stratification. When attention

[9] *The Psychology of Social Classes*, p. 210.

is directed to the hierarchical pattern in politics—to the rise of oligarchy in political parties or parliamentary government, or to the operation of pressure groups—the relation between these and social stratification in general is not the paramount interest.

We can now expand the first of the three questions listed above, introducing some indication of possible answers. Confining ourselves to the three dimensions of class, status and party, we may ask: (1) Has class (in the Marx/Weber sense) been losing importance as a feature of social structure? (2) Has social status been gaining importance as a feature of social structure? (3) Has class been becoming less closely related to stratification? If an affirmative answer were given to question (2) it might assert that the growing importance of social status was absolute, or only that it was relative to the other dimensions. The papers submitted have a good deal to say on these issues, but it will be best, in order to economize in space, to reserve the survey of the evidence until we can at the same time explore the second of the first set of three questions, namely, the extent to which the various dimensions combine to produce multibonded groups. But before we can take up this point we must ask whether any new dimensions have entered the picture.

Among the additional variables listed by Professor Gordon only one, ethnic affiliation, could qualify as a separate dimension, and obviously that is not a new factor in society. Another candidate for consideration, in many respects a similar and a related one, is religious affiliation. It might be expected that, in the period under consideration, these would be factors of diminishing importance in systems of stratification, owing to the movement towards equality of human rights, religious liberty, and the retreat of imperialism (with, of course, certain notable exceptions), and to progressive assimilation of immigrants in countries having a 'melting-pot' character. But one notices recent observations like the following: among Catholics in Elmira 'the religious affiliation (and the ethnic differences it represents) appears to be a stronger influence upon the vote than any other single factor',[10] and 'the most striking fact about Quebec politics is that ethnic solidarity has over-ridden class divisions within the French-Canadian commu-nity'.[11] This suggests the possibility that ethnic and religious affiliations have been, in some cases, of growing significance in community life, not because they have been gaining abso-lutely in strength, but because the competing loyalty to class has become less compelling as a determinant of social action. They may not be, strictly speaking, dimensions of stratifica-tion, but may nevertheless contribute to the confusion and complexity of the stratification system as a whole by providing alternative preoccupations and drives.

Another disturbing factor to which attention is sometimes drawn is the effect of mass media and publicity of all kinds in building up hierarchies of celebrities in the worlds of sport, adventure, radio and cinema and the rest. There is a kind of stratification here which certainly does not fall under the con-cept of class, and does not fit in easily to the pattern of social status, especially if the latter tends to build more and more on local assessments of position on the scale (a point to which I must return later).[12] The point I wish to make here is sim-ply that, if the clear-cut lines of stratification are fading, this may be due, not merely to the growth of more dimensions of stratification, but also to the emergence of more dimensions of social grouping of all kinds—possibly only their emergence from the shadow of the all-compelling class loyalty of the mid-capitalist phase of social history.

We can now bring in the second of the original three ques-tions and ask whether the dimensions have been diverging or converging in their impact on the system of stratification. I have once or twice above spoken of the Marx/Weber concept of class, basing this term on the fact that both of them de-scribed class as economic in character and related to produc-

[10] R. Berelson and others: *Voting*, p. 65.

[11] Dennis H. Wrong, in a paper submitted to the 1955 Congress of the International Political Science Association.

[12] On this whole question see H. H. Hyman: 'The Psychology of Status', *Archives of Psychology*, No. 269, 1942.

tion and the distribution of power within the economic system of production. But on the point before us now they differ. Weber saw class as one of three principles of organization all of which could co-exist in the same society. For Marx class was a unique and dominating principle. It was economic in essence, but 'the struggle of class against class is a political struggle' from which emerges a 'ruling class', and 'the ideas of the ruling class are in every epoch the ruling ideas'.[13] This implies that, as a social system establishes itself, the three dimensions will converge until the economic, political and cultural hierarchies are identical. By a different route Mosca came to a somewhat similar conclusion that 'in all societies . . . two classes of people appear—a class that rules and a class that is ruled'.[14] Finally we must remember the prophecy of James Burnham that managers, having ousted the property-owners from the control of industry, would assert their power over the political machine. Are there any signs in recent history of this trend towards a fusion of two or more of the three dimensions so as to produce something in the nature of a ruling class?

The answer, so far as 'western' democratic-capitalist and/or socialist societies are concerned must be in the negative. The reverse is nearer the truth. As Raymond Aron put it, in a study which goes deeply into this question, 'the fundamental difference between a society of the Soviet type and one of the Western type is that the former has a unified *élite* and the latter a divided *élite*'.[15] A divided *élite* is a collection of persons coming from different social origins and drawing their personal power from different sources; it is the antithesis of a ruling class, for the simple reason that it is not a class. But it would be very rash to generalize about the trend of social change in this respect. For one thing political systems differ too much from one country to another. For another there are

13 Quoted in R. Bendix and S. M. Lipset: *Class, Status and Power*, pp. 30–1.
14 G. Mosca: *The Ruling Class* (1939), p. 50.
15 'Social Structure and the Ruling Class', in *The British Journal of Sociology*, Vol. 1, 1950, p. 10.

some conflicting features about observable trends in recent years. Although David Butler, a close student of British elections, may say that 'class interest by itself is quite inadequate as an explanation of voting behaviour',[16] it is by no means certain that the correlation between class and voting has been weakening; it may even have been getting stronger, especially in the professional and business classes.[17] If it were to do so in the future, and one party were to obtain, for itself or by coalition, a permanent title to govern, this would amount to a return towards a ruling-class situation. It has also been noticed that party officials and members of parliament are usually drawn from a narrower social range than the rank and file of their supporters; there is a tendency towards concentration in the broad middle areas of the social scale. Now Mosca, it will be remembered, said that there must always be a 'second stratum' of the ruling class, more numerous than the first, and containing 'all the capacities for leadership in the country'. The bureaucracy, he maintained, even if nominally open to all, 'will always be recruited from the second stratum of the ruling class'.[18] The concentration of candidates for political and administrative office in the middle ranks of society may be a fact; but the description of this middle section as part of a ruling class does not ring true. Several contributors point out that, in many countries, the middle class has been expanding until it contains nearly the whole population; there is hardly anything left for it to rule. Also, when educational opportunity is equal, it would be as true to say that the middle class is recruited through the bureaucracy as that the bureaucracy is recruited from the middle class. However, it would be worth while to consider whether there are any signs that social selection through an open educational system may produce a new species of 'unified *élite*' in democratic societies, and perhaps in time a new type of ruling class. Could stratifi-

[16] 'Voting Behaviour and Its Study in Britain', in *The British Journal of Sociology*, Vol. VI, No. 2, p. 102.

[17] See Berelson: *Voting*, p. 57, and John Bonham: *The Middle Class Vote*, Chapter 7.

[18] *The Ruling Class*, pp. 404, 408.

cation by education come to dominate, and to oust from the scene, stratification by other dimensions?

Quite different causes for the emergence of a ruling class are discussed by Professor Eisenstadt who writes of stratification in a society which has recently won its political independence or undergone a major revolution. The system here, he suggests, is likely to be 'monolithic' and dominated by the political factor. The 'power variable', he says, 'has an autonomy of its own', and in certain circumstances 'the holders of power tend to establish it as the most important criterion of stratification, to which all other criteria and rewards should be subordinated'. If we accept this view as reasonable and if we infer that the trend towards more multidimensional stratification is characteristic of well-established independent societies, what shall we expect to find in a country which has become settled after a major revolution, for example, in the Soviet Union? One may suggest that the 'dictatorship of the proletariat', operating through the militant arm of the Party, is an example of 'monolithic' or unidimensional stratification dominated by the political factor. But has any tendency towards multidimensional stratification developed as the new social order settled down? It is clear that there is a hierarchy of political power within the Party, even though it may be disputed whether the Party as a whole is a 'stratum' in the sense in which that term may be used of the hereditary aristocracies or feudal 'ruling classes' of the past. Professor Ossowski maintains that economic classes exist, based, for example, on the division between agriculture and industry, but that these have nothing to do with stratification. Granted this use of the term 'class', the conclusion may be accepted. If all power is ultimately political, there can be no stratification on the basis of economic power as a separate dimension. But the intriguing question is whether there is a 'social status' dimension of stratification, arising from a combination of prestige ranking in the political hierarchy, of individual esteem derived from exceptional services, and of the institutionalized inequality of incomes. Of the latter Professor Ossowski says that it is a 'scheme of simple gradation' which cannot produce stratification when there is no private ownership of the instruments of production. This may be true if one thinks of class in terms of power, but does not answer the question if one is thinking of stratification in terms of social status. On this point it might be more fruitful to compare the situation in the Soviet Union with an example of the unfettered private ownership of the instruments of production in an extreme form, such as the northern United States in the days of rapid economic expansion. It may be argued that here there was a 'scheme of simple gradation' based on income, and that, in spite of great inequalities of this kind, all men were treated as of equal worth as men and citizens, and all were supposed to be equally exposed to the chance of rising or falling in the scale of wealth. We have here, perhaps, two rather different examples of the irrelevance of income inequalities to social status.

We might also take note here of two other references to the political factor which occur in the papers submitted. The first is the statement by Professor Heberle that in the southern United States, in which there had been something like a ruling class of planters (though, he maintains, this was not in origin a hereditary aristocracy), there occurred in the early twentieth century 'the growth of a new economic ruling class of top executives and managers, many of whom are not natives of the South'. This class exercised great, and often decisive, influence over local and state government, although its members rarely held public office. This has a distinct flavour of Burnham about it, and it would be interesting to discuss whether this is an exceptional phenomenon in the picture of twentieth-century social change.

The second reference is in the paper by Professor Raymond Aron on the special case of France. He describes how, in the post-war period, the classical form of class conflict between employers and employed yielded place to a permanent battle in which the various competing or conflicting social groups directed their action mainly against the State, a battle 'qui différait essentiellement des notions traditionelles de lutte de classes'. As soon as the State ceased to regulate wages, 'le conflit employeurs-employés est redevenu réel'. But at no

time did the government, which was the centre of this tur-
moil, appear as the representative of a particular class.

From this brief survey I extract two propositions about
unidimensional, or monolithic, stratification in the post-
estate era. First, that a ruling class based on the political
factor is most likely to exist (a) following on revolutionary
change and (b) where political power is centralized and
State action is all-pervasive, i.e. in a planned society. Second,
that a ruling class based on the economic factor is most likely
to exist (a) where the dominating political principle is one of
laissez faire so that state action does not profoundly affect the life of the people, and (b) where government is
decentralized, or federal, and the economic factor can assert
itself over the political in local and regional government. The
first may be rather platitudinous, but the second might have
some value for an interpretation of the last fifty years in the
light of the preceding century.

What I have been saying refers to possible forms of con-
vergence in which the political dimension plays a crucial part.
I must now consider the same theme with reference to the
two dimensions of class and social status, and take up at the
same time the three questions I listed earlier (see p. 143
above) when I asked whether class has been losing importance, whether social status has been gaining in importance,
and whether class has been becoming less closely related to
stratification. It is with problems of this kind that most of
the papers are mainly concerned, and I can therefore deal
with them more briefly and in large part by reference to what
can be read elsewhere in the documents which have been
circulated.

The most general treatment of this theme is that of Professor Jessie Bernard. She contrasts the modern economy of
abundance with former systems based on scarcity. Because,
in modern mechanized civilizations, the prosperity of the
masses is necessary as the basis of the market through which
the few become rich (or relatively richer), Marx's prophecy
of a growing gulf between 'haves' and 'have-nots' is falsified
and reversed and the force of class-consciousness and class-

conflict dwindles. The result is not a homogeneous or wholly egalitarian society, but one in which social status counts for more than class interest as a basis of stratification. Professor Aron follows a similar line of thought when he says that the general trend of progress in capitalist societies has followed the principle of Colin Clark instead of that of Karl Marx; with the growth, in turn, of the secondary and tertiary sectors of the economy the standard of living has risen, and the central gulf in the social order has been bridged and filled by a new and varied collection of middle-class occupations. Professor Aron's purpose is to argue that it is because this development has not taken place in France that French society is marked by conflict and political extremism whereas other societies are marked by peace and political moderation. Professor Girod analyses Swiss history with the use of the same concepts, and Mr Brennan, writing about the British working class, stresses the point (mentioned also by others) that the working class, from being 'regarded as one of the raw materials of industry', has been fully admitted into society in terms both of culture and of actual or potential power. Similarly Professor Ossowski admits that Marx's forecast became inapplicable after the rise of the new middle class and the Welfare State.

One may distinguish three elements in this picture. There is first the aspect of consumption—the rise in the level of consumption as a whole and the compressing of the scale, which becomes at the same time both shorter and more continuous; it is less likely that differences in standard of living will produce self-conscious, antagonized social groups. There is secondly the aspect of the rights of citizenship—the admission of all to full membership of the society, which carries with it rights to freedom, to political power and to welfare. And there is thirdly the structural change in the economy which makes the distribution of property less decisively determinant of the distribution of power, and less important than the distribution of productive forces between the primary, secondary and tertiary sectors.

It should be remembered that Colin Clark's principle of

analysis does not lead, by any means, to any simple generalization about trends in all developing economies during the last half century, and that it may prove less helpful towards understanding the phase of change into which the world is now moving. But, leaving such comments aside, the important point is to consider whether the trends of change about which there seems to be a considerable measure of agreement have led to, and might be expected to lead to, a diminution in the power of class as a social force. Now, position in the production system is not something that could be identified, by a complete outsider, by simple objective tests; it is not definable in terms of the technical function performed, the skill used or the article produced. It is a social concept, as Marx saw very clearly, depending on the relevant relations between men in the production system and on the values attached to them; it has a psychological element. Some factor or factors must come into operation to decide whether the multitude of jobs and occupations is going to split up into three classes, or three hundred, or three thousand. Among the possible factors are invidious comparison and conflict of basic interests. As Marx wrote in *The German Ideology* (1938, p. 49): 'The separate individuals form a class only in so far as they have to carry on a common battle against another class; otherwise they are on hostile terms with each other as competitors.' There is a clear case for arguing that, as extreme poverty, exploitation and 'alienation' diminish, so will the drive towards such a battle grow less strong. One would then expect the classes to break up into smaller functional groups, acting as units in pursuit of their much more specialized interests. But it does not seem that this is what has been happening. At least in the U.S. and the U.K. the quite recent trend has been towards even larger trade union amalgamations. There may have been some pressure in the opposite direction, but it has been counteracted. And this has happened in spite of the strength of the factor to which Professor Aron has referred, the central position of the State as director of economic planning, and its entry into direct relations with each functional group concerned in the operation of its plans. He attributes to this the temporary decline, at least in France, of the classical form of class conflict. A similar tendency may be seen elsewhere, but it seems to have been held in check.

I am suggesting that it would be rash to conclude that class has been losing its importance; but it may be true that it has been changing its character. And it may be that this change consists in a detachment from social stratification in the old sense. Compare the following two pictures. (1) The economic structure of society places a large number of people in fundamentally the same position, so far as the social relations arising out of their productive labours are concerned. This fact, and the common interests arising from it, lead to the formation of a social group, or quasi-group, which becomes conscious of itself in terms both of these interests and of its level in the social hierarchy; it becomes a social class. Out of this group there proceed certain forms of behaviour, both individual and collective. (2) Within the economic structure of society there are many functionally distinct groups, each based on its productive role and the conditions under which it is performed. On some matters the interests of these groups differ; on others they are the same. Associations exist, and spread, for the pursuit of these common interests whenever they arise and with such degree of combination of groups as they demand. The members of these combining groups differ greatly in social level, and the organizations are for them rationally designed instruments for the achievement of certain specific and limited ends, albeit very important ones. In the latter case one need not postulate the existence of the middle term, the 'social class', membership of which induces certain kinds of behaviour. And the associations do not necessarily permeate the whole lives of their members, as social classes do, nor are they always in action; and at times the constituent sub-groups may be more important than the largest aggregate. Perhaps there has been a trend from (1) in the direction of (2), which might be described, not exactly as a weakening of class, but as a detachment of class from stratification—or social class—in the old sense. This might be described as a weakening of class in the Marxian sense, on the grounds that the operative interest-groups are no longer determined by the social relationships within the system of production, that is, primarily by property. This, on the whole, is the view taken by the late Theodor Geiger in his penetrating essay, *Die Klassengesellschaft im Schmelztiegel* (especially pp. 133–6). Or one might maintain that economic interest-groups, standing to one another in a relationship of superiority and inferiority in terms of the normal location of institutionalized power and the day-to-day chain of command, are still important elements in social structure, but that they do not reflect the more generalized and deeply permeating inequalities which determine the system of social stratification. Or, to put it crudely, the differences of social level between such groups may not be much greater than those within each group.

One small point might be added, drawn from Professor van Doorn's paper about the unskilled workers in the Netherlands. It might be thought that the unskilled workers would remain untouched by these mollifying influences, and that class would remain for them a deep and continuing influence closely associated with their inferior general position, that is, with stratification. The evidence suggests that this would be so in the case of some of them at least, because they lie outside the continuum of economic citizens that stretches from the semi-skilled wage-earner to the manager, were it not that they are a heterogeneous, fluctuating, unstable collection of persons with no basis for common consciousness or common action. They are all that is left of the proletariat, thrown back to where it started from. They are, as Professor van Doorn puts it, 'residual groups' forming part of 'a rather isolated social bottom layer, living on the border of social maladjustment'. In a study of the British working class, Dr Dahrendorf uses the same term, 'un groupe résiduel',[19] but applies it to the unskilled workers as a whole, whereas Professor van Doorn is speaking only of the lowest elements among them;

[19] R. Dahrendorf: 'La situation de la classe ouvrière en Angleterre', in *La Revue Socialiste*, No. 89, July 1955.

but the difference of application may be largely a matter of the definition of the term 'unskilled'.

We must next consider the question whether the dimension of social status has been gaining in importance, either absolutely or relatively to the class dimension. Here we might expect to find some difference between the European countries whose past structure was based on estates which, by a process of de-institutionalization, have transmitted a system of social status to the present (which is in turn being eroded by increasing equality of welfare and opportunity), and those countries, most notably the United States, which never had estates and in which social status may have developed fairly recently as economic inequalities became stabilized and linked with cultural values.

As regards the former type, the evidence points to a diminishing real importance of social status in recent years. But this judgement must be qualified in two ways. First, it must be remembered that our period includes the time when the new middle class was expanding and seeking to consolidate its position between the proletariat and the higher ranks of the *bourgeoisie* and was, in the process, acquiring, by imitation of its superiors, a strong and even exaggerated preoccupation with the insignia of social status. Secondly, as the real importance of social status differences diminishes, some sections of society may cling to whatever remains of them, grasping all the more desperately at the shadow because the substance seems to be slipping away.

That something of this kind has been happening can hardly be doubted. One might refer, for views on the fading of status differences, to Geiger's work on Denmark[20] (probably applicable broadly to Scandinavian society as a whole), and, for further views on this and on the survival of status anxieties, to Professor Schelsky's paper on Western Germany submitted to the Liège Congress,[21] and to Professor Bernard's

[20] T. Geiger: *Soziale Umschichtungen in einer dänischen Mittelstadt*, especially pp. 110–12.
[21] H. Schelsky: 'Die Bedeutung des Schichtungsbegriffes für die Analyse der gegenwärtigen deutschen Gesellschaft', in *Transactions of the Second World Congress of Sociology*, Vol. ii, Part 6.

contribution to this Congress. One can also note the point made by Professor Hofstee about the small farmers and agricultural workers in the Netherlands. As the wages of the latter rise above the earnings of the former, 'the feeling of inferiority towards the small farmer is beginning to disappear'. And the sons of the small farmers leave the land, but they do not become industrial wage-earners; they seek places in handicrafts, trade and administration. 'Social position and a certain feeling of freedom and independence seem to count more for them than income.'[22] This warns us to be careful not to exaggerate the change. When some social status differences are obliterated, others may replace them in the lives of the people affected. Similarly, as the prestige attached to hereditary, or ascribed, social status declines, more opportunities may arise for the achievement of social status—though it is important to remember that this in itself involves a considerable change in the structure of stratification. It is safe to conclude that, in the countries of Western Europe during the last fifty years taken as a whole, the real importance of the social status dimension has not increased.

The picture in the United States looks at first rather different. A people, most of whom were untouched by snobbish pride fifty years or so ago, now responds readily and with apparent understanding to the spate of questionnaires on social status with which it is bombarded, as though this phenomenon had become for it a matter of familiarity and consequence. But here again one must beware of exaggeration. The responses, though ready, are not wholly consistent, suggesting that the feelings behind them are not very deep. And part of what is found may be due, as in Europe, to the belated growth of 'status anxiety' in the minds of the new middle class. Professor Mayer points out that 'the image of America as a society where "everybody is middle class" has persisted long after it ceased to be in accordance with economic and social reality', and that in quite recent years economic change has been making the image truer to the facts. And he adds that 'most Americans tend to perceive and interpret objec-

22 E. W. Hofstee: 'Changes in Rural Social Stratification in the Netherlands', in *Transactions*, Vol. II, Part 2, pp. 78–9.

tive economic differences as individual, not as class, differences'. Any considerable strengthening of the social status dimension would be expected to have the opposite effect in both cases.

This brings me to my final point, which is in a sense an amalgamation of two or three points mentioned earlier. Has social status been becoming more local, individual and autonomous in recent years? To save time and space I will again use the expository device of presenting a bold hypothesis. Let us suppose that the social status dimension, as a factor creating nation-wide stratified social groups, closely related to economic classes and therefore to fundamentally economic interests, has been diminishing in force, but that the position of the individual within the social hierarchy of his local community remains a matter of importance and concern to him, and one in which his interest is shared by the members of a rather nebulous and amorphous group clustered round the point in the social scale at which he stands. Let us then suggest that this would solve the problem of reconciling the evidence for the declining real importance of social status with the signs of continued and widespread anxieties about it. It would also explain the point of those 'static' studies of 'status hierarchies in various local communities' to which Professor Mayer referred. We may then add the proposition that class, in the Marx/Weber sense, has been developing into a structure of functional interest-groups, not exactly determined by stratification, and that, in terms of the objective facts of income and standard (possibly also style) of living, most western societies have been developing an enormous middle class (with relatively little above and below it), and that the social status hierarchies just described do not, and cannot, correspond very closely to either of these. In this sense, perhaps, social status has been becoming more local, individual and autonomous.

If we revert to the method suggested at the beginning of this paper of seeking clues in the use or misuse of concepts, some confirmation can be found. The term 'social class' (as distinct from plain 'class' and 'social status') is beginning to sound old-fashioned. It suggests groups possessed both of real and vital common economic interests and of a group-consciousness of their general position in the social scale. In other words it refers to a product of converging dimensions and a system of multibonded groups. 'Social status', on the other hand, does not necessarily imply the existence of groups at all; it could be used with reference to a continuous scale of invidiously valued positions. Nor does it imply a system wholly determined by economic interest derived from position in the productive system; other factors may enter, and traditional values may outlive the economic circumstances to which they originally referred. Another popular term is 'prestige', which is rather less institutional than 'social status' and makes possible the inclusion in the picture of a man's personal qualities as well as the consensus as to the social ranking of the position he occupies. It might include what I have elsewhere called 'personal social status' as distinct from 'positional social status'.[23] And finally, if this were the general trend of social change, then clearly the unique features of the local community would gain in importance as compared with the general characteristics of the total society, since only by reference to them can, in most cases, the more personal factors be weighed and valued.

In conclusion I should like to say that much of what I have written is highly speculative; this represents a deliberate attempt to provide material for discussion. Also, I have tried to suggest the direction of social change during the last fifty years (almost entirely in Europe and North America), but I have not attempted to measure its extent. I do not suggest that these changes have progressed to the point at which a new society emerges; far from it. Nor is it by any means certain that the direction of change will not alter long before such a revolution has been produced.

[23] See Chapter VIII.

CHAPTER VI

THE RECENT HISTORY OF PROFESSIONALISM IN RELATION TO SOCIAL STRUCTURE AND SOCIAL POLICY

The professions, conceived as a select body of superior occupations, have existed from time immemorial, although their identity has often been in dispute. The ancients wrote and argued about them,[1] while Herbert Spencer traced their origin among primitive peoples.[2] The earliest view to which we need here pay attention was that occupations should be judged and valued according to their compatibility with the good life. They were to be tested by their effect on the giver of the service rather than on the recipient. The professions were, in English parlance, the occupations suitable for a gentleman. This idea naturally flourished in societies which distinguished sharply between life lived as an end in itself, and life passed in providing the means which enable others to live as free civilized men should. The professions in such a society were those means to living which were most innocuous, in that they did not dull the brain, like manual labour, nor corrupt the soul, like commerce. They even contained within themselves qualities and virtues which might well find a place among the ends of the good life itself. Leisure, based on the ownership of land or of slaves, was the chief mark of aristoc-

---

[1] See, for example, Otto Neurath: 'Zur Anschauung der Antike über Handel, Gewerbe und Landwirtschaft', in *Jahrbücher für Nationalökonomie und Statistik* (Jena, 1906, Vol. LXXXVII, p. 577).
[2] *The Principles of Sociology* (London, 1896), Vol. III, Part VII.

racy, and here too the professions were but slightly inferior. For leisure does not mean idleness. It means the freedom to choose your activities according to your own preferences and your own standards of what is best. The professions, it was said, enjoyed this kind of freedom, not so much because they were free from the control of an employer—that was assumed —but rather because, for them, choice was not restricted and confined by economic pressure. The professional man, it has been said, does not work in order to be paid: he is paid in order that he may work. Every decision he takes in the course of his career is based on his sense of what is right, not on his estimate of what is profitable. That, at least, is the impression he would like to create when defending his claim to superior status.

This position was a difficult one for the professions to maintain. Their dilemma was indicated by Adam Smith. He wrote:

> We trust our health to the physician, our fortune and sometimes our life and reputation to the lawyer and attorney. Such confidence could not safely be reposed in people of a very mean or low condition. Their reward must be such, therefore, as may give them that rank in the society which so important a trust requires.[3]

The professions, in other words, are respectable because they do not strive for money, but they can only remain respectable if they succeed, in spite of this pecuniary indifference, in making quite a lot of money, enough for the needs of a gentlemanly life. Money must flow in as an almost unsolicited recognition of their inestimable services. Nor did Adam Smith make things any easier for them by classing them as 'unproductive labour', a judgement with which many ordinary men and women, when faced with the necessity of employing a lawyer, are only too prone to concur.

But conditions have changed since then. Leisure is no longer in the same sense the mark of aristocracy, and commerce is no longer a disreputable occupation. Leisure is, of course,

[3] *An Inquiry into the Nature and Causes of the Wealth of Nations*, ed. Edwin Cannan, 5th ed. (London, 1930), Vol. 1, p. 107.

still important as a determinant of social status, but instead of describing a spiritual quality of freedom that pervades the whole of one's activities, it means merely the way one spends one's money when the day's work is done. The way the money is earned is increasingly unimportant. It is the quantity that matters. The business man's leisure is as good as anyone else's, because leisure is simply the antithesis to work.[4] And in addition he can pay apparent homage to the older ideas by purchasing complete idleness for his wife, and by himself becoming a complete and genuine gentleman of leisure when he retires from business. The professional man had to change his ground. He had to admit that his occupation was laborious, like the tradesman's—and even to glory in the fact—but to assert that it was labour of a special and superior kind. In defining its peculiar character the emphasis was shifted from the effect of the service on the giver to that on the recipient, or, more accurately, to the relationship between the two. The idea of service became more important than the idea of freedom. Certain professional types, representing the old view in its extreme form, grew more scarce and are now almost extinct: for example, the man of good family but insufficient means who occupied a sinecure in the service of the State; the humbler member of a similar stock, ill-endowed with brains and character, who drifted through the Civil Service leaving little impression of his passage; the hunting parson and the wealthy ecclesiastical pluralist; the young aristocrat who entered the army as a pastime rather than as a career; the scholar who regarded pupils as intruders disturbing the peace of his academic life; the schoolmaster who felt that he fully discharged his duties by being a gentleman and a sportsman—a type of which some examples may still be found in England today. There was no honourable place for these in the strenuous and efficient life of the nineteenth century. Even in medicine, where the value of training and hard work is most obvious, the standard of scientific qualifications had declined as the profession became recognized as a gateway

[4] See H. V. Durant: *The Problem of Leisure* (London, 1938), Chapter 1.

to social prestige and opportunity. Carr-Saunders, referring
to conditions in England in the eighteenth century, writes:

> The physicians had long established themselves in the
> upper ranks of society, and when scientific inquiry lost
> its novelty, they joined in the ample life of the great
> houses where elegance and wit were pursued. . . . Social
> qualifications became the first requirement for member-
> ship [of the College of Physicians], and it was held that
> the necessary 'morals and manners' could be learnt only
> at the universities.[5]

With the foundation of the British Medical Association
in 1856 and of the General Medical Council in 1858 this
period of lassitude came to an end.

There can be no doubt that, in mid-Victorian England,
the professions were prosperous and respected, and they owed
their position mainly to the work of the professional associations. The principles of their policy are familiar, and there
is no space in this paper to go into detail. In the first place
the association guarantees the technical efficiency of its members, not by supervising their work, but by testing their ability
before they are admitted to practise. This involves an indirect
control of their training. Secondly, it imposes a code of ethics
which includes the duty to offer service whenever and wherever
it is required, to give only the best, to abstain from competition, advertisement and all commercial haggling, and to respect the confidence of the client. Thirdly, it does what it
can to protect its field from invasion by the unqualified—
that is, it enjoys a partial monopoly—and to keep up the
standard of remuneration of its members, and in general to
safeguard the conditions of their work.

It can be argued that all this insistence on service and on
ethical obligations is a mere camouflage to disguise the purely
selfish desire to create an artificial scarcity and to win the
material and immaterial advantages which scarcity can confer.
I do not propose to deal directly with the evidence for and

[5] A. M. Carr-Saunders and P. A. Wilson: *The Professions* (Oxford, 1933), p. 71.

against this view, but to approach the subject indirectly by
asking whether the ethical code is an arbitrary fabrication of
the professional mind or whether it reflects some real characteristics which distinguish the professions from the trades.

Ethical codes are based on the belief that between professional and client there is a relationship of trust, and between
buyer and seller there is not. In so far as the professions pur-
vey services and the trades commodities, the difference is
obvious. The commodity can be inspected before it is paid
for: the service cannot. The principle of *caveat emptor* is at
least plausible when you are buying a horse or a pound of
strawberries: it makes nonsense when you are calling in a
surgeon to a case of acute appendicitis. But there is more to
it than that. Many services can be satisfactorily controlled by
commercial contracts. Some of them, like those of the builder
or the tailor, lead to the production of a commodity which
can be judged by objective tests and rejected if it is not according to specification. But if you engage an artist to paint
your portrait, you must accept—and pay for—whatever he produces. If he says it is his finest work, you are in no position
to contradict him. Other services are so standardized and
impersonal that they can be exactly measured and defective
work can be penalized. Where labour is employed in the mass
on a man-week basis, any failure of an individual workman to
come up to expectations is quickly remedied, without serious
loss, by dismissal. Standardized labour, in fact, can be treated
as a commodity. But with the professions it is otherwise. It
is beyond the wit of man to devise a contract that would
specify, in terms that could be enforced, what it is that the
client expects to receive.

There are two reasons for this. One is that professional
service is not standardized. It is unique and personal. But that
is true to some extent of all skilled labour. The professional
man is distinguished by the further fact that he does not give
only his skill. He gives himself. His whole personality enters
into his work. It is hardly possible to be satisfied with a doctor
or a lawyer unless one likes and respects him as a man. He
is called upon to show judgement and an understanding of

human nature, as well as a knowledge of medicine or law. The best service can be given only when the practitioner knows his client intimately, his character, his foibles, his background and his family circumstances. That is why the British Medical Association is now deploring the way in which specialization and institutional treatment are ousting the family doctor from his key position. These essential qualities cannot be specified in a contract, they cannot be bought. They can only be given. The clients trust to professional traditions and professional ethics to develop and train those qualities and make them available for the service of the public. The mistrust of women doctors, which is not yet quite overcome, was probably due to the feeling that they had not had the chance to imbibe these traditions. During their training they were kept on the fringes of the medical community, while, in addition, the influences of home and school, which had long been directed to producing in boys the virtues demanded by the codes of professional ethics, had ignored the girls or even fostered in them quite different qualities. Any member of the working class who aspires to professional status has to fight against the same difficulties and the same suspicions.

With art, which is also classed among the professions, the case is different. The artist, too, cannot labour in a detached, impersonal way, with his eye on the clock and his mind on his cheque. He, too, must give something that is deeply rooted in his nature, something that cannot be commanded or coerced, or even bribed. But with him it is not his human judgement, his probity, his sound knowledge of life and affairs. It is his creative genius. The attitude of the client to the lawyer is roughly this. 'I am asking you', he says, 'to act as my brain in this matter. I want you to think and judge for me, because I haven't the technical equipment to think and judge for myself. But please do so exactly as I should if I knew the law.' The lawyer, therefore—and I am thinking here of the solicitor rather than the barrister—must have the qualities of the ordinary man undiluted by the ordinary weaknesses. He must be a model of the unshakable middle-class virtues. Eccentricity is fatal, and his private life must be beyond reproach. The artist, on the other hand, is valued because he is different, peculiar. He has the spark that is lacking in the composition of the ordinary man. Eccentricity is an asset. He can thrive on scandal. But the principle of the relationship is the same, for in both cases the professional must be trusted to give what he cannot be compelled or contractually bound to give.

The second reason for the relationship of trust has already been hinted at. It is the ignorance of the client. He often hardly knows what to ask for, let alone how it can be provided. He must surrender all initiative and put himself in his lawyer's hands or under his doctor's orders. That is the great difference between the services of professionals and the services of wage-earners or salaried employees. Authority passes from buyer to seller. It is true that the modern salesman tries to use authority, but with a difference. When the doctor says, 'Take more exercise', it is a command. When the associated greengrocers plaster the hoardings with the slogan, 'Eat more fruit', it is an effort at mass suggestion.

One crucial point has still to be considered before we can sum up this part of the argument, and that is the balance between the duty to the client and the duty to the community. The relationship of trust implies a deep obligation to the client. But an organized profession rightly regards itself as a body placed in charge of an art or science and responsible for directing its use in the interests of society. These two obligations can be reconciled without difficulty if the true interests of society and of the individual are harmonious. A profession proceeds on the assumption that they are. When they seem to be in conflict it is usually because the individual does not know what is good for him. The client, as we have seen, is often ignorant. Authority passes to the professional, who must give him what he needs, rather than what he wants. The client, unlike the customer, is not always right. The guilty criminal wants an acquittal, but what he needs, and what his lawyer must give him, is a fair trial. Now need is a social concept. It can only be assessed in relation to the social order within which the individual is living, and in assessing it the professional must draw on standards that are within his own mind and conscience, placed there by his training and his traditions. Sometimes the State solves his problem by issuing a precise order, as when it forbids a doctor to procure an abortion on an unwilling mother who is physically capable of bearing a child without risk to herself. Sometimes the profession lays down a rule. But often the professional must judge for himself, as when a painter refuses to prostitute his art to the bad taste of the public.

The professions have not always lived up to these high ideals. They have not always struck a true balance between loyalty to the client and loyalty to the community, and they have sometimes treated loyalty to the profession as an end rather than as a means to the fulfilment of the other loyalties. They are often accused of neglecting the public welfare. Doctors, it is said, showed too little interest in public health, architects in town planning, scholars in general education and artists in the culture of the masses. These are sins of omission. Against the lawyers the graver charge has been made that they used their position to defeat the real intentions of the law in order to benefit their clients and themselves. American lawyers, said Theodore Roosevelt, made it 'their special task to work out bold and ingenious schemes by which their wealthy clients, individual and corporate, can evade the laws which were made to regulate, in the interests of the public, the uses of wealth'.[6] There have been many other statements in the same sense, especially, though not exclusively, with reference to lawyers in the United States. Sometimes, however, the charge is found on examination to be, not that lawyers have frustrated the law, but that they have worked to maintain a legal system of which the critic disapproves.

The position of the professions in the recent past was a curious one. They enjoyed, as organizations, varying degrees of group monopoly and developed, in varying degrees, a group spirit and a group conscience. And yet their general attitude was one of intense individualism, which made them unsym-

[6] William Durran: *The Lawyer, Our Old-man-of-the-sea* (London, 1913), p. 50.

pathetic, or at least indifferent, to social planning. But they evinced strong disapproval of competition and unrestricted self-seeking among their members. In estimating the significance of this position it is important to discover the true balance between its individualist and corporate elements. Professor Laski, in a recent article, has laid the main weight on the former. 'The individualistic organization of these professions', he writes, 'is now fatal to the fulfilment of their function. They cannot, I shall argue, give of their best to the civilization in which they play so large a part so long as their members offer their services for private hire and sale. . . . In the present state of civilization the prospect of their fulfilling their end as a profession declines rather than grows.'[7] This suggests that, so long as the professional works on his own for fees paid directly by his clients, his pecuniary interests will prevent him from fulfilling his social obligations, whatever professional associations may do, through their ethical codes, to curb the profit motive in their members.

First let us be clear what these codes imply. They do not assert that a professional man should be indifferent to money and unambitious to extend his practice and increase his income. They assert only that he must do this legitimately, without impairing the quality of his work or withholding those extra personal services which cannot be specifically demanded by the client and are not specifically paid for. Now, the facts do not suggest that this ideal is unattainable while professional men continue in private practice. The cases most commonly cited as evidence of failure are those of the fashionable medical specialist and the successful barrister. The charge has foundation. The opportunities for money-making in such positions are great enough to tempt some to deviate from strict professional standards. But it should be noticed that the specialist differs from the general practitioner and the barrister from the solicitor precisely on the point that they never establish that close relationship with the client that is the foundation of true professionalism. They are called in *to* a

[7] 'The Decline of the Professions', in *Harper's Monthly Magazine*, November 1935, pp. 656–7.

case rather than *by* a client, and the medical profession, at least, is fully alive to the dangers involved. Of the professions as a whole one could not fairly say what Veblen said of business men, that they care only for the vendibility of their product, and not at all for its serviceability.

But individualism may have another foundation, not related to private pecuniary gain. It may mean the belief that the individual is the true unit of service, because service depends on individual qualities and individual judgement, supported by an individual responsibility which cannot be shifted on to the shoulders of others. That, I believe, is the essence of professionalism, and it is not concerned with self-interest, but with the welfare of the client. And this welfare, as I have said, is, and must be, conceived in social terms, even when clients are dealt with one by one as separate units. There is no need to abandon this kind of individualism when the service is offered to a group or to a community. In this sense of the word a prime minister is an individualist, so is a judge or a general in command of an army, and so, too, is any subordinate who clings to the divine right of disobedience. There is nothing in this attitude fundamentally antagonistic to public service or social planning. As one speaker put it at the last conference of the British Medical Association, when discussing the distinction between the private and public medical services: 'The difference was that the medical officer as commonly understood aimed at individual health through communal health, and the general practitioner at communal health through individual health.'[8] They are natural allies, with a common objective, but circumstances have, in the past, been unfavourable to the development of the alliance. There are two main reasons for this. One is a very natural fear of State control. The profession claims to be judge in its own cause. Once the State assumes control it can dictate the standards of service, and enslave the collective conscience of the profession. This means much more than the mere disposal of labour, because, as we saw, the labour of the professional

[8] *British Medical Journal* (Supplement), August 13, 1938, p. 367.

is inseparable from the man. It is no idle fear. Churches have had to fight for religious liberty and universities for academic freedom. Professor Laski urges that the legal profession 'should be a great corporation under government control', as it is in Soviet Russia. But under Hitler, he says, 'a body of learned professors, whose vocation was the disinterested service of truth, were there willing to prostitute their scholarship to ends which hundreds of them knew to be mean and false'.[9] His view appears to be that the State should control the professions, but that the professions should at the same time control the State. And that is not easy, unless State and professions are agreed on the fundamentals of policy.

The second reason for professional individualism is simply this. The professional man cannot spread his services, he cannot, except within narrow limits, distribute his skill through subordinates. He is unable to go in for mass production and is forbidden to offer cheap lines for slender purses. Since he works for a limited market it is not surprising that he should choose one which is solvent and concentrate on the wealthy individual client. In other words, he must find an employer, and the general public was not organized for his employment. The doctors, whose sense of public duty has always been strong, got round this difficulty to a large extent by giving free service to the poor while living on fees taken from the rich, and by organizing unofficial insurance schemes in country districts under which the villager paid his penny a week while he was well and received the attendance he needed when he was ill. But speaking generally this state of affairs led to a maldistribution of professional services in terms of social need, a maldistribution due to economic motives among professional men but not necessarily implying any disloyalty to the principle that service must not be sacrificed to profit. It was this, no doubt, that Professor Laski had chiefly in mind. Big-scale social activities only became possible when the initiative was taken by the State and the local

9 'The Decline of the Professions', op. cit., p. 684.

authorities, by public corporations and rich charities. And by that time the professions had built up their tradition of individualism, which meant not so much the pursuit of individual self-interest as the service of individual clients in a relationship of individual trust. They were therefore disinclined to press for the establishment of corporate agencies for the distribution of professional services and reluctant to work for them when they appeared. But time has wrought a change. There has been a silent revolution in the social services to which the professions are adapting themselves. It is not a painful process, because the adaptation does not involve a surrender of any of the fundamentals of the professional ideal. In my brief description of this change I shall be speaking of recent events in Britain.

The social services were at first directed to the relief of extreme poverty and extreme distress by provision of the minimum necessary for a decent life. What they gave was much what was given by low-grade private enterprise. They did not look at social problems in a new or original way. Inferior quality was implicit in the idea that they were acts of charity to human failures and that they must do nothing to weaken the incentive to self-help. The professions were not expected to be interested in supplying cheap lodging-houses, cheap medicines or cheap education to the indigent. As the political system became more democratic the sense of responsibility for social welfare grew stronger. Public health led the way, because it was soon compelled to treat the environment and not merely the individual. That meant a service to the community and not merely to a class. Gradually the Poor Law Infirmaries are being absorbed into the general hospital system, while medical services, under the National Health Insurance scheme, are extended to the whole of the employed working class and will soon, without doubt, spread further up the social scale. The education authorities came to realize that, even if they provided only an elementary education, it must be the best possible, since they were catering for the vast majority of the children of the nation. Charity schools for the poor belonged to the remote past. Then secondary and technical education were brought within the scope of public enterprise, and through these schools working-class children could pass into State-aided universities. The meagre provision of working-class dwellings grew into slum clearance, town planning and regional planning.

The story is too long to be told and too familiar to need telling. The essential point is that the social services have grown from a cheap makeshift provided for the lowest class in a society built on competitive individualism, into a vast co-ordinated plan for the betterment of the entire community. The social services have lost, or are rapidly losing, their class character. They are inspired by the spirit of professionalism, in the sense that they do not design their work to meet an articulate and effective demand only, but plan it in the light of expert knowledge of the social arts and sciences and of fundamental principles of social welfare formulated on the basis of accumulated human experience. The authority exercised by the social services differs from that of the professions. It rests not only on the superior knowledge of the administrators but also on political power derived from the constitution. A relationship of trust is essential, but it is founded on the principles of political obligation, not on private honour and a traditional ethic.

A vast army of professional men and women is employed in these services without losing professional status, and many more co-operate without becoming employees of the government. There would seem at first sight to be two main differences between these agents of the social services and the independent professions. In the first place they are working for an employer. But if they were reckoned as unprofessional, one would have to strike many of the oldest and most honoured professions off the list: the fighting forces, public administration, the teachers and many engineers, scientists, artists and writers. Secondly they are working for the community and not for individual clients. But this, it has already been argued, is a difference of form rather than of essence.

Admittedly the situation is dangerous when a free profession must work under the orders of a superior. The commands of the superior may clash with the conscience of the profession, and this is particularly serious when the commands are backed by the unlimited power of the State. But I believe that in modern democratic societies this danger is diminishing rather than increasing, because State and professions are being assimilated to one another. This is not happening through the absorption of the professions by the State, but by both of them moving from opposite directions to meet in a middle position. The natural foe of professionalism in private life is commercialism. Its natural foe in public life is politics, in the less reputable sense of that term. Both bring in extraneous motives and scales of value inappropriate to the real business in hand. Now it is a commonplace that the growing technical complexity of the public services is shifting the balance of power from the politician to the administrator. The British social services are not yet above, or beyond, politics, but they are moving in that direction, and other democratic countries are likely in time to follow in the same path. Political controversy still rages over broad proposals for reform and over some provocative details, but there are wide areas of action left to the administrators and the professionals where the voice of the politician is but dimly heard as the distant ineffectual bleating of a wandering sheep. Within that field a clash of ideals is unlikely. Co-operation is close and friendly, and this, in Britain, is largely due to the professional character of the Civil Service. Civil servants are not commercially minded, and politically they are passive. In the past it was said that this left them spiritually eviscerated; they were reduced to a collection of typewriters, calculating machines and rubber stamps actuated by a plausible imitation of human vitality. That is not, and could not any longer be true, because the Civil Service is no longer merely an administrative body. In much of his work, as Dr Robson has put it, 'the official is less concerned to administer the law than to promote energetic and far-reaching projects based on plans which he himself must

create'.[10] These projects are preceded by thorough inquiries
and investigations, in which outside professional help is en-
listed through those invaluable institutions, the Departmental
Committee and the Royal Commission, and in many other
more permanent ways. The quality of official reports is now
so high that most of them could pass the severest academic
tests that a university could impose, because they are the
fruit of the same professional spirit that inspires the work of
the universities themselves. If this were not so, it would be a
pure farce to ask a commission to investigate the causes of
the present distribution of the industrial population and the
probable direction of future change, and to report on the
social, economic and strategical disadvantages of concentration
in particular areas.[11] A great exploratory inquiry of that
kind is neither a political nor an administrative act. It is a
piece of big-scale social research.

In short, the professions are being socialized and the social
and public services are being professionalized. The professions are learning, not merely to recognize their obligations
to society as a whole as well as those to individual clients,
but also to break down the traditional isolation which separated them from one another. They are ready to work as a
team. In fact the value of team work was probably realized
earlier in the public services than in the fields of academic
social research, where it is just as necessary. A recent report
issued by the British Ministry of Health opened with the
following striking passage:

> The skill and experience of the physician, the surgeon,
> the obstetrician, the epidemiologist, the architect, the
> engineer, the lawyer, the statistician, the sociologist, the
> veterinary surgeon and the administrator have all been
> assembled to constitute the science of public health,
> which is thus a compendium of specialized knowledge.[12]

[10] *The British Civil Servant*, ed. W. A. Robson (London, 1937),
p. 19.

[11] Summary of the terms of reference of the Royal Commission on
the Distribution of the Industrial Population, set up in July 1937.

[12] *Annual Report of the Chief Medical Officer of the Ministry
of Health for 1937* (London, 1938), p. 1.

The list is long, but it could easily be doubled.

In the meantime the professions, in their independent capacity, were moving in a similar direction. One might refer to the artists, and cite their greater readiness to give serious attention to some of the more communal forms of art, for the stage, for internal decoration and even for commercial posters, and their highly successful efforts to raise the standard of art teaching in schools of every grade. One might mention the architects, who for the first time have had a chance of devoting their talents to designing homes for the people as well as residences for the rich and who have recently founded a School of Planning and Research in London in which to study the problems of the architect against the background of the social scene. One could claim that the teachers now realize more fully the dignity and the responsibilities of their calling and see themselves as the trustees of a national service instead of the bored drudges of an impersonal authority. Incidentally it is of interest that teachers and education officers up and down the country have voiced their condemnation of the latest Education Act, which raises the school-leaving age to fifteen but allows the release of a child for 'beneficial employment' at the age of fourteen. This is a case of professional standards being invoked to discredit the tricks of political manoeuvres.

But the outstanding example is that of medicine. Many public utterances can be quoted to illustrate the changed attitude of the profession. Here is a simple one from Sir Kaye Le Fleming, spoken at the annual meeting of the British Medical Association last July. Our charge to our students, he said, should be as follows: 'When you go out into practice you have no right to sit alone in your own little niche seeing how much money you can make by attending patients who are ill. You will remember that you have duties to the profession as a whole, to the public as a whole and to the State.'[13] That is a straightforward denunciation of old-fashioned professional individualism. The next is bolder. It comes from the President's address to the same gathering:

[13] *British Medical Journal* (Supplement), August 13, 1938, p. 368.

I have said that this is an age of youth. It is also an age of planning. *Laissez faire*, that principle beloved of our fathers, has done great things but it has outlived its time. All the signs and symptoms point to the fact that, whether we wish it or not, in every field of human activity some form of control, of planning, is necessarily coming. We may not like the thought, but it is useless to kick against the pricks, and it rests largely with us what form that control is going to take.[14]

There is some evidence that these are not mere empty words. For the new attitude towards medical service seems to grow naturally out of the new attitude towards health. In the British Medical Association's scheme for a General Medical Service for the Nation[15]—itself a sign of serious purpose— the first basic principle is 'that the system of medical service should be directed to the achievement of positive health and the prevention of disease no less than to the relief of sickness'. Positive health, according to Sir Henry Brackenbury, means 'not the absence of illness only, but an actual and definite sense of well-being', in pursuit of which medicine must aim at 'the constructive enhancement and perfecting of the communal and personal health'.[16] Positive health is not something clearly and specifically felt by the individual, something for which he can ask the doctor to prescribe in the way that he asks him to prescribe for a pain or a temperature. The ordinary man does not know the possibilities of health. And when positive health is thought of in terms of communal perfection it involves treatment not only of the physical but also of the social environment, a change, perhaps, in social habits, an education in the art of life. Positive health, in fact, is an ideal which can only be defined in relation to an ideal society. That may sound grandiloquent. But

---

[14] *British Medical Journal* (Supplement), July 23, 1938, p. 163.

[15] See the pamphlet with this title published by the Association in 1938.

[16] 'Medical Progress and Society', in *Human Affairs*, ed. R. B. Cattell, J. Cohen and R. M. W. Travers (London, 1937), pp. 125–6.

I am not professing to record an achievement. I am only trying to describe an aspiration.

It has not been my purpose in all this to whitewash the professions. Their faults and deficiencies have been legion. My aim has been to make three points. First, that professionalism is an idea based on the real character of certain services. It is not a clever invention of selfish minds. Secondly, the individualistic bias of the major professions was a product of circumstance. It was not the corner-stone of the building. Thirdly, the professions today are being weaned from this excessive individualism and are adapting themselves to the new standards of social service. The change has been stimulated by outside pressure, but the professions have made an independent contribution of their own and helped to build up the influences to which they themselves are in turn reacting.

There remains the topic of social structure referred to in the title of this paper, but there is time to treat it only in the broadest outline. The most obvious trend has been the weakening of aristocratic prejudices against trade and the consequent amalgamation of the upper levels in the worlds of business and the professions. But society is still somewhat fastidious in picking the commercial positions which it regards as gentlemanly, and it is noticeable that it prefers to bestow, for social purposes, the courtesy rank of professions on precisely those business careers that are furthest removed in character from the professional ideal, in that they are most completely devoted to money values, money profits and speculation. If one were ruminating on the probable alignment of forces in case of a future crisis one would note these social affinities between the upper ranks of certain professions and of financial capitalism, and hazard a guess that capitalist interests would be the dominating influence in the group.

But at a lower social level the picture is different. Here the remarkable thing is the rapid spread of the forms of professional organization among occupational groups which are not professions in the full meaning of the term. The forms which such groups can adopt are: recognized courses of training in a specialized technique, a means of testing efficiency in that technique, the admission of those duly qualified into an association, but building up of the prestige of the association as against non-members, the imposition of certain standards of honourable dealing and the rudiments of a code of ethics. The foundation of the whole structure is the specialized technique, and it is the multiplication of these techniques that has made possible the spread of these organizations. To put it briefly, scientific methods have been introduced into non-manual routine work, like that of the secretary, the accountant, the trade statistician, the advertiser, the office manager. These techniques are not, by older standards, professional. They do not call for creative originality, as in the case of the artist and scientist, nor must they be linked with sound human judgement and the power to inspire trust in one's character and personality, as in the case of the lawyer and doctor. They demand accuracy and efficiency along established lines. They are, in fact, the mental equivalent of the manual craftsmanship of the Middle Ages, and they lend themselves in the same way to the establishment of semi-professional associations. But in many respects these groups are indistinguishable from the great body of the salaried employees of trade and industry, the white-collared workers of the middle class. These workers are far removed from the spirit of what Veblen called 'pecuniary and business employments'. They are not an organ, but only an instrument, of capitalism. They have little experience of those motives and incentives which are reputed to make capitalism work, or fail to work, as the case may be. There is no ideological obstacle to their being professionalized, and if they are not professionalized they will, as is frequently said, be proletarianized. The signs in England today suggest that we shall see a strengthening and consolidating of the middle class on the basis of a modern type of semi-professionalism.

It is important to notice the effects of these changes on social mobility. An organized profession admits recruits by means of an impartial test of their knowledge and ability. In theory they are selected on merit, but it is merit of a particular kind which usually must be developed and displayed in a particular prescribed way. A narrow road leads into the profession through certain educational institutions. How far this favours social mobility depends on whether those institutions are open to the masses, so that merit can win recognition in all classes. Granted the broadening of the educational ladder typical of modern democracies, the system of the official examination is more favourable to mobility than one of arbitrary appointment or casual promotion. But the chance to move comes early, during school days. Once it has been missed and a career has been started at a non-professional level the whole system of formal qualifications makes movement at a later stage well-nigh impossible.

There is another point. In the church or the army, in law or medicine, a man at the head of his profession is on top of the world. He admits no superiors. But many of these new semi-professions are really subordinate grades placed in the middle of the hierarchy of modern business organization. The educational ladder leads into them but there is no ladder leading out. The grade above is entered by a different road starting at a different level of the educational system. Social structure, in so far as it reflects occupational structure, is frozen as soon as it emerges from the fluid preparatory stage of schooling. Mobility between generations is increased, but mobility during the working life of one generation is diminished. That appears to be the direction in which things are moving today, towards the transfer of individual competitiveness from the economic to the educational world, from the office and workshop to the school and university.

This middle-class group of the lesser professions and the salaried employments has many common features. The interests of its members are technical and administrative rather than financial and speculative. Their fortunes are linked, not to profits, but to employment, and if, as Veblen argued, capitalism is bound to sacrifice the latter to the former, they should be unfriendly towards capitalism. The competitive aspects of the concerns in or for which they work hardly touch them, and competition in their private lives is, as we have just seen, weakened by the spread of professionalism. Their desire is for security in the enjoyment of the status their education has won them. Therefore, although socialism would have no terrors for them once they could get over their fear of the word, communism is anathema, because it means destruction of their middle-class status. If, as seems likely, they shrink from an alliance with the workers, to whom will they turn for leadership? Not, probably, to their capitalist employers and clients. Not, I think, to that competitive professionalism, typified by the medical specialist, the successful barrister, and the fashionable architect, which has such close affinities to the world of finance. The natural place for them to look is in what might be called administrative professionalism, of the type described in our discussion of the social services. It is surprising that Veblen did not pay more attention to this group of occupations. He denounced the destructive activities of business, guided by its interest in 'the vendibility of the output, not its serviceability for the needs of mankind', and administering that 'tissue of make-believe' called credit and finance. He turned for salvation to the realism of the engineer, 'trained in the stubborn logic of technology', and believing that 'nothing is real that cannot be stated in terms of tangible performance'.[17] But the engineer, though a realist, is not well equipped to judge of human needs. It cannot be assumed that the welfare of mankind will be promoted by giving man everything that machinery makes possible. As Professor J. M. Clark pointed out when reviewing one of Veblen's books, no one has ever shown 'how social efficiency can be organized on a technical basis alone'. Progress 'calls for an evolution of our scheme of values, not for a "technocracy" which ignores value'.[18] Veblen should have put the professions as a whole in the position he assigned to the engineers. They too are realists, they are rela-

[17] Thorstein Veblen: *The Theory of Business Enterprise* (New York, 1904), p. 51, and *The Engineers and the Price System* (New York, 1921), p. 75.

[18] Joseph Dorfman: *Thorstein Veblen and His America* (New York, 1934), p. 491.

tively free from the spirit of 'pecuniary and business employments', and in addition it is their business to study human
needs and to construct a scale of human values. Social efficiency, as distinct from both business efficiency and mechanical efficiency, should be, and to an increasing extent is, their
objective. In spite of all their faults, it rests with them, more
than with anyone else, to find for the sick and suffering democracies a peaceful solution of their problems.

CHAPTER VII

THE NATURE OF CLASS CONFLICT

If the subject of this Conference[1] means anything at all, we must assume that an interpretation is being given to the word 'class' which implies that all group conflicts are not class conflicts. We are discussing a particular kind of group, whose nature is indicated by the phrase 'social stratification'. The groups, that is to say, lie one above the other in layers. It is the business of this Conference to discover whether such groups exist and, if so, how they behave. It is my special task to distinguish and classify the different forms of conflict that occur between them. Conflict between two firms or two nations does not enter into the classification, although it may play a part as evidence helping us to understand—or perhaps to dismiss as an illusion—conflict between social strata.

We think of 'a class' as a group of people. But we can also think of 'class' as a force or mechanism that operates to produce certain social attitudes. I like to begin my definition of class in this second sense by saying that it is a force that unites into groups people who differ from one another, by overriding the differences between them. It may sound paradoxical to stress in this way the differences within classes instead of those between classes. But I believe it is salutary to do so. If you take in turn the class criteria that we have already discussed, income, property, education and occupation, you will find that every class contains within itself per-

[1] On 'Class Conflict and Social Stratification', held under the auspices of the Institute of Sociology in September 1937.

sons differently endowed in respect of each one of them. But the institution of class teaches the members of a society to notice some differences and to ignore others when arranging persons in order of social merit. In a word, social classes could not exist unless certain inequalities were regarded as irrelevant to the determination of social status. It follows that there are two main roads to the classless society. One leads through the abolition (as far as possible) of the social differences between individuals—which is roughly the way of communism —and the other proceeds by rendering all differences irrelevant to social status—which is roughly the way of democracy.

It is, of course, equally true that a class system notices, even emphasizes, certain forms of inequality, and uses them as a barrier to divide the classes. With respect to the points thus selected for attention members of the same class *are*— or believe they are—identical. But it is important to remember that they always differ in other respects. It is futile to argue that, because groups within a class are unlike in their circumstances or their interests, therefore the class itself is an 'artificial' group, or that because there is conflict within a class, therefore conflict between classes is 'unreal'.[2]

Antagonism, as Delevsky has argued at unnecessary length, is relative.[3] Those who are antagonists for one purpose may be colleagues for another. Our first task, then, is to classify the main forms of antagonism, in order to see which are most compatible with co-operation in other fields. The analysis will be confined to the types most important in the study of class conflict.

First, there is competition, where two or more persons offer the same service or desire the same object. This shows us at once that we cannot group people according to their resemblance to one another. In the case of competition it is simi-

[2] Such words have only a relative meaning. All group attitudes must be based, not only on facts, but also on the social meaning given to them. An attitude is only 'unreal' if the meaning is excessively far-fetched or if, as in some types of propaganda, it is based on deliberate misrepresentation.

[3] J. Delevsky: *Antagonismes sociaux et antagonismes prolétariens.*

larity that divides; but let the competitors become partners, and the very same similarity will prove to be a bond of union. Secondly, there is the conflict that arises out of the division of labour, conflict, that is to say, over the terms on which co-operation is to take place, as illustrated by a wage dispute between employer and employed. The division here is a secondary product of a unity of interest based on difference. Thirdly, there is conflict over the system itself upon which the allocation of functions and the distribution of benefits are based, as when a bargain about wages is converted into a revolt against capitalism.

Antagonism between competitors is clearly not incompatible with a community of interest between them. In fact such a community of interest is implied in the term 'competition'. For competition is a social process conducted through the medium of institutions which are equally indispensable to both competitors. The very existence of the service that is offered and its value in exchange are due to a social system and a civilization that are a common possession. The power of this common interest to produce common action will vary according to circumstances, but the interest always exists. In the second type of antagonism co-operation between the antagonists is part of the definition. It is sometimes suggested that the co-existence of the two relationships is illusory, on the grounds that the antagonism is not real and that the true interests of the parties are identical. But this is absurd. It is true that he who drives a hard bargain may injure himself by ruining his opposite. Nevertheless, a bargain is in essence a wrangle within limits set by the need to continue the offer of the service bargained for. There is no more difficulty in admitting that buyer and seller are at the same time friends and enemies than in asserting that bowler and batsman have a common interest in helping one another to play cricket, although their views as to the most desirable fate of each ball bowled are diametrically opposed. More important is the question how far co-operation between, say, employer and employed is an obstacle to the solidarity of labour *vis-à-vis* capital. That it *is* an obstacle is obvious, but this does not mean that it is the more real interest of the two. Here again we have the fact that labour is united by its common position in relation to the institutions through which the bargain of co-operation takes place. And to this I would add that, whereas the co-operative function of production by division of labour is sectional and specialized, the antagonism which is inherent in every bargain expresses itself in terms which are general to the class, in terms of wages and hours and the basic conditions of bargaining power.

To sum up: competition within the ranks of labour (or capital) does not render impossible or unnatural a conscious unity of labour (or capital), and sectional co-operation between labour and capital does not render impossible or unnatural a general antagonism between labour and capital.[4]

It is only in the third type of conflict that the common interest shared by the rivals dwindles to vanishing point. In extreme cases conflict of this kind becomes civil war, which is not a social process and in which, as the world knows only too well, little regard is paid even to the accepted rules of warfare. I suggest that we might well reserve the term 'conflict' for cases in which the presence of this last type of antagonism can be detected. Neither competition nor bargaining is conflict in this refined sense, but when either party feels that the process of competing or bargaining ought not to take place at all, or that it is of necessity being conducted under conditions of injustice, then conflict appears and may grow to revolution. Conflict therefore, implies, not merely disagreement as to what is to be done next, but dissatisfaction with what already exists. Two parties in parliament disagree as to policy, but conflict begins when one denounces parliamentary government. Two parents may disagree about the education of their child, but conflict begins when the father denies that the mother has any say in the matter and the mother replies, 'I wish I had never married you'. And feelings of this kind may run as an undercurrent in the stream of disagree-

---

[4] For an opposite view, see L. von Mises: *Socialism*, Part III, Section 1, Chapter 4.

ment for a long time before conflict breaks out, as has happened more than once in the history of trade unionism.[5]

I have been speaking so far, not about social classes, but
about economic groups. I do not believe that the two are the
same. I do believe in the reality of those social levels, distinguished by their culture and standard of living, which we
discussed at our first two meetings. But differences of level
are less likely to lead to conflict than differences of group
interest. To that extent I accept the Marxian analysis of the
nature of class conflict (though not the theory of its historic
role), but I deny that it exhausts the subject of social stratification. Simplifying for the sake of brevity, I should say that
class conflict occurs when a common interest unites adjacent
social levels in opposition to more distant social levels. When
the levels united by a common interest are not adjacent, as
in international war, the conflict is not a class conflict. The
fusion of levels is facilitated when the divisions between
them are of unequal depth, when, for instance, the gulfs
between levels one to four are shallower than that between
levels four and five. There is another cause of fusion. Class
conflict arises over social institutions. Often the same institutions dominate the division into levels. In such cases the
two types of cleavage play into one another's hands. I imagine
this was the case in feudal society. It is arguable that it is less
true today. The wage-earner with savings finds that his social
level urges him to defend the rights of property while his
interests as a wage-earner prompt him to invade them. The
issue depends partly on the nature of the conflict of interests, and on this point the analysis can be carried a stage
further.

That resentment against inequality which is characteristic
of class antagonism may spring from three processes, which
I shall call comparison, frustration and oppression. Comparison sustains both the sense of superiority of the rich over 'the
great unwashed' and the sense of resentment in the poor

[5] The General Strike showed well what confusion of mind results
when the forms of bargaining are used for the purposes of conflict.

against 'the idle rich'. Such feelings may be shared by any number of persons from a single individual to a whole nation, and they are therefore most uncertain in their group-making effects. Yet they are the main force creating social levels, and they do this, not so much by provoking antagonism, as by perfecting the individual's awareness of himself and the group's consciousness of its own character. They are foundations of self-esteem. Perhaps that is why men seem to prefer to concentrate on comparing themselves with their inferiors. It is said that there is no caste in India so low that it cannot point to another beneath it. Comparison does not make contacts, it breaks them. It leads to isolation rather than to conflict. But if conflict is brewing, the attitudes born of comparison will stimulate it, and, when it matures, embitter it, and they are always there, ready to convert into a class struggle a dispute which is in essence no more than a disagreement about the terms of co-operation.[6]

Frustration adds to comparison a stronger motive for conflict by definitely imputing to the superior class responsibility for the injustice under which the inferior suffers. It arises, of course, wherever privilege creates inequality of opportunity. But more important, because more distinctive, is the case where two classes represent, as it were, two different economic systems or two incompatible conceptions of social life. Pirenne has suggested that this is the normal way of economic progress. The creators of the new order rise up alongside of, not among, the decaying champions of the old.[7] The result is a lateral conflict, in which the old order appears more as an obstacle than as a tyrant. The process can be seen most clearly in the history of the *bourgeoisie* from the beginnings of the decline of feudalism to the perfection of capitalism in the nineteenth century, and especially in France. In the early days, says Pirenne, the *bourgeois* 'merely desired a place in the sun, and their claims were confined to their most in-

---

[6] Subject, of course, to the reservations made above about the effect of social levels on class unity.

[7] H. Pirenne: *Les périodes de l'histoire sociale du capitalisme.*

dispensable needs'.[8] Subsequently it became clear that concessions to the *bourgeois* involved sacrifices by the aristocrat.
Later, says Henri Sée, the *bourgeoisie* 'a intérêt au nouvel
ordre de choses, à une organisation plus régulière, à la destruction des privilèges des deux premiers ordres, à la recon-
naissance de l'égalité civile'.[9] Privilege was an obstacle because it was a cause of administrative inefficiency and financial
mismanagement. How confused were ideas at the time of the
Fronde as to the relations between social strata appears from
the fact that the government's first act, when it realized the
danger of disturbance, was to call on the *bourgeois* militia to
stand by, while the revolutionary *bourgeoisie* organized a
mercenary army of *compagnons* to relieve their portly selves
of the burden of drilling and carrying arms.[10]

It might be argued that the position today is similar. The
new middle class, composed mainly of the salariat and the
lesser professions, is not writhing under the heel of a tyrant,
but it is uncomfortably aware that the realization of its great
ideal of a quiet life lived in security and with full enjoyment
of the arts of civilization is being prevented by the incessant
wranglings of capital and labour, which seem to it to be an
essential part of the social system of the last century, and by
the obsession of men's minds by a restless longing to specu-
late and to bargain in a ceaseless striving for profits. Either
capitalism or socialism alone would be preferable, because
both must use the services of this middle class in much the
same way. But the conflict between the two is enough to goad
it into revolution, with the natural, though not entirely wished
for, result of Fascist dictatorship. Conflict against frustration
is likely to include moral denunciation of the old order as
corrupt, perverted or decadent. The modern middle-class
movement shows this strain. It denounces materialism and

[8] H. Pirenne: *Economic and social history of medieval Europe*,
p. 51.
[9] *La vie économique au xviiie siècle*, p. 173.
[10] Charles Normand: *La bourgeoisie française au xviie siècle*, p.
349. In general see Joseph Aynard: *La bourgeoisie française*, Chapters 8 and 9.

the lack of a sense of social brotherhood, and, perhaps, the failure to appreciate the value of the artists and intellectuals. Fascism offers a new mind and a new spirit. 'The Fascist State . . . is a force, but a spiritual force, which embodies in itself all forms of the moral and intellectual life of man. . . . Its principle . . . implants itself in the heart of the man of action, the thinker, the artist and the scientist alike—it is the soul of the soul.'[11] This is not exactly what was asked for, but it may serve for a time.

Oppression describes a conflict between two parties engaged in unequal co-operation, the inequality being a product of the institutions of a stratified society. The word is not meant to define the motives or methods of the upper class, but only the situation as it appears to the lower. Whereas comparison breaks contacts and frustration produces contact by collision, oppression implies contact as an organic process. Obvious instances are the relations between serf and lord or labour and capital. When conflict breaks out, the attack is made against a group of persons wielding power. They may be referred to as 'the governing class'. This phrase is loosely used. The feudal aristocracy was literally a governing class. The modern capitalists are not. And yet the words express a truth. The implication is that the capitalist is using in the economic field a power that is partly political, in that it is derived from the laws and institutions of the society. If a class is strong enough to secure or to preserve those institutions that favour its activities, it may be said to be 'governing' to that extent. But, as we saw, in the modern world interest in the essential institutions is not confined to the capitalists who meet labour as employers. It is perhaps for this reason that the attack comes to be directed less against a group of persons than against an impersonal system. Relations between the co-operating groups relapse into bargaining. Conflict deals in theories. One would expect this to result in a decline in the influence of trade unionists, who bargain, as leaders of a working class, in favour of communists, who

[11] B. Mussolini: *La dottrina del Fascismo*, Section 12.

theorize. An alternative consequence may be an increase in what might be called 'level-consciousness' as compared with 'class-consciousness'. This seems to be what is happening in England.

Space remains for only one more point. We can ask whether conflict is more likely to arise in a static or a dynamic society. This involves contrasting estate with class, status with contract. In a society stratified into estates inequality is based on an accepted scheme of differential status and differential standards of living. One class is utilized for the benefit of another, but within the limits of a plan of co-operation approved by custom. Disagreement over the terms of co-operation can hardly arise, since the terms are not open to question. Where status rules, bargaining, which belongs to contract, cannot prevail. Antagonism can find no expression except in conflict.[12] There is no middle course between acquiescence and rebellion. It might be argued that this must render conflict more likely, because there is no milder alternative. But it may equally be urged that the gravity of the step will act as a deterrent. It is easier to drift into danger than to jump into it. In addition, the very nature of a society based on estates is such as to favour the development in each group of the type of mentality suited to its position. Revolt is paralysed from within.

In a free contractual society disagreement as to the terms of co-operation is normal and chronic. It is implied in the bargaining process out of which the contract emerges. We notice, too, that the idea that every station in life has its proper standard, that every class has its culture, is at its weakest. Acquiescence is positively discouraged by the prevailing belief in the virtue of social ambition. Democracy professes to believe in equality and capitalism extols competition. A uniform standard for all kills competition, while differential standards deny equality. Capitalist democracy, therefore, at first accepts no standard, taking what is given it by the free play of economic forces. The English pauper was not to be

[12] Cf. K. Bauer-Mengelberg: 'Stand und Klasse', in *Könerl Vierteljahrshefte für Soziologie* (1923).

fed according to the needs of the human body but according to what could be bought with a little less money than capitalism vouchsafed to the free worker. When the standard enters once more, as it did in the later nineteenth century, it enters as a minimum, above which infinite variation is allowed and expected. In capitalist democracy, then, we have a perpetual state of friction between classes combined with a destruction of the psychological forces favouring acquiescence. Is there, we should ask, any positive force turning antagonism into conflict which is absent in the static society? I see a possible answer in the idea of exploitation.

In both types of society there appears to be utilization of one class by another for the benefit of the latter. But whereas in the society of estates it is according to plan, in the contractual society it is at will. To distinguish between these processes we may say that the second is exploitation and the first is not. The benefits accruing to lord and serf under feudalism cannot be compared, because they are different in kind. Those accruing to capital and labour seem to be measured by their money incomes, and they are manifestly unequal. A contract is ideally an agreement to co-operate for equal advantage. When it habitually produces unequal advantage, exploitation is suspected. The idea appeals strongly to the exploited, who quickly conclude that the power that is defeating them resides, not in the personal superiority of their oppressor, but in the unfair advantages he derives from the system. If the system renders contract a sham, the system must be changed.

Some people hold that social mobility affords a safety valve and helps to avert the threatened conflict. Although this is true up to a point, I think its importance can easily be exaggerated. Where individual mobility is automatic, or nearly so, class loyalty develops with difficulty. If every apprentice has a reasonable hope of becoming a master he will form his associations on the basis of his trade or profession rather than of his social level. Again, where a whole group can rise in social estimation and economic value, leaving no stragglers, the alliance of groups into classes is more difficult. This is no doubt

the effect of the recent rise of many skilled occupations into
the ranks of the professions. But where mobility is individual
and not automatic, but depends on the results of competitive
striving, I am doubtful whether the same result follows.
When the race is to the swift, the slow, who are always in a
majority, grow tired of their perpetual defeat and become
more disgruntled than if there were no race at all. They begin to regard the prizes as something to which they are entitled and of which they are unjustly deprived. They declare
that no man ought to be made to race for his bread and butter, and the argument is not without force. Especially is this
so when society shows itself indifferent to the condition of the
losers on the ground that the road to better things is ever
open before them.[13] The use of mobility as an excuse for
inequality is usually associated with a measure of self-decep-
tion. But, if I were to pursue that theme, I should be tres-
passing on the subject to be discussed at the next session of
this Conference.

[13] Cf. C. H. Cooley: *Social Organization*, Chapter 27.

CHAPTER VIII

THE NATURE AND DETERMINANTS
OF SOCIAL STATUS

In recent years there has been a veritable spate of argument and discussion, in homes, common rooms and scientific journals, about the true nature of social class and social status. Although considerable progress has been made, it cannot be claimed that the problem has been solved or that full agreement has been reached. The dispute has been as much about words as about facts, with the result that, especially in informal discussion, it is often impossible to get beyond the 'it depends what you mean by social status' stage. This is very tiresome and frustrating. One is liable to get bogged down in arguments about the definition of terms and to be led further and further away from a study of the real facts of the situation. All one really needs to start with is a first approximation sufficient to indicate what one is talking about; the fuller and more exact description should emerge later as the investigation progresses. But it is difficult for the sociologist to offer even this first approximation, when the words at his disposal mean one thing to some people and another to others. However, the task cannot be evaded.

Social status refers to one aspect of the phenomenon of stratification in society, and it will be best to deal with the more general concept before turning to the more limited one. Stratification, as the word implies, means the division of a society into strata, or layers, lying one above the other. It is a concept which belongs to the study of social structures, and

we discover stratification by identifying those parts of the
structure which have this character of superimposed layers
and by seeing how they are related to one another and to the
working of the social system as a whole. Each part, or stratum,
is composed of large numbers of people who occupy the same,
or closely similar, positions in the social structure.

There are, and have been, many different kinds of stratification in human societies, and there is fairly general agreement
among sociologists that they can usefully be classified into
three main types: Caste, Estate and Class.

The most perfect example of Caste is found in India—not
in our present age, but at that point in the past when the
caste system was at its height. Its principal characteristics can
be briefly summarized. Marriage takes place between members of the same caste, and the children belong to the caste of
their parents; these are the principles of endogamy and heredity. Membership is normally lifelong; there is, in other words,
practically no social mobility. Caste members are united by
distinctive social customs and separated from other castes by
rules limiting contact or enjoining avoidance. These include
the restrictions on intermarriage, and also limitations on eat-
ing together, accepting food and drink from, and even (in
some cases) coming into close proximity with members of
other castes. These are the outward expressions of social distance. Castes form a hierarchy, being arranged in an order of
superiority and inferiority, which is associated with ideas of
purity and impurity. Each caste, also, is linked with a limited
range of permitted occupations (in some cases with one only),
and the classification of occupations also brings in the idea of
purity and impurity, especially at the extremes of the scale.
The prestige order of castes is not based on wealth.

Clearly this is a very rigid system. It is also one which pene-
trates deeply into the lives of the members of society. There is
no room for any other principle of stratification or social ranking to exist side by side with it or to challenge its supremacy.
If the caste system is in full vigour, caste membership is an
indisputable and unalterable fact by which a man's position
in the social structure is wholly determined. And, in addition

to this, the system as a whole is not regarded as something freely invented and constructed by man, which may be changed by him or which can be made different by the spread of different ideas. The basic beliefs are upheld, not because they are traditional, but because they are true. As a modern authority says: 'The general Hindu feeling about the caste system is that it has been "established by divine ordinance" or at least with divine approval.'[1] It is rooted in the divine plan and in the nature of man and the universe. This is clearly seen in the doctrine of *Karma*, according to which 'a man's condition in this life is the result of his conduct in his last incarnation; his high or low caste is therefore the reward or punishment of his past behaviour', that is, of his behaviour in a previous life on earth.[2]

The Estate system, too, is marked by rigidity, but less complete and of a different kind. It is more difficult to find a perfect example of an estate system, but its principles can be recognized in the middle period of feudalism and the aristocratic societies of Europe in the seventeenth and eighteenth centuries. An estate may be defined as a group of people having the same status, in the sense in which that word is used by lawyers. A status in this sense is a position to which is attached a bundle of rights and duties, privileges and obligations, legal capacities or incapacities, which are publicly recognized and which can be defined and enforced by public authority and in many cases by courts of law. The word is today so widely used by sociologists with a broader and less exact meaning[3] that, in order to avoid confusion, it is best to speak of 'legal status' when we refer to status in its original sense—the sense which has just been roughly defined above. We must add, also, that many legal statuses have little to do with stratification, for instance such statuses as those of minor, doctor, innkeeper or married woman. We are concerned here only with those which distinguish a social stratum or at least a substantial part of one.

[1] J. H. Hutton: *Caste in India*, p. 164.
[2] ibid., p. 109.
[3] See below, pp. 196–7.

The most important status distinction of this kind in medieval society was that between the free and the unfree. We may say that the serfs constituted an estate because their legal status was marked by a lack of rights, especially the right to personal liberty and the right to own property. We may also say that in England the greater barons who established their claim to be personally summoned to the King's Council, and who developed into the hereditary peerage sitting in the House of Lords, had a distinctive legal status. In pre-revolutionary France the nobility were distinguished, not only by the use of titles, but also by the enjoyment of certain legally recognized rights or privileges affecting in particular taxation and landholding, and by separate representation as an estate in the national assembly. We can also recognize the power of the estate system in Germany, where 'members of different estates could not intermarry at all, and later could at best enter into no marriage of full effect', and where 'military [knightly] life, civic industry and rustic field work were mutually exclusive occupations in the law of status'.[4]

Castes, as we saw, were endogamous and hereditary. Endogamy within estates was the normal practice but enforced more often by social custom (which could be defied) than by law. The French aristocrats, like the English, were not strictly endogamous; one of them cynically observed that 'to marry beneath oneself is merely taking dung to manure one's acres'.[5] Children inherited the position of their parents, except in so far as primogeniture restricted the full right of inheritance to the eldest son. But mobility was possible. It was, however, controlled. Status being legal and official in character, change of status must be by a legal or official act, as when a serf was liberated or a commoner ennobled. The sense of social distance was strongly marked, and each estate was linked with a limited range of permitted, or at least appropriate, occupations. Though at the lower levels this might operate as a disability, at the higher levels it represented a valuable monopoly. The estate system, then, reveals a precise and fairly rigid

---

[4] R. Huebner: A History of Germanic Private Law, pp. 91–3.
[5] L. Ducros: French Social Life in the Eighteenth Century, p. 61.

stratification, but in no case can it be said to give us the whole picture. Legal status rights did not permeate the whole of social life, and a description of stratification in terms of these rights alone is jejune and artificial. Our purpose here has been only to explain the nature of the principle.

The third type of stratification is Class, and its basis is economic. The concept has been widely used, notably by Karl Marx, and with various shades of meaning. It is not, in fact, and never can be, a very precise term, but it is an indispensable one. 'Classes', says Max Weber in one place, 'are groups of people who, from the standpoint of specific interests, have the same position in the economic system'.[6] The combination of the terms 'position' and 'interests' implies that positions are to be regarded as the same if the lives of those occupying them are governed by the same forces and influenced in a similar way by the same circumstances—if they have, in Weber's phraseology, the same life chances within the economic system. A class system is a social structure in which stratification is dominated by this principle. And it is enough for our immediate purpose to recognize that capitalist society is an example of such a structure. That certain positions in a capitalist society have a hierarchical character is obvious. There is the hierarchy of power within the firm from the management down to the wage-earner, and the hierarchy of the corresponding groups in the society at large, in which power brings wealth and wealth buys power. But, although the outlines of the structure are clear, the details are not. And, although we may feel certain that economic positions rank themselves in terms of wealth, power and opportunity into something which looks like a system of superimposed strata or layers, we find it difficult to say exactly what these layers are and exactly who belongs to them. Here, too, the picture is incomplete, and in order to fill it out we may have to introduce some principle other than the objective test of position in the economic system.

All three systems have a certain objectivity, although the

[6] H. H. Gerth and C. Wright Mills: *From Max Weber*, p. 405.

use of this word is fraught with the peril of misunderstanding. Caste membership is an indisputable and unalterable fact about which there is no room for differences of opinion. Estate, in its pure form, is equally factual; a man either possesses the rights or he does not. If the matter is in doubt, it is settled by a public authority, not by public opinion. Differences of class, in the technical sense in which we have been using the term, are also factual. That certain people occupy the same position in terms of wealth, economic power and opportunity is something which an outside observer might discover even though the people themselves were not aware of it. It is this that we shall have in mind, and no more than this, if we refer to the objective facts of stratification in the course of the discussion of social status on which we must now embark.

It will be recalled that, when discussing estate systems, we noted that sociologists today make frequent use of the term 'status' (without any qualifying adjective), and that they do not mean by it the same as the lawyer does when he uses the word. Legal status is a position distinguished by publicly enforceable rights and duties, capacities or incapacities, which are relevant to the position and its function in society. Status, as used by sociologists, is similar but is extended to include characteristics of the position which are not legally determined. It covers all behaviour which society expects of a person in his capacity as occupant of the position, and also all appropriate reciprocal behaviour of others towards him. In saying this we are really describing status in terms of what many sociologists call its 'role', that is to say its active aspect. And, in fact, it is very difficult to conceive of status except in terms of action. The rights and duties of legal status are rights and duties to do something or to have something done to one —they are, in fact, legally sanctioned behaviour. When we extend the concept beyond the legal sphere the corresponding notion is that of socially expected behaviour. A father, in his capacity as such, has certain legally recognized rights and duties with regard to his family which constitute the legal status of father, but there are also many other forms of action relevant to his status which, though not legally prescribed, are socially expected. But status in this extended sense, like legal status, is not necessarily connected with stratification. Only when it refers to a position in the social hierarchy or to membership of a social stratum do we call it 'social status'.

By social status, then, we mean a man's general standing *vis-à-vis* the other members of society or some section of it. 'General' is inserted to indicate that we refer to something more all-embracing than a specialized standing as an expert in something, such as the maintenance of motor-cars, though such expertise may contribute something to social status. Secondly, social status, like stratification, carries with it the idea of superior and inferior. If we compare the social status of two people, we ask whether they are equal or unequal, and, if unequal, which is the higher and which the lower. And in such a comparison we are concerned not only with the objective facts, such as rights, wealth or education, but also with the way in which the two people regard each other, that is to say with reciprocal attitudes expressed in reciprocal behaviour. The attitudes spring from a valuation or assessment of relative positions, which is reached by valuing or assessing the relevant objective facts which are known or can be observed. Among the most relevant facts are those which we have noted in studying stratification. The relevant facts may be called the evidence, the indices, or the symbols of social status, and in that sense its determinants. They are the immediate cause of the attitudes and the resultant behaviour. But behind them lie determinants in a different sense, namely the factors which determine how these relevant facts come to appear where they do. If wealth is one of the determinants in the first sense, then the forces controlling the distribution of wealth are determinants in the second. There is yet a third level which is the most difficult to explore. We may wish to discover what determines the values which society attaches to the various types of relevant fact. It is with determinants in the first sense that we are chiefly concerned in this article.

The reference to society raises an important point. Social status, we have said, is standing or position in society, and it may be misleading to describe it in terms of the relationship between two individuals. For social status rests on a collective judgement, or rather a consensus of opinion within a group. No one person can by himself confer social status on another, and if a man's social position were assessed differently by everybody he met, he would have no social status at all. In other words, social status is the position accorded in terms of the social values current in the society. It has, one might say, a conventional character. And it is a position having relevance for certain attitudes and forms of behaviour, not for all. It is so difficult as to be almost impossible to define what these are. One can only give crude examples. A doctor, for instance, may treat all his patients with equal care, regardless of social position, without inviting them all indiscriminately to dinner. Or, looking at it from another angle, the assessment of social position is not the same as the assessment of personality. Both affect reciprocal attitudes and behaviour, and it is very difficult to disentangle them. One might suggest that the best measure of social status in its pure and undiluted form is the preliminary and provisional judgement of social position based on 'paper' evidence (such as family, schooling, income, occupation) and on the impression gained by a brief contact in which such overt indices as speech and manners can be observed. On this evidence a person may be recognized as a representative of a particular group or social class. It is obvious that it is only in terms such as these that we can speak about the social status of a group, for instance of teachers. But an individual teacher may, by virtue of personality and attributes not characteristic of the group, acquire a rather different social status within a community in which he is well known. We might call the first 'positional social status' and the second 'personal social status'.

We have now identified three different levels. First, the actual social position as accorded by the attitudes and behaviour of those among whom the individual lives and moves —which we have called personal social status. Secondly, the social position accorded by the conventional values current in the society to the group or category of which the individual is representative—which we have called positional social status. And thirdly, the position in the system of stratification which is a feature of the structure of the society—which we have been rash enough to refer to as an objective fact. These three levels present us with two questions of interrelationship. First, how much freedom is there for the establishment of a personal social status differing from that indicated by positional social status? And in asking this, we must realize that, if personal social status were completely independent, positional social status would be a meaningless concept. This, it must be admitted, is a question of the greatest difficulty and complexity, and we can do little more than draw attention to the problem. Secondly, how tightly is positional social status tied to the system of stratification? It will be noticed that this question, as formulated, implies that it is bound to be tied fairly tightly but may have a certain measure of autonomy.

We need not pause long to put this question in the case of a caste system. It has already been suggested that so powerful, rigid, and all-pervading a system can leave little room for any other principle of stratification. 'Everywhere in India', writes an Indian scholar, 'there is a definite scheme of social precedence among the castes, with the Brahmin as the head of the hierarchy.'[7] 'Social precedence' means the same thing as 'social status'. On the deep penetration of caste into individual lives another authority says: 'From the point of view of the individual member of a caste the system provides him from birth with a fixed social milieu from which neither wealth nor poverty, success nor disaster can remove him. . . . He is provided in this way with a permanent body of associations which controls almost all his behaviour and contacts.'[8] We may conclude that, to all intents and purposes, social status is a mere reflection of caste membership, except, perhaps, for distinctions of personal social status within a local caste group.

The estate system deserves more attention, partly for its intrinsic interest, and partly because certain features of the es-

[7] G. S. Ghurye: *Caste and Race in India*, p. 6.
[8] Hutton: op. cit., p. 97.

tate system have survived into the age of class. It has already
been pointed out that estate rights, in the strictly legal sense,
had a limited significance, and that the lines drawn through
a society by estate differences were usually few, so that each
estate was a very large group capable of further differentiation. Three developments demand our attention.

First, where an estate was firmly entrenched, the legal
rights were extended by a body of privileges so firmly rooted
in social custom as to have in effect the force of law, or, one
might say, to be official rather than merely conventional in
character. Social status was firmly tied to estate status. The
prestige of a German noble, for instance, was in all its aspects
as unchallengeable as his legal rights. Secondly, we find sub-
division of estates proper into sub-estates based not strictly on
distinctive legal rights but on official position. Here we might
instance the division in seventeenth-century France between
the ancient noble families of chivalry, the *noblesse de l'épée*,
and the more recent recruits to nobility by office, the *noblesse
de la robe*, and the further division of the latter into the
grande, moyenne and *petite robe*.[9] Thirdly we find, also in
France, distinctions within the Third Estate which reveal
what can best be described as culture groups. The urban
bourgeoisie contained, not only oligarchies of office, but also
layers united by a common economic position, that of trade
as distinct from manual labour (we might call this a class
within an estate), but also by a consciously cultivated culture, which in some cases, but not in all, succeeded merely in
being a ridiculous imitation of the culture of the aristocracy.
Such groups strove to create a social status, not based wholly
on estate or class, but sustained by value judgements which
they hoped would become part of the conventions of the society.[10]

But the best example comes from England, a country in
which the outlines of the estate system were generally more
weakly drawn than on the Continent. As Professor Namier
has said of the English class system: 'Classes are the more

[9] C. Normand: *La bourgeoisie française au xviie siècle*.
[10] J. Aynard: *La bourgeoisie française*, Chapters 8 and 9.

sharply marked in England because there is no single test for them, except the final, incontestable result; and there is more snobbery than in any other country, because the gate can be entered by anyone, and yet remains, for those bent on entering it, a mysterious, awe-inspiring gate.'[11] The 'final, incontestable result' is acceptance or rejection by the common estimation of the group. It is 'mysterious' because it is not governed by rules, is not bound to follow the shape of any other official or objective status system, and cannot therefore be convicted of delivering a false verdict. Social status is judged in terms of social status alone.

The most perfect illustration is the peculiarly English figure of the gentleman. There is here no basis of politico-legal status; there are no distinctive enforceable rights, no title, no office—nothing but the 'final, incontestable result' of a number of factors. The word 'gentle' and its derivatives did at one time have a certain flavour of estate about them, because they referred to those entitled to bear arms. But 'gentle' also connoted a way of life associated with ideas of chivalry. In the post-feudal age the 'gentry' were a group below the nobility but above, or at least distinct from, the *bourgeoisie*, but the word 'gentleman' could be applied to nobility and gentry combined. And this section of the population had never constituted an estate. It contained the whole of the top estate and a part of the middle one. Nor could it be wholly identified with a class, since it contained the greater and lesser landowners, the professions, and some selected members of the business community. The surprising thing is, not so much that this particular social status was so autonomous and was not rigidly tied to any other system of stratification, as that the assessment was so definite and unhesitating, and that gentlemen so clearly formed a group or social class whose members enjoyed in a very real sense equality of social status, although important inequalities were superimposed upon the fundamental equality. In nineteenth-century England one might, after hearing a long description of a man, ask: 'Yes,

[11] L. B. Namier: *England in the Age of the American Revolution*, p. 15.

but is he a gentleman?' and expect, and receive, the answer yes or no. The same was true of the title 'lady', as can be seen from Trollope's description of Mrs Dale, the impoverished widow whose grandfather had been 'almost nobody'.

> That she was a lady, inwards and outwards, from the crown of her head to the sole of her feet, in head, in heart and in mind, a lady by education and a lady by nature, a lady also by birth in spite of that deficiency respecting her grandfather, I hereby state as a fact—*meo periculo*. And the squire, though he had no special love for her, had recognized this, and in all respects treated her as his equal.[12]

The factors which figured as determinants of this social status of gentleman are easy to recognize, 'determinants' being taken to denote those attributes whose presence won recognition of the status. The most obvious necessary attributes were birth and culture. The two were easily reconciled as criteria as long as it could be maintained that the second was transmitted by the first. Transmission might be by biological heredity or family influence, and there is evidence of belief in both. But birth and family atmosphere were not enough. They required to be reinforced by education. The seventeenth-century author of *The Gentleman's Calling* went so far as to assert that men's minds are by nature of the same clay; education is the potter which moulds them into vessels of honour and dishonour.[13] This is a rather extreme view. More typical, probably, is that expressed in the opening scene of *As You Like It*. Orlando is denouncing the treatment he has received from his elder brother. At first he claims equality by birth and blood: 'I have as much of my father in me as you.' Then he says: 'My father charged you in his will to give me good education: you have trained me like a peasant, obscuring and hiding from me all gentleman-like qualities.' A gentleman was recognized, then, by his family and his education,

[12] A. Trollope: *The Small House at Allington*, Chapter 3.

[13] R. B. Schlatter: *The Social Ideas of Religious Leaders*, 1660–1668, p. 50.

with this difference—that a 'good' family counted, even if its influence was not apparent in its product, but education (before universities and schools became a field for competitive snobbery) was judged by its results. To these we must add enough money to live the life of a gentleman and an occupation compatible with the ethos of that life, or no occupation at all.

There emerges here a point of some general importance. It might be said that, in the case of the gentleman, birth determined social status, and social status in turn determined culture; it created a right to the appropriate culture and was normally accompanied by the means with which to acquire it. But there were exceptions to this perfect correlation between birth and the appropriate way of life. The question then arises, can the reverse process take place? Can the way of life, adopted without the advantage of birth, determine social status? This question has been debated in England, often with great heat, for at least four centuries. The point at issue, however, has not been whether the simple answer should be yes or no: it must undoubtedly be yes. The argument has been rather about the time required to complete a change of status by these means—whether in one generation, or two, or more—and the degree of cultural assimilation necessary to confirm it. Protests against social upstarts and their too-ready acceptance into good society were rife in Elizabethan England, as witness the well-known passage from Sir Thomas Smith:

> As for gentlemen, they be made good cheap in England. For whosoever studieth the laws of the realm, who studieth in the universities, who professeth liberal sciences and, to be short, who can live idly and without manual labour and will bear the port, charge and countenance of a gentleman, he . . . shall be taken for a gentleman.[14]

Satire is a favourite weapon of an aristocracy unable to stem the flood of invasion from below, and satirical attacks

[14] See A. L. Rowse: *The England of Elizabeth*, Chapter 6.

on the *bourgeois gentilhomme* are found in England as well as in France. The first words of Sogliardo, the *nouveau riche* in Ben Jonson's *Every Man Out of His Humour*, are: 'Nay, look you, Carlo; this is my humour now. I have land and money, my friends left me well, and I will be a gentleman whatsoever it cost me.' More subtle, perhaps, in spite of its apparent crudity, is Shakespeare's thrust in *The Winter's Tale*, which seems to strike both at ludicrous ambition and at exaggerated pride of birth. The shepherd, who fathered Perdita, and the clown, his son, have been honoured for their services and hailed as 'brother' by the king and his son: they meet Autolycus:

> *Clown:* You denied to fight with me this other day, because I was no gentleman born . . . give me the lie, do, and try whether I am not now a gentleman born.
> *Autolycus:* I know you are now, sir, a gentleman born.
> *Clown:* Ay, and have been so any time these four hours.

Notice the test of gentle status—the right to avenge an insult. The theme can be followed right down into the nineteenth and even the twentieth century, through the fortunes of Meredith's Evan Harrington, the cultured son of a tailor, and in the pages of *Punch*, where we can laugh at the solecisms of the upstart in the hunting-field and lament over the boorish antics of the war-profiteer in his Scottish castle. The tone changes from mirth to bitterness as the defences of aristocracy fall before the invader.

This peculiar phenomenon survived into the class system of modern England, and the English gentleman has often been the object of the curious attention of foreigners. He is the symbol of English snobbery and class-consciousness. But that is not all. A similar social-status group took shape in the level next below him, the lower middle class, with its black coats and white collars, suburban villas, exclusive social circles and genteel clubs. One might be tempted to regard this as the result of imitation, were it not for the fact that something of very much the same kind appears to have happened in the United States, where the gentleman never existed at all. At one time the preoccupation with social status as something distinct from, though not independent of, position in the hierarchy of estate or class, was regarded as peculiarly English. But today this concept is being widely used in sociological investigations in America, and it is in some of the Scandinavian countries, rather than in the United States, that one will find those who look with mild surprise on the English idea of social status as a quaint anachronism. Professor Geiger, who recently studied stratification in a Danish town, held that preoccupation with hierarchy and prestige was 'an ideological vestige of estates-society, and only appropriate in a class-society in so far as this continues to manifest estate residues'.[15] This may be true of England, but it cannot be true of the United States.

We may find the clue to this problem by looking at the earlier phase of capitalist society in America, the golden age of the independent *entrepreneurs*, those sturdy individualists whose successors are today referred to as 'the old middle class'. In the last quarter of the nineteenth century they comprised about one-third of the working population, but they had a symbolic value out of proportion to their numbers. The independent *entrepreneur* was the ideal type of the American citizen in a competitive capitalist economy, holding a position to which every citizen aspired and which it was believed that every citizen worth his salt could achieve. This idealized picture of a world open to talent and enterprise was based on a belief in fundamental social equality in sharp contrast to the ethos of caste, estate or social snobbery. And social relations largely conformed to this belief. The only significant differences were those measured by success and the simple, obvious and incontrovertible fact of wealth. There was little room in such a society for an independent or autonomous set of social values to assert itself. The plain facts of economic inequality were accepted for what they were worth—but not for more; they were not invested with any mystical meaning such as might make rich and poor appear as different species of hu-

---

[15] J. Floud: 'Social Stratification in Denmark', *The British Journal of Sociology*, June 1952, p. 174.

manity. There was no place for a snobbish preoccupation with
social status.

But the situation changed. The proportion of independent
entrepreneurs fell, the chances of achieving independence,
still more of retaining it, dwindled, while the fortunes of
those belonging to this sector of the economy were more and
more controlled by the power and policies of the big capitalists and organized labour. But the ideal persisted, enfeebled
but still alive, and we are told that today the independent
entrepreneur 'has become the man through whom the ideology of utopian capitalism is still actively presented to many
of our contemporaries'.[16] Meanwhile there was a steady
growth of the 'new middle class', composed chiefly of the
lesser professions and salaried employees, who occupied a permanent middle position in the capitalist hierarchy. It is in
their ranks that we find the clearest evidence of a preoccupation with social status similar to that which had long been
typical of the English.

Careful study of these two pictures, the English and the
American, leads to the apparently paradoxical conclusion that
preoccupation with social status may be stimulated both by
fluidity and by rigidity in the social system. When a section of
society is threatened by invasion from below, as the English
gentlemen were in varying degrees from the sixteenth century
onwards, they protect themselves by constructing barriers
out of those attributes and symbols of social differences which
are most difficult to acquire. Conspicuous expenditure can be
copied by those who get rich quick, but correct manners, the
right accent, and the 'old school tie' are esoteric mysteries
and jealously guarded monopolies. And it was in the nineteenth century that these symbols gained their great ascend-
ancy in English life. Similarly, those who climb successfully
from below seek by the same means to proclaim and consolidate their position, while the partially successful may devise
comparable methods of identifying the half-way house which
they have managed to reach.

[16] C. Wright Mills: *White Collar*, p. 34.

But in America it is generally felt that social structure has become more rigid and that status consciousness in the middle ranks springs from a sense of frustration. The road upwards has been blocked, that is to say, the road that leads from one position in the economic system to another quite different one (e.g. from worker to manager), and also the road that leads up to wealth. Exaggerated importance, therefore, may attach to those minor shifts and distinctions which are still possible within the same stratum of the economic structure —such as the shift which brings the clerk within the orbit of the boss or the saleswoman in touch with higher-class customers. Thus fluidity and rigidity may have, in this respect, the same result. They may also exist together in the same social pattern—as they in fact do in contemporary society. The opportunity to move to a social level different from that into which one was born is concentrated mainly into the years of education and training. It is here that all those with just the average amount of ambition get their chance, and it is by this process that the defences of the status-conscious middle and upper layers are penetrated from below. But thereafter, once the starting-point in public life outside home and school has been found, the regular road is clearly marked ahead, it is only the exceptional who can get away from it, and its terminus is visible not very far away. A cynic might observe that modern man, having striven during childhood and youth for the realities of life, proceeds to struggle for the shadows and the symbols after he has reached years of discretion. But that would be to exaggerate the role of status consciousness in our society today.

A great many studies have recently been made, both in England and in the United States, in an attempt to discover what that role is and what contemporary man means by social class. The results are not as yet very conclusive, partly because the investigators have not always been quite certain what they were investigating. In order to avoid misunderstandings a distinction has been made between 'subjective status', a man's status as assessed by himself, and 'accorded status', or a man's status as assessed by others.[17] But 'subjective status' is an unfortunate term. In its original meaning status is essentially something which no man can bestow upon himself; it is always 'accorded' by the society of which he is a member. No doubt a man's estimate of his own position is an important social fact which will influence his opinions and his behaviour, but the use of the word 'status' to describe it leads to confusion. When people are questioned about 'subjective status', it is difficult to interpret their answers. Some may try to express what they believe to be their own ultimate and absolute value, judged by some personal standard of their own; others may describe the position they think they ought to have, as judged by the standards current in their society; others may say what they believe is the position they occupy in the eyes of others—they may give, as it were, the subjective view as to what is the accorded status. It is impossible wholly to disentangle these elements in the answers.

This may be illustrated by two examples. The first, a familiar one, refers to self-assignment to a group or class. In two polls taken in the United States in 1939 and 1940, in which people were asked to assign themselves to the upper, middle or lower class, the percentages choosing the middle class were 88 and 79.[18] But in a subsequent inquiry in 1945, which offered the 'working class' as an additional option, the middle class percentage fell to 43, and in a follow-up study in the next year to 36.[19] Now it so happened that the interviews for this inquiry were taking place at the time of the British General Election, and the news of the Labour victory broke on July 26. The percentages of those assigning themselves to the working and lower classes fluctuated according to the date of interview as follows:

[17] H. H. Hyman: 'The Psychology of Status', *Archives of Psychology*, No. 269, 1942.

[18] See, for these and some similar inquiries, G. D. H. Cole: 'The Conception of the Middle Class', *The British Journal of Sociology*, December 1950, p. 276.

[19] R. Centers: *The Psychology of Social Class*, p. 77.

Before July 26, 51; on July 26, 67; after July 26, 54.[20]

These figures suggest that to some people 'subjective status' is a matter of political outlook and sympathy, and their sympathies with the working class were aroused or fortified by the Labour victory. And, in fact, when people were asked what, apart from occupation, was the most important thing to know about a person in order to assign him to a social class—family, money, education or beliefs and attitudes—47.4 per cent. chose 'beliefs and attitudes' and only 29.4 per cent. education, with the other criteria lagging behind.[21] But this may mean a number of different things. If a socialist son of a professional family assigns himself to the working class, he thereby tells us very little about his social status, either subjective or accorded.

The second example comes from the study by H. H. Hyman. He defined status as 'the position of an individual relative to other individuals', and he used the term of positions in several 'dimensions', that is, related to several different attributes or activities—such as intellect, athletics, culture, social standing, personal looks and so forth. He asked his subjects to place themselves on a scale of prestige in relation to these dimensions, and he naturally found that they used different scales, or derived their standards from different 'reference groups'. One man's 'subjective status' as an athlete might be based on comparison with the village club, and another's with the heroes of county cricket (this is not, of course, an actual example). It was found that the commonest practice was to rate status by reference to friends, and standards drawn from the total population were used more rarely. But, when they were, they were more reliable under repeated tests than ratings by reference to friends. This may indicate that rating by reference to the total social structure is less personal, in fact less 'subjective' in the true sense, and brings in the factor of common estimation or, in other words, of accorded status. The extreme case of personal rating was the

[20] ibid., p. 139.
[21] ibid., p. 91.

woman who 'phrases her "status" in comparison with herself. She has her own idea of where she should be and asks herself if she is doing as well as she can.' The whole study, though only exploratory, is most helpful and illuminating.

We might suppose that the idiosyncrasies of personal judgement would be diminished or even disappear when, by asking people to assign themselves to a named social group, we gave them an external and independent standard to work to. We might go on and suggest that the first example quoted above supports this view. When the term 'working class' was introduced into the question, the distribution of self-assigned class corresponded pretty well to what one might expect on the assumption that social class is at least related to occupation and income, even if not exactly determined by them. In other words, if you ask the right questions, people talk sense. Unfortunately this picture is not sustained in other parts of the inquiry. The subjects were asked to assign occupations to social classes. It was then found that only just over half (53 per cent.) of the self-styled middle-class members said that office workers belonged to the middle class, while very nearly half of the self-styled working-class members claimed them for the working class.[22] And, be it noted, 'office worker' in this context excluded big-business executives, store and factory managers, and small-business owners; it was practically equivalent to 'white collar', an occupational group which, one might have thought, is more unequivocally middle class than any other.

There are two ways of studying accorded status by means of interrogation. One is to ask people to classify individuals of whom they have some personal knowledge. This method has been most elaborately employed by Lloyd Warner and his associates.[23] The objection to this method is that each informant knows only a limited circle, and he does not know all those within this circle equally well. His information is not of uniform value, and it may be coloured by personal likes and dislikes and moral judgements. Lloyd Warner has been criticized for the undue reliance he has placed on informa-

[22] op. cit., pp. 82–3.
[23] See his book, *Social Class in America.*

tion which may be unreliable or a-typical, and also for the arbitrary way in which he converted a multitude of individual assessments into a tidy pattern of six distinct social classes.[24]

The second method, which has been much more widely used, is that of asking people to assess the social status of certain clearly defined groups or types of persons, for instance, occupations. A great many studies of occupational ranking have been made recently.[25] The results show that, when a wide range of occupations is offered for ranking, there is a high measure of consistency and uniformity in the answers. That is to say that the results do not vary much from one inquiry to another, and that the rank order is much the same whether the respondents are male or female, old or young, members of the upper or lower levels of society. But it is also noticed that agreement is closer about occupations at the top and the bottom of the scale than about those in the middle, and that the agreement in terms of average opinion conceals a good deal of individual disagreement. This is very much what we should expect. There exists a genuine social judgement, or common estimation, about the broad relationship between occupations and social stratification, but the consensus of opinion disappears when we try to make detailed comparisons. This is sometimes due to the ignorance of the respondents about the nature of some of the occupations in the list. In other cases the cause is just the opposite. A man's judgement of occupations closely associated with his own may be influenced by personal loyalties and rivalries. In one inquiry, for instance, in which students of medicine, law and engineering were asked to grade twenty professional and ancillary occupations, each group put its own profession at the top and, whereas the medical students put the nurse fifth, the lawyers put her nineteenth.[26]

[24] S. M. Lipset and R. Bendix: 'Social Status and Social Structure', *The British Journal of Sociology*, June 1951.
[25] For a survey of these, see A. F. Davies: 'Prestige of Occupations', *The British Journal of Sociology*, June 1952.
[26] W. Coutu: 'The Relative Prestige of Twenty Professions as judged by Three Groups of Professional Students', *Social Forces*, Vol. xiv, May 1936.

The mass of evidence suggests that occupation is generally regarded as an index of social status, probably the most important single index though not an infallible one. The disagreement referred to above about the assignment of office workers to a social class does not necessarily imply disagreement about their place in the scale of social status. It was probably due rather to differences of opinion as to the points in this scale at which to draw the dividing lines between social classes. But an occupational ranking cannot be arrived at by the mere recognition of objective facts, as in the case of ranking by income. There must be a value judgement, and it is based on the conventional values current in the society. In societies which have much the same occupations but different ideologies, the ranking will differ. This was shown by a modest study made in Russia in 1927. There were three groups of respondents—younger children, older children and textile workers. All put ministers of religion near the bottom with bankers and business men; the negative lesson had been well learned. But the street cleaner was also near the bottom, which suggests a survival of *bourgeois* ideology. But most remarkable was the disagreement about the places higher up. The young children put the peasant first, followed by the aviator and the member of the Central Executive; but the older children put the latter first and the peasant fifth. The textile workers placed mechanics and engineers very high, the Central Executive member tenth and the peasant seventeenth. It would seem that in 1927 the revolution of ideas was not complete and common estimation was in a state of flux.[27]

However, even in the assessment of occupations there is room for the expression of personal idiosyncrasies. This is particularly apparent when the questions are couched in terms which seem to invite almost a moral judgement. We sometimes find, for example, in the introduction to the questionnaire, phrases such as the following: we tend 'to look up to' some occupations and 'down on' others: we may even 'be

[27] Jerome Davis: 'Testing the Social Attitudes of Children in the Government Schools of Russia', *American Journal of Sociology*, Vol. XXXII, May 1927.

ashamed or proud of our relatives because of their occupation', and so forth. In the inquiry among professional students mentioned above, all respondents put the osteopath bottom, presumably because his practice was regarded as unprofessional. Another type of inquiry is sometimes used which is especially likely to bring out personal feelings. It attempts to measure 'social distance' by asking respondents to classify occupational types as eligible for admission to marriage, club, street, church, the country (as citizen), the country (as visitor). In one such inquiry it was found that students training as teachers or clergymen rated film actors, vaudeville performers and jazz musicians low in the scale, while students of commerce and dentistry rated them high because they 'add zest to life'.[28] In a similar inquiry carried out among 861 students, the highest score for marriageability (obtained by the teacher) was 691, the doctor coming next with 647, while twelve students voted for the total exclusion of ministers of religion from the country.[29] In such cases there would seem to be some blending, or confusion, of the two concepts of positional social status (the status accorded by society to the occupation) and personal social status (the status accorded to typical representatives of the occupation by the individual respondents). The effects of this confusion of thought are noticed by another investigator, who says of the status of teachers in the United States: 'On the one hand, the teacher represents a group well above the average citizen in intelligence, culture and socially desirable conduct. . . . Along with this, however, goes a reputation for economic incompetence, personal futility and inadequacy in community affairs.'[30]

The second obvious objective test of social position is income. There is, of course, a measure of correspondence be-

[28] E. S. Bogardus: 'Occupational Distance', *Sociology and Social Research*, Vol. xiii, 1928.

[29] Forrest Wilkinson: 'Social Distance between Occupations', *Sociology and Social Research*, Vol. xiii, 1929.

[30] George W. Hartmann: 'The Prestige of Occupations', *The Personnel Journal*, Vol. xiii, 1934–5.

tween income and occupation, since the standing of an occupation depends to some extent on the income it can yield.
But the correspondence is not exact. Some light has been
thrown on this question by an analysis made by Professor
Hadley Cantril of the results of an inquiry by the Office of
Public Opinion Research.[31] Respondents were asked to say
both to which income group and to which social class they
thought they belonged. We find that 15.4 per cent. assign
themselves to the upper or upper-middle social class, but
only 8.3 per cent. to the upper or upper-middle income
group, and that 50.6 per cent. assign themselves to the lower-
middle or lower income group, but only 18.8 per cent. to the
lower-middle or lower social class. Professor Cantril comments:

> The higher the social class, the more is it likely to be
> founded on non-economic criteria. . . . Persons in the
> low social class are there in large measure because they
> are poor with all that poverty implies, while people who
> feel they are in the upper social class are not necessarily
> there because they feel they are well off.

The results can be summarized in another way by saying that
54.3 per cent. rated social class and income group at the same
level, 42.5 per cent. rated social class above income group and
only 3.2 per cent. rated it below.

At this point it is necessary to attempt to sum up the conclusions reached by this survey. This is a difficult task, because
the situation we have been studying is full of confusion and
contradiction and is not governed by any one clear-cut principle.

Social status in contemporary Western society is related to
the broad pattern of stratification, that is to say to class structure in the technical sense described above. The dominant
elements in class structure are wealth, occupation (or function) and power, it being understood that 'power' includes,
not only power over the lives of others, but also power over
one's own life, i.e. independence. But social status is not

[31] 'Identification with Social and Economic Class', *Journal of
Abnormal and Social Psychology*, Vol. 38, 1943.

rigidly tied to class structure. Frequent anomalies occur, and there is room for much differentiation of social status within each broad economic stratum. Social status has a measure of autonomy, and that is why it is today a subject of such intense interest both to social scientists and to the general public.

This autonomy derives from the fact that social status is in the main a cultural concept, so that a social-status group may be referred to as a cultural sub-group of the total national culture group. The three most important factors contributing to the formation of social-status groups are family influence, formal education and the cultural quality of an occupation regarded as a way of life. But the autonomy is only partial, because culture depends to a great extent on the material resources available, while the cultural quality of an occupation is one aspect of its role in the class structure of the society.

Owing to the part played by family influence, and by the influence of the circle into which the family gives entry, there is an hereditary element in social status. And this element is particularly powerful because family influence begins at birth, and what is not obtained in this way can only with great difficulty, if at all, be acquired later in life. Therefore parentage remains an important determinant of social status.

The role of education has undergone great changes in the course of history. There are two ways of assessing the social value of education—first, by the actual results, that is to say, the knowledge and skills acquired, and secondly, by the symbolic value of the institutions in which the education was obtained. In medieval England education was judged primarily by its results. The man who could read and write was valued for the services he could render and entered his allotted place in the social structure in the church, in administration or, later, in the other professions. And, so long as the structure of the estate system survived, he did not seriously challenge the position of those at the top. But in the eighteenth, and still more in the nineteenth, centuries, when positions at the top were no longer secured by legal rights but depended on social privilege, and when the educated man from the middle classes could challenge the supremacy of the upper classes, a new emphasis was given to the social significance of particular places of learning which the aristocracy converted into a close preserve of their own, thus frustrating the purpose for which they were founded. It was enough to have been to one of the best schools and universities, even though you might have profited little from the instruction provided in them. Thus the 'snob-value' of the universities and public schools operated as a powerful defence of a precarious social status. With the movement towards equal educational opportunity (a goal which has by no means yet been reached) the position changed again. Once more it is the results that count, the examinations passed and the diplomas won. But, in so far as the human material is effectively sifted according to its native abilities, and in so far as those abilities are successfully developed in appropriate institutions, the results achieved should correlate closely with the schools and other places of education attended. If, in such circumstances, we classify people as 'secondary modern', 'grammar school', 'technical college' or 'university', we are in fact referring to the expected results in terms of knowledge and skill acquired, although we do this by naming the parts of the educational system in which these results were, or should have been, obtained. This favours the use of collective rather than individual valuations, that is to say, classification into groups rather than individual ranking on a scale.

As regards the cultural aspect of occupation, it has already been pointed out that this is based on value judgements which are conditioned by the ideas current in the society. A long list could be made of the elements which are relevant to these judgements—the contribution made by the occupation to the ends of the society, the amount of skill involved and, in consequence, the training required, the physical conditions of work, such as dirt or its absence, clothes ('white collar' and 'black coat' and similar phrases point to this), the relative share of brain and brawn, the amount of freedom enjoyed in planning the work as compared with rigid routine, the security of tenure, consideration shown by superiors, amenities enjoyed and, of course, the income earned. Wright Mills points out that the social position of the white-collar workers in the United States, which rested on distinctions of this kind, is being threatened by economic changes, which he sums up as follows:

> Lack of differences between wage-worker and white-collar income; white-collar unemployment, as during the 'thirties; the breakdown of the white-collar monopoly on high-school education, the inevitable reduction of the claims of white-collar people for prestige based on their not being 'foreign-born, like workers'; the concentration of white-collar workers into big work places and their down-grading and routinization; the mere increase in the total numbers of white-collar people.[32]

He also points out that, as the job provides a less and less satisfactory index of social status in itself, there develops a 'leisure ethic', or tendency to judge the job by the kind of leisure activities it makes possible.[33] And thus we come back to the idea of culture sub-groups moulded by these three factors—the influence of family and the immediate social circle, education and the total character of the occupation. When we speak of social classes today, we have such culture sub-groups very much in mind. For we may claim, with some justification, to be able to recognize, at least as types, an upper-middle, lower-middle and working-class way of life each with its distinctive pattern of expenditure. And the patterns of expenditure may retain features of difference even when the actual incomes have become the same. The outlines of the picture cannot be clear, because the structure of stratification changes, as do also the ideas on which value judgements are based. Some occupations rise in social prestige by developing new technical skills which require a higher level of education and training, while others, which do not develop in this way, lose prestige by comparison. Trades are transformed into profes-

---

[32] C. Wright Mills: *White Collar*, p. 312.
[33] ibid., p. 236.

sions, while old skills, formerly honoured, sink into obsoles-
cence. When this happens, there is an interplay between the
changing character of the job and the change in the type of
person, as judged by family and education, who takes it up.
In the days of Florence Nightingale nursing was a despised
occupation performed by untrained women of low origin, except in so far as it was practised by religious orders. The introduction of a system of training and of better conditions
of employment gradually transformed nursing into a profession which then began to attract recruits from higher social
levels. These then demanded, and were regarded as entitled
to, still better conditions—and so the process may continue. A
similar development has helped to raise the status of teachers. It is thus possible by deliberate action to raise the social
status of an occupational group, partly by altering the objective character of the job, and partly by changing the attitude towards it.

Finally, when the outlines of social structure lack precision
and when the categories to which people can most easily be
assigned are not in fact homogeneous, preliminary assessments
of positional social status lose much of their force and can
more readily be modified by consideration of individual attributes. In other words, personal social status wins a degree
of autonomy from positional social status, at least within the
smaller community in which persons can be judged for what
they are. There may, for example, be a rough general judgement, or common estimation, of the social status of teachers,
but in a narrower circle distinctions are made between teachers
of different grades and different schools; and also between
teachers of outstanding personality and culture who wield
great influence within a local community, and teachers who
lack the qualities necessary to rescue them from being finally
classed as representatives of an occupational type.

It may be permitted to end with the observation that, when
a social structure is in a state of flux, when the essentials of
civilization are being more equally distributed, and when
mobility of groups and individuals is increasing, it is not un-

natural that there should be great preoccupation with social status, a preoccupation increased by puzzlement as to what it is all about, although the real importance of social status, and of the *mystique* of social inequality, may be steadily diminishing.

CHAPTER IX

A NOTE ON 'STATUS'

The purpose of this note, in addition to that of associating the author with a tribute to a distinguished scholar, is to protest against the growing abuse of a potentially very valuable word. I say 'abuse' rather than 'misuse', because the latter would imply the breach of a linguistic canon, and I would not claim that any such canon exists today. But 'abuse' refers to mishandling of the kind that damages and eventually destroys. We can recognize it by its results, without having to lay down the law as to which usage is correct and which incorrect. If a word is being tossed around in such an irresponsible way that no consistent meaning remains to it and it is losing its value as a tool of exact thought, then obviously something is wrong.

The fault does not lie in the concept itself, for that is something with which we cannot dispense. It needs to be refined and sub-divided, but it cannot be abandoned. It has a part of special importance to play in social theory and that is why the abuse of the term, which threatens to make it unusable, is so serious. Status provides the link between the structural study of social systems and the psychological study of personality and motivation. The desire to explain the relation between social systems and the mental processes is as old as sociology itself but, as social science develops, the synthesis demands new categories of thought and new methods of research and exposition, the perfection of which is one of the major tasks of sociology today. The twin concepts of status

and role have been offered as one means of bridging the gap
—often far too wide—between sociology and psychology. As
Michael Argyle has said in a recent article,[1] the great popularity of the concept of role in recent literature may be due
to the fact 'that it links psychology in its study of individual
behaviour with sociology and anthropology in their study of
positional and situational determinants of behaviour'.

We see the same idea at work in the 'situational' approach
of W. T. Thomas and above all in Talcott Parsons' *General
Theory of Action*. The basic unit of social systems, says Parsons, is the act. The next unit of higher order is the status-
role. A person's status is 'his place in the relationship system
considered as a structure, that is a patterned system of parts'.
Thirdly, the actor himself is a unit of the social system. In this
sense he is 'a composite bundle of statuses and roles. But this
social actor must be distinguished from the personality as
itself a system of action.'[2] Personality cannot be subsumed
under status, but status is, as it were, the lowest *common*
denominator in the analysis of both structure and personality.
In the composite book, A *General Theory of Action*, Samuel A. Stouffer stresses this point of linkage, when he writes:
'One of the significant ideas in the system outlined in this
volume is the concept of role. This is not a new concept, but
its possible utility in unifying personality and societal theory
has perhaps not before been seen so clearly' (p. 480).

But Stouffer, in this context, refers to role rather than to
status, and so does Henry A. Murray in a similar but more
elaborate (and very confused) passage a few pages earlier in
the same volume (p. 450). This fact may serve to introduce
the first danger to which the term 'status' is exposed—the danger of being swallowed up by 'role' and then pocketed by those
psychologists who regard 'role' as their private property. T. M.
Newcomb is not one of these; he is scrupulously careful to
retain the distinction between the structural and the personal. Using the word 'position' in lieu of 'status', he writes:
'The ways of behaving which are expected of any individual

[1] *Sociological Review*, Vol. XLIV, 1952, Section 3, p. 1.
[2] *The Social System*, pp. 24–6.

who occupies a certain position constitute the role associated
with that position';[3] and then: 'roles and prescribed roles,
therefore, are not concepts which refer to the actual behaviour
of any given individual. Role behaviour, on the other hand,
does refer to the actual behaviour of specific individuals as
they take roles.'[4] And, very naturally, role behaviour, and the
taking and playing of roles by individuals in certain circumstances is of the very greatest interest to social psychologists.
There is consequently a tendency to forget the starting-point;
'role' comes to be used for 'role behaviour'; from this, which
still relates to behaviour adjusted to a specific role, one can
easily pass to the total behaviour of an individual while occupying a role. For example, if we consider the status of father, we can see three levels at which the term role might be
applied: (1) The behaviour expected of fathers in that particular society; (2) The behaviour adopted by Mr X (consciously or unconsciously) in playing the role of father; (3)
The total behaviour of Mr X in so far as it enters into his
relationships as father. For instance, Mr X may have developed various oddities of behaviour before he married—personal
peculiarities of speech, dress or manner, which persist and
become for his children symbols of 'father' and important
ingredients in the child-father situation. But such action is
not part of the role nor of the role behaviour, and has no immediate reference to social structure. If, therefore, 'role' is
carried off into this area of exploration of unique personality
problems, and drags status with it, then status will lose its

[3] *Social Psychology*, p. 280.
[4] *Social Psychology*, p. 330. The opposite view is taken by Kings-
ley Davis who defines 'role' as 'the manner in which an individual
actually carries out the requirements of his position', and claims
(wrongly, as I believe) that in this he is following Linton. ('A Conceptual Analysis of Stratification', *American Sociological Review*, Vol.
VII, June 1942, p. 311.) Marion Levy (*The Structure of Society*, p.
158) maintains that this definition is accepted, not only by Linton,
but also by Parsons. This is definitely not the case. Levy proposes
to replace the terms 'status' and 'role', as allegedly used by Linton
and Parsons, by 'ideal role' and 'actual role', but this would be
clumsy and confusing.

value as a bridge between social structure and personality studies, because it will have been wholly uprooted from the soil of structure.

Although confusion between role, role behaviour and total behaviour is clearly to be condemned, it is possible to make a case for the merging of status with role. It will be remembered that Linton, to whom most writers refer as the author of the modern terminology, said that role 'represents the dynamic aspect of a status' and that the distinction was 'only of academic interest'.[5] And Parsons, as we have seen, links the two with a hyphen. The main argument for the merger is that a status, conceived as a position in a social system, can be imagined only in terms of relationships, and the substance of social relationships is expected behaviour—or in the famous words of Max Weber (Parsons' translation) a 'social relationship thus consists entirely and exclusively in the existence of a probability that there will be, in some meaningfully understandable sense, a course of social action'.[6] It can be argued, therefore, that if the dynamic aspect of status is removed, nothing is left except a fallacious conception of a position in a social system as a static objective thing. Certainly the temptation to fallacious reification is present; but it is present whenever one thinks about social structure at all, and it should be possible to resist it. Status leans towards structural analysis and a high level of abstraction, and role towards individual behaviour and concrete situations. If this is kept clear, then 'role' can, with appropriate qualifying adjectives, be used in the study of unique personality problems, provided it keeps a firm grasp of the hand of status, which must remain planted on the other side of the fence. Briefly put, status emphasizes the position, as conceived by the group or society that sustains it, and role emphasizes the person who occupies the position. Status emphasizes the fact that expectations (of a normative kind) exist in the relevant social groups, while role emphasizes the items which make up the behaviour that is expected.

[5] R. Linton: *The Study of Man*, p. 114.
[6] R. Linton: *The Theory of Social and Economic Organization*, p. 107.

Status is your idea of the plant whose seeds you are sowing, and role is the picture on the seed-packets.

It must be admitted that the apparent need for both terms is sometimes due to slovenly thinking. We may say, for instance, that we know what a policeman is (status), but have a very imperfect idea of what he does (role). This distinction is not legitimate because status should be as precise a concept as role. It should embrace all that distinguishes the position as an element in social structure, whether the facts are known to the general public or not. The slovenly use described above will, if permitted, lead to a concept of status as the meaning attached to a position by other members of the society in general; this is then translated into something like 'the popular assessment' of the position, and soon 'status' is (as we shall see) hopelessly confused with 'social status', 'rank' and 'rating'.

What has just been said does not imply that 'status' cannot be used at different levels of generalization, and therefore with differing completeness of attributes or contents. For instance, we may discuss the status of father in the upper middle classes of twentieth-century England, or we may speak of father-status as something found in all human societies. In the latter case the breadth of generalization is made possible by the paucity of attributes included in the definition of the concept. But at each level of generalization there is a role corresponding to the status. However, because (as noted above) role leans towards individual behaviour and concrete situations, we may find ourselves saying, for example, that 'the father-status is found in both societies X and Y, but the father-role is different in the two'. But if the latter part of the sentence is true, then the father-status, at the more restricted level of generalization, must also differ.

Undoubtedly the retention of the two concepts has its disadvantages. But the advantages are considerable and, I think, outweigh them. I have already spoken of the major advantage, that 'status' is less likely than 'role' to become detached from the structural side of the picture and carried off into the territory of personality-studies. Another advantage is that the use of the two terms enables us to distinguish between role and one of the meanings of function. Because status stands as a link between structure and the individual, therefore it has two dynamic aspects, one relating to structure and the other to the individual. The function of a status is the part it plays in the system of social structure, its role is the action on the part of its individual occupant which enables this function to be performed. The distinction is important, and is missed by Murray in the passage referred to above, where he first identifies 'group' with 'social system' and 'role' with 'function', and then refers to respiration and excretion as roles of the 'self-and-body', and to hierarchical organization and the recruitment and training of new members as 'social roles' of the group.[7] The retention of 'status', and the attachment of 'role' firmly to it, might help to prevent confusions of this kind.

Let us, then, retain the concept of status to denote a position in a social system. Parsons calls it 'a place in the relationship system'; Linton, after using a similar phrase, adds that it is 'simply a collection of rights and duties'.[8] This suggests my second point, that the popular emphasis on role and expected behaviour (without it being specified who 'expects') has caused one of the earliest uses of the word 'status' to fall gradually into disuse. I refer to the lawyer's use, illustrated by Maine's famous dictum about the movement of progressive societies 'from Status to Contract'.[9] The most positive rejection of this use comes from Benoît-Smullyan who calls it 'an older usage' which is 'no longer popular', and is 'defective' because it presupposes a complex society.[10] Why a usage should be rejected because it is old, or deemed defective because it applies to relatively complex societies, is not clear. In reality the usage is valuable, and even necessary. C. K. Allen defines status as 'the condition of belonging to a particular

[7] A *General Theory of Action*, p. 450.
[8] op. cit., p. 113.
[9] H. S. Maine: *Ancient Law* (1878), p. 170.
[10] A. Benoît-Smullyan: 'Status, Status Types and Status Interrelations', *American Sociological Review*, Vol. IX, April 1944.

class of persons to whom the law assigns peculiar legal capacities or incapacities, or both'.[11] The concept is a legal one,
and sociologists are quite right to extend it, but the extension
need not cause us to abandon the older meaning or even to
lose sight of the significant difference between it and the extended meaning. The extension from legally established capacities and incapacities to socially recognized rights and
duties and so to socially expected behaviour within the frame
of specified relationships is perfectly natural and proper. But
the concept of legal status need not be discarded, nor the
distinction between it and what sociologists mean by plain
'status' ignored. It is a matter of very great importance to
know whether the power of an upper class is based on legally
enforceable rights or not, and whether labourers have the
legal status of slaves or not. It is impossible to make comparative studies of the family if one does not pay attention to the
shifting borderline between the legal rights and the socially
approved and expected conduct of the husband-father or the
wife-mother. Let us, then, retain the 'older usage', but bow
to necessity and attach the adjective 'legal' to the noun 'status'
when we wish to make use of it.

My third and last point relates to the confusion between
status on the one hand and social status and ranking on the
other. 'Status', as used by Linton, Parsons and others, has
no direct or necessary reference to position on a scale or in a
hierarchy. It embraces all relationships, not only those of
superiority and inferiority. But 'social status' is now in general use to denote position in the hierarchy of social prestige.
It is in effect very nearly what Linton meant by 'the status' of
an individual (as distinct from 'a status' occupied by many
individuals) and he described it as 'the sum total of all the
statuses which he occupies'.[12] The hypothesis that there is
a 'general status' which is the sum total of all special statuses
was investigated by Hyman, whose results appeared to support it.[13] I find it impossible to do the required sum. How

[11] *Legal Duties and other Essays in Jurisprudence*, p. 42.
[12] op. cit., p. 113.
[13] H. H. Hyman: 'The Psychology of Status', *Archives of Psychology*, No. 269, 1942.

do you add together, for instance, doctor, father, councillor, wicket-keeper, church warden and husband to get a unitary result? But, although these statuses cannot be added up, they all contribute to the determination of social status, which is the position of the individual (envisaged in his totality) within the community (conceived as a social whole). Functional specialization is here pushed into the background, and it is not unreasonable to regard the superiority-inferiority dimension as entitled to appropriate to itself the use of the status concept in this setting.

But this annexation of 'social status' by the prestige scale should leave 'status' unaffected. Unfortunately this has not been the case. We can again refer to Benoît-Smullyan who states categorically that status means position in a hierarchy—economic, political or prestige.[14] And when M. Sherif cites and accepts this view without realizing that it diverges sharply from that of Linton (which he also professes to accept, though the passage he quotes from Linton as an explanation of status is in fact a comment on ascription), the results are disastrous.[15] For Sherif places the main emphasis on the hierarchical positions within groups, such as trade unions, gangs, professional bodies, universities, etc., and therefore ignores the primary concept of status as the fact of membership itself. The distinction (in England) between Harley Street specialist and country general practitioner is important, though not only in terms of hierarchy. But we must not ignore the status significance of the broader categories of professional man and doctor (which may include elements of legal status), again not only in terms of hierarchy. Then, having given this slant to the argument, and pointed out that 'the scale of status positions is a stimulus for the would-be member', Sherif proceeds to consider the relative roles attached to the statuses of father and mother. But obviously this is not a question simply of position in a hierarchy, and we can hardly imagine an individual being stimulated by status aspirations to become a father rather than a mother.

H. H. Hyman, in his important study of the psychology of

[14] op. cit., pp. 151–2.
[15] M. Sherif: An Outline of Social Psychology, p. 297.

status, defined status as 'the position of an individual relative
to other individuals', but confined his investigation to the
particular relationship of higher and lower on a scale. And
when a girl's rating of her attractiveness on a scale of, say,
one to ten is described as 'subjective status', it is obvious that
we have moved a long way from the concept as used by Linton
and Parsons. In fact it becomes clear that 'position relative to
other individuals' implies only comparison, whereas 'place in
the relationship system' implies interaction.

The conclusion to this note is bound to be unsatisfactory.
For comparison is important as well as interaction, and hierarchical structure is not only of interest in the case of total
communities to which the term 'social status' can be applied,
and, though the distinction between legal and social rights is
a necessary one, we must not sacrifice equally necessary distinctions in order to find words in which to speak of it. Our
terminology is in a tangle, and it will take time to straighten
it out. My own preference is for the retention of the term
'status' as used by Linton and Parsons, that is without any
necessary reference to hierarchical position. The chief objection is that the hierarchical connotation is already so firmly attached to the word that it may be impossible to detach it.
But against this are the arguments that, if we keep it, we can
(1) also keep 'legal status' and go on discussing Maine's dictum; (2) retain the marriage of status and role, which may
save 'role' from going to the bad from the sociologists' point
of view. If we follow Newcomb and replace 'status' by 'position', I fear that the concept will lose its power and value. I
would accept 'social status' for hierarchical position in a total
community—but only in a community. And I would confine it
to positions that are largely unstructured. Structured hierarchical positions are better referred to as 'ranks'. And 'rank'
can also be used with reference to associations—e.g., army,
civil service, university, etc. The chief difficulty is to find a
word for hierarchical positions which are not sufficiently structured to be called ranks and which exist within associations
(which precludes the use of 'social status'). I might say of a
man: 'He likes his job, but is worried by his status.' Status

here is local to the organization, and is not his social status, though it may influence and be influenced by it. It is not wholly structured as a position in an establishment, but includes elements of prestige, which are rather fluid. Society today is full of people who worry about their status in this sense, in the office or the village or the club and so forth. Personally, I should prefer the word 'standing' in order to preserve the more precise and technical sense of status. And where no more is meant than comparative value in terms of some allegedly measurable attribute such as intelligence or good looks or skill at tennis, I should say 'rating'.

Let us take, as a summary example, a University Librarian or senior administrative officer such as Registrar or Bursar. His *status* differs from that of a Professor, because his *role* and the *functions* of his post differ from those of a Professor. But his university *rank* may be the same. He may, however, have a lower *social status* in the community at large than most Professors (perhaps because of his family origins), and a rather low *rating* for intelligence or general culture or social graces. In consequence of all these factors his *standing* in the university is not quite what he would like it to be.

But I have no wish to impose a terminology on anyone. The main point is to agree as to the concepts we wish to use and the nature of the distinction between them. If we can do that, then perhaps we shall eventually agree about their names.

CHAPTER X

WORK AND WEALTH

In the third chapter of the book of Genesis is written the story of the fall of man and the curse of God. The Lord said to Adam: 'Cursed is the ground for thy sake; in sorrow shalt thou eat of it all the days of thy life. . . . In the sweat of thy face shalt thou eat bread. . . . Therefore the Lord God sent him forth from the garden of Eden to till the ground from whence he was taken.' That, so we are taught, is how work first came into the world. But today we talk about 'honest sweat' and the 'dignity of labour' and argue that work is necessary for man's happiness. Now, one of the favourite terms of modern psychologists is 'rationalization', which means that we believe, or profess, what is convenient and soothing in the light of our guilty conscience, our moral weakness, or the imperfections of this wicked world; so it might be that our reverential attitude towards work is a mental trick designed to conceal the true facts, namely, that work is a necessary evil and that men are by nature bone idle. Frankly, I believe that there is a good deal of wishful thinking on this subject. Undoubtedly utter laziness, a desire literally to do nothing at all, is contemptible by any human standard, and it is rare; most of us need to be active in order to be happy. But aversion from work may spring from a desire to be doing something different rather than from an unwillingness to do anything, and we must admit that, if we were free from all compulsion and obligation, we should not—most of us—spend our time exactly in the way we now do. We might choose a different or more varied occupation; we might like to enjoy greater freedom from control by the boss or from subservience to the demands of the client or customer; we might prefer to work a little less hard or for rather shorter hours. But we carry on. The direct pleasure we get from our work may be great or small, but however great it is, only very rarely will it suffice by itself to make us do all that is required of us. We have ulterior motives that drive us on, and we *must* have them if the work of the world is to get done.

Work Motives

I do not use the word 'ulterior' in any derogatory sense. I do not mean that these motives are in any way inferior, unworthy, improper or dishonest. I mean only that they differ from the pleasure obtained directly by doing the job and relate to something that happens as a result of the job being done. Now, all paid work produces two after-effects: income for the worker, and goods or services for the consumer; and each of these may provide a motive for individual industry. It is tempting to call these the motives of self-interest and service. But this would not be quite accurate, and the words carry a flavour of praise and blame. In the first place a worker does not spend his earnings on himself alone, but on his family, and the support of a family is a form of service. Secondly, self-interest is not in itself reprehensible, provided it is not pursued at the expense of others. We give praise to those who strive to excel, and we do not withdraw the praise when we find that they were fully aware that their excellence would be rewarded. If personal advancement is won by rendering a service to society, then we do not blame a man if he is spurred on by the desire for advancement. In such a case it is impossible to disentangle the motives of self-interest and service or to decide what part has been played by each. But it would be possible, by changing our social system, to eliminate one form of self-interest, namely, the pursuit of material gain. We could make income entirely independent of the value of service rendered by adopting the principle of 'to each according to his needs'. This would mean applying to everybody the methods of public assistance and the means test, or, if you prefer it, the system of sharing that prevails in every happy and well-regulated family. It would involve a revolutionary experiment which has not been carried through even in Communist Russia. So let us, for the present at any rate, accept self-interest as a respectable incentive to work.

At the other end of the scale is the motive of service to the community. Recent experience during the war has shown us that this can be a very powerful and fully conscious motive in times of national emergency. But we should not assume that it operates only in emergencies and only in response to moving appeals for a special effort. It is alive in us even when we are not fully aware of it. We are, all of us, very conventional at heart, and have a strong instinct to conform to social custom—in our clothes, speech, manners, recreations, and in the code of conduct that governs our way of life. And work is an important part of the pattern; the duty to work, and to work to a certain standard, is part of the code. In the past this weaving of work into the texture of social life was outwardly expressed by ceremonies, many of which had a religious character. The driving of the first furrow, the sowing of the seed, and the gathering of the crop were events of vital meaning to the whole community. To withhold one's labour at such a time was tantamount to going into voluntary exile, to becoming an outcast, a man without fellows. Such practices flourished most naturally in small local communities devoted to agriculture, for here the common interests of all and the consequent duty of each were most clearly visible. They could not survive in a modern mass society with its infinite variety of occupations. The social occasions which draw us together into a self-conscious community seem to be associated less with going to work than with getting away from it—with Saturday afternoons and Bank Holidays. When we go back to work we split up again into our innumerable groups.

Work as a Social Bond

Have we, then, nothing to put in the place of these primitive rites and medieval gild ceremonies and the like, no out-

ward and visible expression of the truth that work is a function of social life, an attribute of the membership of society?
No, we have nothing quite like them. In this, as in other matters, abstract ideas must deputize for ceremony. And the relevant idea in this case is the democratic conception of citizenship. Today all workers are citizens, and we have come to
expect that all citizens should be workers. Service to the community is an obligation which can be freely recognized by
those who enjoy full rights as members of the community,
rights which include, not only the vote, but equal justice,
freedom of speech and social security. It has been said many
times that it was for this idea that the war was fought and by
this idea that the war was won, and that is as near to the truth
as any simple statement on a great issue. But the idea was
not born in the war, though it is harder to find clear evidence
of its power in the years of peace. As I was pondering on this
point it occurred to me that one might learn something of
what work meant to a man by seeing how he was affected by
the loss of it. So I took down a book published in 1934 called
Memoirs of the Unemployed—a collection of first-hand personal stories by all sorts and conditions of men—and turned
over the pages. I will let the men speak for themselves:

A Young Engineer: 'After prolonged unemployment the
victim feels that society has no real use for him, and in an
introspective person this produces a morbid sense of inferiority. In some cases it produces an apathy which develops into
vicious idleness.'

A Colliery Banksman: 'For myself the dependence on the
State for money without having honestly earned it has made
me creep within myself, losing faith in everything except my
own capabilities. . . . In fact it has made me, who once
prided myself on my generous and self-sacrificing nature—a
real follower of Christ—a selfish person.'

A South Wales Miner: 'What effect has unemployment had
on me? It has definitely lessened my interest in politics, because it has led me to believe that politics is a game of bluff,
and that these people do not care a brass farthing for the

bottom dog. . . . The same applies to the trades unions;
when it comes to a real test they are hopeless.'

A *Business Man:* 'During the last twenty years I have been
an active worker in the Socialist movement. . . . Now my interest in politics has completely vanished. I am embittered
against all politicians of all parties. I am still a Socialist, but
am not prepared to speak unless for money.' He then refers
to an article he had published and says: 'I dared not write
what I thought of governments and politicians. I sold my soul
—God forgive me—for money.'

A *Skilled Engineer of Middle Age:* 'The one important
thing is to get hold of money. I'd steal if I could get away
with it. I'm disgusted with my former political and trade
union associates.'

And some did steal:

An *Electrician turned Burglar:* 'When I look back over the
last five years I feel I am in some way justified in hitting back
at society. It's when I don't look back that I feel uncomforta-
ble. I feel I belong to a race apart and wonder what the end
is going to be. . . . I have plenty of good food, clothing and
shelter, and strange though it seems I feel I am *somebody,*
and I certainly never felt that during my two years of honest
idleness.'

Now we might have expected most of that, but, taken together, these extracts have a flavour that is illuminating. A
man who has lost his job has lost his passport to society. It is
not only that idleness is boring and the dole a mere pittance.
What hurts most is the knowledge that his service is not
wanted. His work is rejected, and that means that he himself
is rejected, as a man and a citizen. Two results follow. He
loses interest in politics. Politicians are a race apart; they belong to another world, the world of citizens, of which he is no
longer a member. The same is true of his old social groups—
his neighbours, his trade union. He is isolated, and therefore
nobody. Even a burglar is somebody, because he belongs to
a gang. Secondly, he becomes selfish—'the one important thing
is to get hold of money'—and there is a note of surprise at the
sense of degradation that follows. Now that is interesting. All

these men worked for money before, and we cannot suppose
that they were indifferent as to how much they earned or
were never moved by a desire to increase their income. But
then self-interest harmonized with service. Their work was
wanted; it was a contribution to a joint social effort to produce. They were in partnership with their fellows. Unemployment dissolved the partnership and substituted the law of the
jungle, each for himself. It might turn a man into a lone
wolf, preying on society. I would not suggest for a moment
that this experience was general. But the fact that these things
could happen reveals the strength of work as a social bond.
It shows how motives which move in harmony within a social
order dissolve into clashing discord when that order is dis-
rupted; in a word, that loss of work disintegrates social man.

Social Groups within the Community

Before I try to draw any practical conclusions from this general analysis, there is another point I must make—an important one. I have spoken of the motives of self-interest and
service to the community. Between the individual and the
community stand groups of various kinds, including groups of
fellow workers. Loyalty to the group may provide a motive,
not merely to work, but to work up to a prescribed standard.
The most familiar examples are the medieval gild, the professional association, and, though with a difference, the trade
union. The gild was a body of master craftsmen, officially
recognized, which was entrusted with the task, not only of
protecting the interests of its members, but also of guarantee-
ing their service to the community and the standard of their
work. The same is true of the profession. Even though it may
have been given by law a charter and privileges amounting to
monopoly, it does not regard itself merely as the agent of the
State. It claims a special authority as trustee, on behalf of the
community, of an art or science that serves the community.
Professions have, as we know, sometimes opposed the State,
and claimed to do so in discharge of this trusteeship, though
possibly in fact the motives have not always been entirely

disinterested. The trade union, I said, is different. Members of a profession are as a rule their own masters and their external relations are primarily with the client. Members of a trade union are not their own masters and their external relations are primarily with the employer. It is natural that the motive of self-protection should loom large in the history of their development, and it is inevitable that measures taken to prevent exploitation should sometimes take the form of measures restrictive of production, and such measures can be carried too far. But the element of trusteeship is present too, and the more firmly established the unions are, and the more successful in their efforts on behalf of their members, the stronger it can become. In a recent speech Mr Arthur Horner (as reported in *The Times*) said: 'They were trying to build up a new morality depending on voluntary discipline and the goodwill of the men. If a lodge was satisfied that individuals were persistently refusing to do their clear duty, then those individuals would have to be informed that they could no longer count on the support of the rest of the men if they found themselves in difficulties.' That is the spirit of the gild, and it is Mr Horner, not I, who has called it 'a *new* morality'.

The picture I have drawn is, I know, an ideal one, but it serves to demonstrate the function of these groups. No man can stop, daily or hourly in the course of his work, to ask himself, 'what must I do in this case to serve the interests of the community?' and expect to find the answer in his own mind. But the gild or the profession or the trade union can, through its traditions and its rules, give him clear guidance which he can follow, and, if all is well, he should be able to feel confident that, by following it, he will discharge his duty to society. Thus the lesser loyalty embraces the larger.

Now I can draw my first general conclusion. In our working life we obey many motives, acting at different levels. We have loyalties to ourself, our family, our fellow-workers, the community, and possibly even humanity itself. It is in the nature of society that this should be so. Sometimes these loyalties appear to clash, but it would be wrong to seek to remedy this by eliminating all the loyalties but one. In the crisis after

Dunkirk it was possible to appeal to the workers to forget everything except the nation's peril, to strive for one thing only, the production of munitions of war, and to discard all their peace-time customs and traditions and work till they dropped. But you cannot do that all the time. You may launch a crusade for single-hearted devotion to the common good, but other motives cannot be completely stifled. You will be asking each man to find the true balance for himself, and that is too heavy a responsibility for him. The result, before long, will be conflict—conflicts between groups and classes, and conflict within each individual man. Society's task is more subtle and more complex than this. It is to create conditions in which the various natural motives and loyalties of social man can operate in harmony. Admittedly all problems will not be solved in this way and no adjustment can be perfect or immutable. But, with a firm foundation of spontaneous order, doubt and controversy can be focussed on those established customs which have come to act as a barrier to progress.

The Conditions Needed for Social Harmony: Ends Worth Working for

And now the time has come for me to be more practical and to indicate, if I can, some of the conditions necessary for the achievement of this harmony of motives. You will not expect me to exhaust this subject in twenty minutes, and the most I can hope to do is to give some illustrations drawn from different spheres of life.

The first condition is that it must be generally believed that the game is worth the candle. Work, as I have said, involves some sacrifice. The production of munitions in 1940 was worth any sacrifice; the production of wealth in time of peace is not. Wealth has been produced in the past at the price of health, happiness, and even life itself. Today we should condemn such a bargain. It is not that we have only just discovered that well-being is not based on material wealth only, but also on personal qualities which can be crippled by over-work and need leisure for their full development and enjoyment. This has been known ever since civilization began. But it is only recently that we have recognized that the right to develop and enjoy these qualities belongs to all classes of the community. There has been going on, especially in the last fifty years or so, a steady fusion of class civilizations into a single national civilization, although there still remains a substantial section of the population at the bottom of the scale that has been little affected by the change. There was a time when the culture of each class was, as it were, a unique species. Peasants had their own style of clothes, houses, furniture, art and amusements—many of them of such good quality that surviving examples are coveted by rich collectors. Mass production destroyed this isolation, with the result that the articles made for sale to the poor became cheap and tawdry imitations of those made for sale to the rich—gimcrack furniture, jerry-built houses, ugly ill-fitting clothes, and so forth. Now we have passed into another phase. We have seen the rapid flowering of that 'new civilization of the crowd' which Masterman observed at the beginning of the century[1] and which has since then transformed the quality of life of the lower middle and upper working classes. Its effects can be seen in clothes, especially women's clothes, the designs of newly erected dwellings and factories, in transport—by train, bus and tube—in the appointments of cinemas and popular restaurants, in household conveniences, radio sets, and so on. A great spur has been given to the movement by the war, through the rationing of food and clothes and the production of utility goods. There has been a progressive equalization of the quality of material culture so that, even though great differences remain between the top and the bottom, they are variations on a single theme and are linked in a continuous scale.

Now what follows from this? First, the production of wealth becomes more worth while, because wealth is more widely distributed. The masses become customers, whose tastes and

[1] C. F. G. Masterman: *The Condition of England*, 1909.

comfort are considered, not merely consumers into whose homes a certain quantity of commodities must be shovelled to keep them alive and working. And secondly, luxury goods do not move in a closed circle, but filter downwards, and the skill evolved in their production quickly fertilizes the processes of manufacture. But thirdly, as higher quality goods move down the social scale, so hands reach up towards them from below and voices are lifted demanding a speedier rise in the standard of living. Now, economic ambition may provide a strong incentive to work. In eighteenth-century England, when economic ambition was lacking in the rural working class because there were no goods or services to spend extra money on, it was said that, if wages rose, men only worked long enough to cover their customary expenditure, and production declined. The sole elastic demand was for drink. The same thing may sometimes happen even today, especially in wartime when wages are high and consumer goods are scarce. But it is not characteristic of modern society. Nevertheless it certainly does not follow that the livelier desire for a higher standard of living will make men work longer hours, for long hours lower the standard of well-being. In fact we must expect demands for higher wages and shorter hours to go hand in hand. It is quite proper that they should, and that the fruits of economic progress should be distributed in such a way as to produce these twin effects. It is futile to imagine that a rigid stratification of cultures can persist in our society, or to think that there is something shocking or immoral in a working man wanting to own a car. But a limit is set by the fact that you cannot distribute the fruits until they have been grown and gathered, and that no nation can consume more than it produces, unless it receives alms from its neighbours.

Faith in Government

The second condition is that citizens should have faith in the honesty and efficiency of the system of government. The fact that economic and social life are increasingly affected by political decisions is patent to all and, if citizenship is to provide a basis for the motive of service, it is essential that those decisions should be respected. In a democracy this means that loyalty to the State must be above loyalty to party, and I believe that is the case in this country. Although it is a little early to judge, the reception given to the Labour Government seems to confirm this view; both the general public and the dockers appear to be behaving very much as they would do under a Conservative or a Coalition Government. But we must not grow too complacent and think there is no room for improvement. Nothing is more destructive of the true essence of citizenship than the existence of a gulf between the governors and the governed. Many people have observed that the Germans habitually speak of their rulers as 'they' and of German policy as 'their' policy, keeping 'we' to denote the people as distinct from the State. That is not our manner of speech or of thought. We do not regard our politicians as remote and unapproachable strangers for whose doings we have no responsibility. We are not disposed either to worship or to assassinate them; they belong to us. But there is a real danger of a gulf forming between the administrators, whether civil servants or local government officials, and the public. I see two main lines of action to prevent this. First, through selection and training of officials. The net of recruitment should be thrown wider, especially for the higher posts, and if our educational system still restricts unduly admission by examination, then more scope should be provided for entry later into positions where experience outside official life is of the greatest value. In training social workers we insist on both practical work in the field and theoretical study of social structure, forces and problems. When interviewing candidates for our new course in personnel management, I was struck by the number of those who felt, quite spontaneously, that they wanted not only technical training in the job, but education in the social sciences. Civil servants and officials need similar training, either before or after appointment. The second line of action is publicity. I fully realize how difficult it is for officials to explain exactly what they are doing and to take the public fully into their confidence. It requires infinite patience and the temper of a saint. But much can be done centrally by public relations departments, and it may be that there is a task here for a Ministry of Information of a new kind. We must not allow the bad repute into which propaganda has fallen to blind us to the necessity of keeping the people fully and accurately informed about public affairs.

Harmony within and between Social Groups

My third point is group loyalty, and it is a very difficult and controversial one. I need only remind you of the attitude of the medical profession on the question of a national health service and of the attitude of the dockers towards their union leaders. The problem is, from the point of view of the individual, how to harmonize loyalty to the group (whether employers' association, professional body, or trade union) with legitimate self-interest and duty to the community. The first condition is that the status of the groups should be fully recognized. When trade unions were fighting for the right to exist it was natural that they should claim an exclusive and aggressive loyalty from their members. Recognition should cut the roots of antagonism, though it cannot entirely eliminate conflict. But if functional groups win recognition from the State they must also accord it to one another. They must judge the actions of groups of other kinds by the same standards that they apply to themselves, and that is not always easy. Nations are perhaps the worst offenders, and diplomacy bristles with examples of the pot calling the kettle black. The second condition is that groups should be consulted on matters that concern them. We have made great progress here, in particular through our admirable system of *ad hoc* committees and Royal Commissions and permanent advisory bodies. The third condition is that, if groups are fully consulted, they should not claim political power; political influence, yes, by the ordinary means of argument, discussion and propaganda. But not power; otherwise group loyalty and citizenship are bound to clash.

Next, I would apply to groups the principle I have already

laid down for political life: that there should not be a gulf between leaders and led. This means that the practices of democracy must be followed within the group and that members must be fully informed about its affairs. An association in which interest, activity and power are confined to a small irresponsible clique is a public danger. And lastly, organized groups must realize that they exist to give as well as to get— to give something *to* the community as well as to get something *from* the community for their members. Their power to serve is derived ultimately from their expert knowledge and experience, and it is important to remember that these are diffused throughout the group and varied in character. National associations are apt to become over-centralized, through fear of disintegrating, and in consequence over-political in their outlook. The war has shown us that immense vitality can be generated in the small group, and how valuable it is as a unit of co-operation. We saw it in the A.R.P. services, the Home Guard, the W.V.S. and many other movements, all of which were highly decentralized. At this level, the level of the village, the neighbourhood and the street, the 'human factor' became a friend and ally instead of a mysterious and rather terrifying bogey.

And that brings me to my fourth and last point: the conditions needed to produce a harmony of motives within the factory. I have kept it to the end in order that it may serve as a link between my broad sociological approach to the subject of this Conference and the more practical treatment which it will receive from the speakers who are to follow me. It would be an impertinence for me to attempt to lay down the law on such a matter before such an audience, and I shall confine myself in the main to making a general analysis of the problem.

Conditions for Harmony within the Factory

First then, I think there is a real analogy between the political and industrial problems. The small group is a social microcosm, or miniature reproduction of the large. I have stressed the importance of the idea of citizenship and argued that it is not a purely political conception but signifies full membership of a community. It affects the industrial problem in two ways. If the worker is to be happy in his work he must have confidence in the Government and its handling of industrial issues, and in particular in the measure of social security that it grants to him. He must know that he enjoys the full rights and dignity of a citizen. But there is also a sense in which the idea applies to the industrial unit in which he works, a sort of citizenship in the microcosm of the factory. Here too the worker must have confidence in the efficiency and disinterestedness of the management, and he is in many respects a good judge of efficiency. He must not feel that his incentive to serve is frustrated by incompetence at the top nor that his legitimate self-interest is thwarted by the excessive self-interest of his employer. He must be assured that by serving the immediate aims of his firm he serves also the larger aims of the economic system. Secondly, membership of a factory community means more than the mutual fulfilment of a wage contract for, though labour certainly is a commodity, the labourer is not. Since the man himself is inseparable from the work that he sells, his human needs both in and outside working hours must be considered. Security and continuity are vital elements in citizenship, in the sense that membership of the community is permanent and uninterrupted, but industrial security—security in the job—cannot be as complete as political. It is easy to say that, if a workman fulfils his duties, then his employer incurs an obligation which goes beyond the terms of the immediate contract of employment, but it is by no means easy to define just how far it should go, and I shall not attempt to do so. I will only point out that this is a case where the two levels of citizenship can supplement each other—security in a particular job can be supplemented by the general 'right to work'. I should guess, too, that holidays with pay have great psychological as well as physical value because, to reverse Maine's famous dictum, they express clearly the development from contract to status, the status of continued membership of a social group.

Four Degrees of Co-operation

I think we should all agree that our aim is to secure co-operation in industry, and that the essence of the problem is to adjust the methods of co-operation to a distribution of authority and responsibility suited to the nature of the actual task in hand. In the case of industry I suggest that there are four possible degrees, or grades, of co-operation.

The first is *information*. By this I mean that managers take their employees into their confidence by explaining just what they are doing and why they are doing it. The value of this practice is widely recognized. You will find it in the Army. The other day I asked an officer whether the old idea of 'theirs not to reason why' still survived at all; he replied at once that it did not. There had, he said, been a revolution in the army in the past five years, and officers were now made to explain fully to their men the nature of a coming operation; this had had an excellent effect on morale. However, the men, though informed of decisions, have no share at all in the making of them.

The second grade is *consultation*. This means that employees are not only informed before a decision is taken, but have an opportunity to express their views on points that concern them. These views may or may not be taken into account when the decision is made; there is no transfer of authority. But often the effect is the same as if there were. Where relations of confidence and respect prevail between the parties, the influence exerted by the views of subordinates on matters of which they have expert knowledge and in which they are vitally interested can be very great indeed, and in fact often normally decisive.

The third grade is *delegation*. When employees have been informed and consulted and their views have been taken into account in formulating a plan, then they, or small groups of them, may be asked to work out the details for executing part of the plan and to carry on under their own steam. Delegation, of course, figures in every administrative set-up, through a chain of officials each responsible to the man above him. The Nazis call this the 'leadership principle'. But I mean something rather different, namely delegation to a group which then enjoys, in its particular task, a large measure of autonomy. The method can be most easily used for tasks which lie on the periphery of the main work of a concern and are to some extent detached from it; the war-time examples I have already cited of A.R.P. and fire-watching are cases in point. But I believe it is capable of further application, although its use raises technical problems which must be carefully examined in each case.

The fourth level of co-operation is *joint control*, under which the workers are represented on the management. The advantages and disadvantages of this method have been much discussed. I would only say this: the hopes sometimes placed in it may prove illusory. A man may chafe under factory discipline and believe that the root of the trouble lies in the unrepresentative and irresponsible character of management. But in fact it may lie in the actual nature of the job he is doing or of large-scale production as such. The presence of workers on the management would make little or no difference to his daily experience in the workshop. Joint control is a piece of machinery whose adoption will not automatically alter the real texture of working life itself—and that is what matters. Let me quote Mr Arthur Horner again. Speaking of nationalization of the mines, he said: 'Their view was that, while the pit was working, the manager must have as much definite authority as the captain had over a ship at sea. They would not stand for any duality of responsibility for the operation of the pit. The manager would be in complete control. He would be expected in pit committees to listen to, and often to apply, ideas which the workers put forward, and would be liable to criticism, but while the pit was working no person would have the power to countermand a lawful order.' So Mr Horner, you see, puts his faith in information and consultation.

I would say that, of the four methods of co-operation I have listed, the first two, information and consultation, should be used everywhere in the largest measure possible. That the third, delegation, appears to be a fruitful expedient, but that one cannot generalize about it; there is need here for further experiment and research. The fourth, joint control, has limited possibilities and is not such an improvement on the others as is sometimes imagined. In any case it is not a substitute for them. I would rather see the other three methods used without joint control than joint control without the other three.

The Contribution of Social Science to Industrial Relations

I have only one more thing to say. You may think that I have led you by a long and devious route to the real subject of this Conference, but this was deliberate. I am, as you have been told, concerned in organizing a university training scheme for personnel officers. I therefore wished to show you what is, in my view, the specifically academic contribution that universities can make to this training. I feel that the problems I have discussed are all relevant to the work of personnel management and that some consideration of them should figure in the training. I am not suggesting that this should occupy the major part of it. These subjects provide a background, and I can assure you that even universities are capable of getting down to brass tacks, and are very ready to invite outside practical experts to help them. There is another point. I hope I have enabled you to see how imperfect and incomplete is our knowledge of these matters and also how important it is to increase that knowledge by scientific research. Industrial relations cannot be handled by common sense and intuition alone. Science must lend a hand, and great contributions have been and are being made by industrial psychologists and other scientific experts. This work must go on, and I should like to see more done in the way of sociological, as distinct from purely psychological, research. I am tempted to hope that university-trained personnel officers might, while still fully discharging their official duties, act as research workers in this field. To some extent they must do so if they are to be any good at their job. They should be expected to make constructive suggestions for the solution of the problems that confront them. But that is not quite enough. Now, I am far from endorsing the sentiments of the Cambridge toast recently quoted by Lord Samuel on the Brains Trust: 'Here's to the higher mathematics, and may they never be of any use to anyone.' But it is a fact that research is hampered if it is too much tied to immediate action. To solve a particular problem it may be necessary to stand back and study a much wider problem in order to arrive at fundamental causes. And this requires thought and planning, and what I would call an academic spirit of detached and objective inquiry. And, in the social sciences, it usually requires team work, to pool results and analyse them as a whole, and to direct a number of separate inquiries on to a single problem which is not only urgent but also offers good hopes of getting results. Is it too much to hope that a group of personnel officers, who occupy a key position in this matter of industrial relations, might work on research as a team under central direction and guidance, in the provision of which the Universities might play an important, though not the sole, part? Would that be contrary to anybody's interests? One thing the Universities always strive to do is to inculcate a spirit of impartial scientific inquiry, and nobody should be afraid of that, provided, of course, the individual agents are competent for the job. But perhaps the idea is a crazy one. If so, you can do no worse to me than tell me so.

CHAPTER XI

PROPERTY AND POSSESSIVENESS

This paper was one of four contributed to a Symposium held under the auspices of the Medical Section of the British Psychological Society and the Institute of Sociology in December 1934. The first of these two organizations was represented by Dr Ian Suttie and Dr Susan Isaacs, and the second by Professor Morris Ginsberg and myself. The only one of the other papers I had seen before I wrote mine was Dr Suttie's. In it he described saving as an irrational activity and an 'economic illusion' and acquisitiveness as 'a special technique for the maintenance and development of social rapport'.

Dr Suttie gave me the privilege of reading his paper before the meeting, and I found, partly to my pleasure and partly to my dismay, that I was in substantial agreement with him. I too had arrived at the conclusion that the essential problem was to discover the relation between property and the desire for security and the fear of isolation and destruction. But there are certain differences between us as regards the analysis of this fact, not so much because of disagreement as of divergence of interest; we approach the question from slightly different angles. This is largely because I have no shadow of a claim to be called a psychologist.

I propose to distinguish three things: first, the desire for security in the enjoyment of the means to life and happiness and the anxiety lest loss of these may cause one's destruction;

secondly, the desire to have what I will call a status among one's fellow men, that is a position of membership in an organized society which entitles one to benefit by the organization; and thirdly, a desire to be in a stronger position than one's neighbours. And I propose to ask in each case, how far does this desire find satisfaction through property; and is the relationship unalterable, or is there a possibility of conversion into another form?

I put the question like this because it seems to me that this desire for security is ineradicable, and that it is not in any sense anti-social. Trouble does not arise unless the social situation is such that people believe security can be found for themselves only by a means which denies security to others. Even the third desire, the spirit of emulation, does not necessarily imply this. It is at least an arguable hypothesis that the evil element in property as a means to security lies in its stimulation of a competitive acquisitiveness which is not really necessary for the fulfilment of the end in view and is definitely anti-social in its effects.

We seek satisfaction by obtaining access to material things, and one form of that access is property. These are the things that we use. But why should we own them? It is obviously possible to use things that we do not own. There is a rational explanation. Ownership gives security. We can get at the object whenever we want to, it is the object with which we are familiar and it has not been damaged by other users. But this is *not* rational if applied universally. Why do I hire a gas oven from the Company? Because I need not then have a *particular* gas oven, which may get ruined, but I have an anonymous, an immortal gas oven endowed with the blessing of perpetual youth. When we think of it, we realize to what a large extent our access to the means of enjoyment is not provided in property form, and how adaptable we are in that respect. There is, first, all the enjoyment we get from services rendered by others, our travel, our amusements, our cinemas, our hotels, our public houses, the hospitals in which we are born, the cemeteries in which we are buried. Secondly, we may remember how subtly the whole system of relationship to land has varied through history, how difficult it is to say who owned land in the Middle Ages, how independent security of tenure may be from property. Next we see that the concept of property is not really applicable in full to consumable goods, not because it is impossible to own them, but because it is impossible *not* to own them. Even the food given to a pauper in the workhouse must become his property at some point during the journey from the plate to the mouth. It may be relevant to ask whether the book I am reading belongs to me. It is irrelevant to ask whether the piece of bread I am chewing belongs to me. Finally we notice how the system of access varies according to the article in question. Take the case of the musician. A violinist owns his violin. A pianist probably owns a piano, but never plays on his *own* piano at a concert. An organist may own an organ, but it is not considered a disadvantage to be without one.

Of course the title to obtain these non-property satisfactions may itself come from property. You may even refer to the title itself as property. But it is property two stages removed from the end it serves. There is an important difference between gaining security for welfare in old age by accumulation of property and by being entitled to a pension. The former has social by-products from which the latter is free. Yet both give security. I am suggesting that, whatever the psychological basis of this anxiety, of this desire for security, it does not (in the aspects I have so far examined) necessarily demand satisfaction through property. It is doing so less and less and it is evidently adaptable. The desideratum is the security itself. It is not hopelessly bound up with a particular *form* of satisfaction, a particular means that has come to be substituted for the end.

And yet there does seem to be an irrational delight in ownership. We do like to own books and furniture—and, when we really *ought* to hire it, Mr Drage finds it fairly easy to persuade us to accept the compromise of hire-purchase. I do not pretend to know what this sentiment is. It seems to be a feeling of affection, a projection of ourselves into our possessions, an enlargement and externalizing of the self which gives a sense of importance. In part its object is social prestige—on which I have a word to say later. But it is not only that. Members of the male sex feel it less towards their best clothes than towards their oldest clothes. It may be in part the value we set on a long association which establishes friendly relations with the external world, found in the familiarity that never breeds contempt. This might be described as a form of security, but it is not essentially a product of property. We feel it towards a neighbourhood. I know a lady who has no difficulty in appropriating St Mark's, the Doge's Palace and the entire Grand Canal in this way whenever she meets an English friend in Venice.

My point is this. Income, or the claim on goods and services for current use, does not belong to a category quite distinct from property, but it differs in some essentials from capital, or accumulation. The difference is important because income, being directly related to use, is more governed by the rational principle. For the great mass of the people today it is the only known basis for security of access to goods. For the remainder it is of increasing importance, since there is a growing tendency to save through insurance companies or building societies, with a view that is, to concrete future satisfaction through income for use, not to accumulation for power or prestige.

We have next the question of social status. Property is or may be the certificate of membership of society. It establishes useful contacts and relationships with other persons. It creates rights and obligations. The property-less man is an outcast, a parasite, a tramp. The man of property has a stake in the country, and if his property is in land he almost feels that he has helped to *create* his country by contributing his acres to the national total. It may be that the link between property and the vote and the gradual extension of the franchise through widening circles of property owners, is not merely a result of economic power, but the reflection of a deeper social fact. The most obvious way in which property serves this purpose in the purest form is by the exchange of gifts, to which Dr Suttie has referred. It is hardly necessary to remind a mid-December gathering that this custom is not confined to primitive savages. Dr Suttie spoke of the change from a basis of 'good will' to a basis of 'good faith', that is, of binding contracts. We are now approaching the season of 'good will', but the principle of enforced reciprocity is not completely lacking in an English Christmas, and is, as Dr Malinowski has shown, markedly to the fore in the customary gifts of the primitives. Property may act as a social cement defeating the dread of loneliness. We may use it for social exchange among equals, or we may regard it as making us part proprietors of the civilization that the community has created. If 'an Englishman's home is his castle', it is largely because he regards the police as his servants and not as his masters. It is a castle from which he writes letters to *The Times* abusing the government—*his* government. It is not a lonely castle. The significance of property in determining social attitudes is enormous, not because of the income it yields, not because of the power it gives in business and in politics, but because it is a guarantee of the right to enjoy the blessings of civilization. It means that we shall not be cast out into the social wilderness, it shows that we are solid and to be trusted to fulfil our obligations, and that we can therefore move freely and securely in the heart of a great society.

Now this is security again, in another form, but it differs, I believe, from the motive of emulation. It is not *necessarily* competitive. Nor is it *necessarily* linked with property. In our society property is becoming less and less important in this respect, as more and more is added to the status of citizenship, or to the status of wage-earners. It is possible that it is *because* it has been linked with property that it has been merged in competitiveness. By nature it is a desire for equality. But if the slope is slippery, it may be hard to get a footing on the hill except at the summit, and property in a competitive society is a slippery slope.

Thirdly we have the use of property as a means of social competition, as a source of prestige. The manner of use varies according to the pattern of social behaviour and scale of social values. It may take the form of accumulation or of destruction, of stinginess or generosity. It is important to realize that social competition has many forms, that in a society where accumulation of property is abolished there could still be a competition for the right to live at a high standard of material comfort, as is very markedly the case in contemporary Russia. There is also the possibility of developing the value of the prestige of social approbation, as through the 'socialist competition' so strongly advocated by Stalin.

My point is simply this. I cannot see that this represents the pure quintessence of the unconscious urge towards property accumulation. In the first place it is not demonstrably irrational. It achieves its very definite end. Even if Dr Suttie's presentation of the problem of general saving is accurate, which I doubt (many highly rational economists are fighting like cats over the intricacies of the question), it does not prove irrationality in the individual. Saving is a possibility, anyhow for some. It does not seem to me to be irrational for fifty people to enter for a competitive examination when there are only five vacancies, and I cannot give the palm for rationality to the Caucus Race in *Alice in Wonderland*, at the end of which the Dodo remarked, 'Everybody has won, and *all* must have prizes.'

We might be inclined to think that if there does exist a quintessence of the unconscious urge to acquire, it is shown in the irrational desire to own, when ownership is not necessary for satisfaction of use or security, for example, in the tender love of an old maid for her precious knick-knacks or, in an extreme form, in the miser. But the miser's use of property is not merely an exaggeration or a perversion of the social use. It is a direct contradiction. He does not satisfy material needs, he starves; he does not get security, since he refuses to spend for that object; he does not get social contacts, he gets social isolation; he does not get prestige, he earns contempt. The sociological approach *does* suggest that the psychological explanation of the pathology of the miser will not lead us to the psychological basis of property in society. It does support the view that the excretory, or some such hypothesis might explain the former, while the mother-need of the infant may explain the latter.

My difficulty is, however, in understanding why the anxiety-security complex of the mother-need situation should *necessarily* lead to irrational competitive acquisitiveness. It stresses the demand to have access to material goods, but is not obviously bound to seek this through accumulation in the form of property. It breeds a desire for acceptance within a social group, but not obviously one with a competitive flavour. The position of the child at the breast is not competitive. The breast is not withheld in the interests of a rival child. Competition enters later. Is it not possible, then, that the particular form taken by this desire in a competitive property-owning society is a product of the social situation, and that the desire itself need not necessarily create that situation? Admittedly an appropriate situation may arise in any unorganized crowd—as in a free group of schoolchildren or in a nursery. But must we assume that what Dr Isaacs has called the 'hard lesson of taking turns', that is of sharing, involves the conquest of this basic urge? If property exists as a social institution, this anxiety-security complex is likely to lead to competitive acquisitiveness. But different types of property show different degrees of compulsion towards this end. I have tried to show that the property situation is highly adaptable to real social ends. I believe that the anxiety-security complex is inescapable. I see no reason for trying to weaken it. I suggest that it is by no means impossible to educate it.

CHAPTER XII

SOCIAL SELECTION IN THE WELFARE STATE

It is a great honour, which I highly appreciate, to be invited by the Eugenics Society to deliver the Galton Lecture,[1] and it is an honour which may, I think, appropriately be bestowed upon a sociologist. But for a sociologist who, like myself, is ignorant of biology and genetics and unskilled in those statistical techniques, now so widely and expertly used in social surveys and psychological investigations, it is also an embarrassment. What subject should I choose? I pondered over this for some time before I felt sure I could accept the invitation. Social selection seemed to be the most promising general field, but I knew it was one in which I should have to walk warily. For I should find in it signposts pointing in directions in which I must on no account allow myself to travel—signposts bearing such words as 'Nature and Nurture', 'Fertility and Intelligence', or perhaps the mystic letters g, F and k pointing the way to certain shady paths in and around the garden commonly known as 'I.Q.'.

So I devised a title, a rather elaborate one, which would keep me out of danger and also make it fairly clear what I intended to talk about. But it had two disadvantages. It was too long to get on to the cards and notices of the lecture, and it might have committed me in advance to a task which I should later find it impossible to execute. So I decided to

[1] The Galton Lecture delivered at a meeting of the Eugenics Society on 18 February 1953.

seek refuge in brevity and obscurity, with the result that you have before you: 'Social Selection in the Welfare State'. This title gave me no pleasure, partly because 'Welfare State' is a term for which I have developed a strong dislike, and partly because the subject indicated was obviously far too big for a lecture. But when I began to consider it more carefully, I found it was better than I had expected. I think it really does mean something, which is a great relief. But I shall have to spend a little time explaining what it is that I think it means.

There need be little ambiguity about 'social selection'. I take it to refer to the processes by which individuals are sifted, sorted and distributed into the various positions in the social system which can be distinguished one from another by their function, status, or place in the social hierarchy. I shall be considering, in this lecture, social selection through the educational system.

The Principles of the Welfare State

The Welfare State is a tougher proposition, because it would be difficult to find any definition acceptable both to its friends and to its enemies—or even to all its friends. Fortunately I needn't try to define it; I have only to explain what are the characteristics of the Welfare State which seem to me to provide a distinctive setting to the problem of social selection. I take the most relevant aspects of the Welfare State, in this context, to be the following.

First, its intense individualism. The claim of the individual to welfare is sacred and irrefutable and partakes of the character of a natural right. It would, no doubt, figure in the new Declaration of the Rights of Man if the supporters of the Welfare State were minded to issue anything so pithily dramatic. It would replace property in those early French and American Testaments which speak of life, liberty and property; this trinity now becomes life, liberty and welfare. It is to be found among the Four Freedoms in the guise of 'Freedom from Want'—but that is too negative a version. The welfare of the Welfare State is more positive and has more substance. It was lurking in the Declaration of Independence, which listed the inalienable rights of man as 'Life, Liberty and the Pursuit of Happiness'. Happiness is a positive concept closely related to welfare, but the citizen of the Welfare State does not merely have the right to pursue welfare; he has the right to receive it, even if the pursuit has not been particularly hot. And so we promise to each child an education suited to its individual qualities, we try to make the punishment (or treatment) fit the individual criminal rather than the crime, we hold that in all but the simplest of the social services individual case study and family case work should precede and accompany the giving of advice or assistance, and we uphold the principle of equal opportunity, which is perhaps the most completely individualistic of all.

But if we put individualism first, we must put collectivism second. The Welfare State is the responsible promoter and guardian of the welfare of the whole community, which is something more complex than the sum total of the welfare of all its individual members arrived at by simple addition. The claims of the individual must always be defined and limited so as to fit into the complex and balanced pattern of the welfare of the community, and that is why the right to welfare can never have the full stature of a natural right. The harmonizing of individual rights with the common good is a problem which faces all human societies.

In trying to solve it, the Welfare State must choose means which are in harmony with its principles. It believes in planning—not of everything but over a wide area. It must therefore clearly formulate its objectives and carefully select its methods with a full sense of its power and its responsibility. It believes in equality, and its plans must therefore start from the assumption that every person is potentially a candidate for every position in society. This complicates matters; it is easier to cope with things if society is divided into a number of non-competing social classes. It believes in personal liberty because, as I choose to define it, it is a democratic form of society. So although, of course, like all States, it uses some compulsion, it must rely on individual choice and motivation for the fulfilment of its purposes in all their details.

How do these principles apply to selection through the educational system? The general social good, in this context, requires a balanced supply of persons with different skills and aptitudes who have been so trained as to maximize the contribution they can make to the common welfare. We have, in recent years, seen the Welfare State estimating the need for natural scientists, social scientists and technicians, for doctors, teachers and nurses, and then trying to stimulate the educational system to produce what is required. It must also be careful to see that the national resources are used economically and to the best advantage, that there is no waste of individual capacities, by denying them the chance of development and use, and no waste of money and effort, by giving education and training to those who cannot get enough out of them to justify the cost.

On the other side, the side of individualism, is the right of each child to receive an education suited to its character and abilities. It is peculiar, in that the child cannot exercise the right for itself, because it is not expected to know what its character and abilities are. Nor can its parents wholly represent its interests, because they cannot be certain of knowing either. But they have a rather ambiguous right at least to have their wishes considered, and in some circumstances to have them granted. The status of parental rights in the English educational system is somewhat obscure at the moment. There is no reason to assume that the independent operation of the two principles, of individual rights and general social needs, would lead to the same results. The State has the responsibility of harmonizing the one with the other.

So far I have merely been trying to explain the general meaning which I have discovered in the title of this lecture. As I have already said, I shall first limit this broad field by concentrating on selection through the educational system. I shall then limit it further to the two following aspects of the problem. I shall look first at the selection of children for secondary education and try to see what is involved in bringing it into harmony with the principles of the Welfare State. I choose this particular point in the selection process partly because of its intrinsic and often decisive importance, and partly because so much has recently been written about it. I shall look in the second place rather at the social structure and consider how far it is possible to achieve the aims of the Welfare State in this field—particularly the aim of equal opportunity—in a society in which there still exists considerable inequality of wealth and social status. In doing this I shall be able to draw on some of the still unpublished results of researches carried out at the London School of Economics over the past four years, chiefly with the aid of a generous grant from the Nuffield Foundation.

Selection for Secondary Schools

We are all, I expect, aware that for some time past educationists (both teachers and administrators), and psychologists and statisticians (I sometimes find it hard to distinguish the one from the other) have been hurling themselves at the problem of selection for secondary schools with a determination and a ferocity of purpose which are positively terrifying. A good general survey of the campaign can, I think, be extracted from four sources. There is first the Report of the Scottish Council for Research in Education, *Selection for Secondary Education*, presented by William McClelland in 1942. This is an impressive document which might be described as a bold and challenging advance by the forces of pure science and exact measurement. It was met and held in check by a counter-attack delivered by the National Union of Teachers in its Report *Transfer from Primary to Secondary Schools*, published in 1949. Meanwhile there had opened, in June 1947, a friendly contest conducted under strict tournament rules in *The British Journal of Educational Psychology*, in the form of the 'Symposium on the Selection of Pupils for Different Types of Secondary Schools', which continued until February 1950. It was richly informative, and contained a little bit of everything. Finally we have the two Interim Reports of the Committee of the National Foundation of Educational Research: *The Allocation of Primary School Leavers to Courses of Secondary Education*, published in 1950 and 1952. It is too soon to say exactly what position this new detachment will take up on the battlefield, but the wording of its title is highly significant when compared with that of the Symposium. 'Selection' has been replaced by 'allocation' and 'types of secondary school' by 'courses of secondary education'.

The first point to note is that, in this matter of selection for secondary education, the State is in full command of the whole situation. It provides the primary schools which prepare children for the examination, it designs the secondary school system for which they are being selected, and therefore determines the categories into which they are to be sorted, and it invents and administers the tests. Such power is dangerous. It is easy in these circumstances to make sure that one will find what one is looking for, and it is, no doubt, gratifying to discover that one's artistic masterpiece has been faithfully copied by Nature. I find it unfortunate that, just as there are three main types of secondary school, so there are three types of ability with which educational psychologists juggle—g or general, F or technical and k or spatial. I am afraid people may come to regard this as evidence of collusion, when in fact, of course, the two trinities do not correspond.

The second point to note is that the principles of the 1944 Act, which I take to be the principles of the Welfare State, have not yet been put into effect. The Act, according to the N.U.T. Report, 'has given the problem of transference from the primary to the secondary school an entirely new form', which necessitates a thorough reassessment of our old methods of selection (p. 16). The profound change referred to is that from competitive selection of a few for higher things to allocation of all to suitable schools, or, as Kenneth Lindsay phrased it nearly twenty years before the Act, from 'selection by elimination' to 'selection by differentiation'.[2] When allocation is working fully, says the N.U.T., 'the situation ought not to arise in which it is impossible to send a child to the school most suited to his needs because there is no place available for him in a school of this kind' (p. 20). We are still a long way from this, and 'for the time being the sole certain indication for a modern school is unsuitability for a grammar or technical school' (p. 18).

I see danger lurking here too. If too long a time passes during which an ideal cannot be realized, it may become unrealizable--a myth, as it were, which has lost contact with the world of experience, and which has never been through the testing which must lie between the blueprint and the finished machine. There is a danger, too, that we may imagine we are preparing the instruments for use in the new operation when in fact we are only perfecting those which are suited for use in the old. In the first Interim Report of the National Foundation there occurs the sentence: 'It is the procedure of competitive entry to grammar schools that has been responsible for the undue importance which has been attached to objective tests and to external examinations' (p. 62). Note 'external examinations', for there is something pretty fundamental there.

But the principle of allocation is not a new idea. It was implicit in the Act of 1918, which stated that sufficient provision must be made to ensure that no children are 'debarred from receiving the benefits of any form of education by which they are capable of profiting through inability to pay fees', and it has been steadily developing since that date. And the importance attached to objective tests and external examinations is not an old phenomenon which happens to have survived into the new age. It has grown side by side with the growth of the idea of allocation, and continued to grow after the passing of the 1944 Act.

The movement in the field of ideas towards allocation instead of selection, and the movement in the field of practice towards uniform general standardized testing have been con-

[2] *Social Progress and Educational Waste*, p. 28.

temporaneous. I think, too, that any reader of the Symposium must be struck by the intense interest shown in the possibility of devising objective tests accurate enough to be used for allocation on the basis of special aptitudes, as well as for selection on the basis of general ability. There are, of course, signs of movement in other directions among education authorities, such as the greater use made of cumulative school records and so on; and, as regards the Symposium, it must not be overlooked that Sir Cyril Burt opened boldly with the statement that the problem was 'administrative rather than psychological'.[3] This sounded very much like the old-fashioned rebuking the newfangled, and no doubt some psychologists thought that he was letting the side down.

In all this I seem to see evidence of a clash between what I earlier referred to as the collectivist and individualist elements in the Welfare State. Allocation, interpreted along N.U.T. lines, represents unqualified individualism. The right of each child to receive the education best suited to its unique individual needs should not be inhibited by reference to the cost of providing the necessary schools and teachers nor to the demand in society at large for particular numbers of persons educated and trained in particular ways. But to the collectivist principle these limiting factors arise from rights of the community as a whole, which the Welfare State cannot ignore. And they may favour a provision of grammar school places which is less than the provision needed to accommodate all who could benefit from a grammar school education. As long as this happens, competitive selection will remain with us. How long that will be, I do not propose to guess. But, when selection is competitive, the authorities must reach a decision somehow, using the best means at their disposal. And they must be able to enforce the decision negatively (that is to say, the decision not to admit) against the wishes of the parent. When faced with the necessity of filling the last five places in a grammar school from twenty applicants, all backed

[3] *The British Journal of Educational Psychology*, Vol. XVII, June 1947, p. 57.

by ambitious and determined parents, you may feel that the best means of selection are either to follow the mark order or to toss up. The public may prefer you to follow the marks, even though you know that in this border zone the verdict of the marks has no real validity. So the use of imperfect selection methods can be justified by the inadequacy of the educational system, as judged by the ideal of allocation.

But in my view, if allocation replaced selection, then no amount of improvement would make the tests sufficiently exact to carry the weight of decisions enforceable against parental wishes. For the question to be answered in each case would not be: 'Is this child better suited to a grammar school than the other applicants? If so, we must tell the others we are full up.' But: 'What, as judged by absolute standards and without reference to competing claims, is the education best suited to this child's needs?' I feel convinced that, in the majority of cases, questions in this form will remain unanswerable by tests and examinations—unanswerable, that is, with the degree of assurance necessary before the answer can be made the basis of administrative action. So we should find, I think, that instead of allocation in the sense of the definitive assignment of each child to an appropriate school or course, we should have something more like an advisory service which left the responsibility of decision to the parents. And that, I understand, is what happens now in so far as the principle of allocation already enters into our system. And in support of the view that it *should* be so, I can quote, from the Symposium, Mr Dempster of Southampton, who writes: 'The wishes of the parents are possibly the best guide at present available to selectors in deciding between grammar and technical school education.'[4]

This sounds in many ways a very attractive prospect, though we ought to know a little more about how parental wishes work before we acclaim it, and I shall have something to say on that later. But I fancy it conflicts with another aspect of

[4] ibid., Vol. xviii, November 1948, p. 130.

the collectivist element in the Welfare State. The principle I have in mind is the one which says that all should be judged by the same procedure, as impartially and impersonally as possible, that favouritism and privilege must be eradicated, and also the effects of differing social environments on the critical turning-points in life. So far so good. The principle must be allowed to have full weight. There is one obvious point at which it favours objective tests. Because children come to their examination at 11+ from schools and neighbourhoods of very different quality, they cannot be judged by their attainments only; an attempt must be made to discover natural abilities which may have been frustrated by circumstances but may still be able to come to fruition if given a fair chance. But latent capacities are concealed, and something more scientific than a teacher's judgement or a school record is needed to reveal them.

But the collectivist principle goes farther, and sometimes assumes shapes which are more open to question. The doctrine of fair shares and equal opportunity sounds admirable, but it may become so distorted as to merit the cynical comment that fair shares means 'if we can't all have it, nobody shall', and that equal opportunity means 'we must all have an equal chance of showing that we are all equally clever'. And the present situation may encourage this type of distortion, if it leads us to regard competitive selection as a necessary evil. If the Welfare State is to bring its two principles into harmony, it must conceive of the basic equality of all as human beings and fellow-citizens in a way which leaves room for the recognition that all are not equally gifted nor capable of rendering equally valuable services to the community, that equal opportunity means an equal chance to reveal differences, some of which are superiorities, and that these differences need for their development different types of education, some of which may legitimately be regarded as higher than others. The notion, therefore, that selection, even competitive selection, can be eliminated from our educational system seems to me to be a pipe-dream and not even a Utopian one.

Obstacles to Equal Opportunity

I will defer making any general comment until I have considered my second question, to which I now turn. This relates to another dilemma or antithesis inherent in the principles and structure of the Welfare State. It is the problem of establishing equal opportunity without abolishing social and economic inequality. I say this is inherent in the nature of the Welfare State because it is my opinion—which I do not propose to argue here—that the Welfare State, as we know it, must necessarily preserve a measure of economic inequality. This problem, therefore, is a permanent and not a transitory one.

One of the most striking passages in Kenneth Lindsay's well-known and far-sighted study of this question in the inter-war period is the quotation from Lord Birkenhead which runs: 'There is now a complete ladder from the elementary school to the university, and the number of scholarships from the elementary to the secondary school is not limited, awards being made to all children who show capacity to profit.'[5] This fantastic illusion was blown sky-high by Lindsay's book, and later studies showed that equality of educational opportunity was still a distant ideal at the outbreak of World War II. The research carried out at L.S.E. during the past four years, to which I have already referred, has drawn in more firmly the outlines of the picture and added some details. We can see pretty clearly what the situation was when the Welfare State took over and what were the obstacles it had to overcome.

This research included a 10,000 sample survey of persons aged 18 and over in Great Britain in 1949. Mobility was examined on the basis of the seven-point scale of occupational status, widely known as the Hall-Jones scale, which had been prepared for this study. Groups 1 and 2 include the professional and managerial occupations, and groups 3 and 4

[5] Kenneth Lindsay: *Social Progress and Educational Waste*, p. 9.

the supervisory and clerical—to give a rough idea of their character. Together they comprised about 30 per cent. of the sample, which can be called the middle-class section (the upper class is too small to appear in a sample of this size). Group 5, including routine non-manual and skilled manual jobs, was a very large one comprising 40 per cent., while groups 6 and 7, semi-skilled and unskilled manual, provided approximately another 30 per cent. Of the general picture I will say little; I would rather wait for the papers to be published with full statistical tables. But one or two points may be noted. We find that the social forces holding a son to the occupational group of his father are significantly strongest in groups 1 and 2 and weakest in group 5. We can summarize crudely by saying that money and influence count for most at the top, and life's chances lie most widely open, for good or ill, in the melting-pot in the middle of the scale. This is interesting, because it is at this middle point in the scale that we might expect to find many families ambitious for their children's future and ready to forgo their earnings while they get secondary and further education, but not in a position to pay fees. It is precisely among such families that the building of an educational ladder is likely to have the greatest effect.

The second point of relevance in the general picture is that the returns show what to many may be a surprising amount of downward movement. There is a common saying, which in the United States has had the force of a political dogma, that 'there is plenty of room at the top'. And one remembers benevolent members of the upper layers of society who have strongly advocated the building of a social and educational ladder under the impression, apparently, that it could carry one-way traffic only, and that the ascent of the deserving from below would not have to be accompanied by a descent on the part of any of their own children to make room for the new-comers. But, if we take all the male subjects in the sample, we find that 35.2 per cent. had the same occupational status as their father, 29.3 per cent. had risen and 35.5 per cent. had fallen. These figures probably exaggerate the falls because they include the young men in the sample who had not yet reached their final occupational level, and, of course, they tell us nothing of the distance risen or fallen, which is an important factor. The believers in one-way traffic thought that upper- and middle-class jobs were increasing faster than jobs in general, while upper- and middle-class families were producing fewer children than families in general. But it seems clear, and the 1951 census sample confirms this, that this was true, as regards middle-class jobs in general, only of women's employment. The proportion of occupied men in such jobs showed no significant increase from 1911 to 1951, while the proportion of occupied women in such jobs rose approximately from 24.5 per cent. to 45.5 per cent. There was some increase in clerical jobs for men, but even here the spectacular advance was in the employment of women. In 1947, to quote one illustrative case, of those leaving secondary grammar schools at the age of sixteen to go straight into jobs, just about 43 per cent. of the boys went into the 'clerical and professional' category and of the girls 68 per cent., or, if nursing is included, nearly 77 per cent. Since there was an expansion of grammar schools during this period, and since grammar schools were largely an avenue to middle-class jobs, these facts are interesting. There may have been many boys who hitched their wagon to a white collar without realizing that their most serious competitors were their own sisters.

The educational data in the survey confirm and extend the picture presented in 1926 by Kenneth Lindsay. The most interesting general lesson to be drawn is that it is harder than one might suppose to ensure that the new opportunities created go to the people for whom they are intended, provided the fundamental principles of a free democracy are preserved. The survey covered the period of the introduction and expansion of the Free Place system in secondary schools, and its successor, the Special Place system, and it is possible to compare the experience of the first wave of entrants following the Act of 1902 (those born from 1890 to 1899) with the last pre-war wave (those born from 1920 to 1929). In the period covered by this comparison the percentage of boys in families belonging to the top three occupational groups who went to grammar schools rose from 38.4 to 45.7, and the corresponding figures for group 5 (the skilled manual and routine non-manual workers) are 4.1 and 10.7. The percentage increase for the working-class group is much greater than for the middle-class group, but the inequality that remains is enormous. And it is still greater if one includes boarding schools. The reason for this was not only that the total provision was insufficient, but also that a considerable part of the benefit went to the middle classes. It is true that the proportion of children in grammar schools who are occupying free places increases as you go down the social scale. But the proportion of the whole company of children of an occupational group who hold free places in grammar schools is highest at the top, 13.2 per cent. in status groups 1 and 2 (upper middle class) and 5 per cent. in group 5 (upper working class). I have picked these pieces of information from the analysis which Mrs Floud has made of this part of the survey and which contains many more points of equal interest.

My point is this. It may look at first sight as if the *bourgeoisie* had, as usual, filched what should have gone to the workers. But, in the circumstances, that was bound to happen in a free democracy and is bound to go on happening in the Welfare State. For the Welfare State is not the dictatorship of the proletariat and is not pledged to liquidate the *bourgeoisie*. Of course more and more middle-class families made use of the public elementary schools as the quality of these improved, and of course more and more of them competed for admission to secondary schools through free and special places. And since the children were backed by a better educational tradition and stronger parental support, because more of their families could afford to forgo the earnings of the children, because they came from more comfortable homes, where it was easier to work, and from smaller families, they were certain to be more successful. And when it came to deciding as to remission of fees for special places, many of the middle-class families had a genuine claim. Today, with the 100 per cent. free place system in maintained schools, there can be no question of discriminating against middle-class families, and the competitive advantages of social and economic status can operate without check. Other inquiries conducted at the L.S.E., either within or in close relation to the main project, have begun to throw some light on the nature and extent of these competitive advantages.[6]

That there is a greater preponderance of working-class children in the modern schools today and of middle-class children in the grammar schools is a fact which no one is likely to dispute. In an article in the March 1953 issue of *The British Journal of Sociology*, Messrs Halsey and Gardner produce evidence to show that, in the London areas they studied, this uneven distribution could not be attributed solely to the intelligence of the children, but must be in large part the result of social forces. When, for instance, comparison was made of two groups with the same mean I.Q., one of which had been assigned to a grammar school and the other to a modern school, it was found that the middle classes were heavily over-represented and the working classes, especially the unskilled families, heavily under-represented in the grammar school group. It is also interesting that of working-class children in grammar schools in the areas studied 63 per cent. came from small families with one or two children and 37 per cent. from larger families with three or more. Among working-class children in modern schools the proportions were almost exactly the reverse, and among middle-class children there was no significant relation between type of school and size of family. No known correlation between fertility and intelligence could possibly explain this, and it is clear that powerful social influences are at work. And they show themselves in other ways. A similar, though less marked, correlation with size of family appears when we ask how much thought parents give to their children's school career, how much interest they show in their work and progress, and how ambitious they feel about their

[6] The work has been done by Dr Hilde Himmelweit, Mr Martin and their associates. Since the information has been collected in intensive local studies it cannot be used for generalization of any kind as yet.

future. Here, then, is a social factor causing what might be called 'unfairness' in social selection about which the Welfare State can do very little. Positive action, by improving the physical conditions in poorer families and by stimulating greater interest and ambition among apathetic parents, can only be a very slow process. Family differences will continue to have their influence as long as the family is the basic cell in the social structure.

Social Ambition and Educational Achievement

The interest of parents may be shown by their giving thought to the matter of secondary schooling for their children. In one county area parents of children about to sit for the examination for secondary schools were asked whether they had thought a lot, a little, or not at all about the matter. The proportion claiming to have thought a lot declined steadily as one moved down the social scale and was little over a third among the unskilled workers. But the preference for a grammar school education, though it showed the same trend, did not fall so low. The lowest proportion preferring the grammar school was 43.4 per cent. and the highest preferring the modern school 23.9 per cent.—these figures being those for unskilled workers. But over two-thirds of the unskilled worker parents preferring the grammar school did not want their child to stay there after the age of sixteen. Their ambitions were limited. And about half the professional and a quarter of the clerical families said that if their child did not get a grammar school place they would not send it to a modern school.

The picture is slightly distressing. It suggests that those who care about education, and some who do not care much, almost automatically aspire to a grammar school for their children; but the aspiration may vary from the desire of a steady job, with good prospects, to be entered at sixteen, to the hope of admission to a university and a professional career. There cannot be much homogeneity of purpose in a grammar school population. And, looking at the other side of the picture, we find a low opinion of the modern school which to many appears as a catastrophe and a disgrace. Talk of 'parity of esteem' is a little premature.

Now these likes and dislikes owe something, no doubt, to real or supposed differences in the quality of education received in the different types of school. But I doubt whether most parents are following the advice of the N.U.T. to concentrate on the 'present educational needs of the child' and not to think too much 'what these needs may be at some later stage in his development'.[7] They are thinking of what the school may lead to in the way of employment or further education, and perhaps of what it stands for in terms of social prestige. This last point is one on which it is extremely hard to get reliable information, since much of the mental process involved may be only semi-conscious. If social status is not offered by the questioner as a possible reason for aiming at a particular school or job, it is not likely to be put down spontaneously; if it is offered, it may score a fair number of votes, but less than such job attributes as good prospects, security and interesting work. Another cause of difficulty is the lack of uniformity in the use of class names. People differ widely in the way they classify themselves or typical occupations as middle or working class, and it is clear that the term 'lower middle class' is becoming abhorrent. But, in spite of this, there is fairly close agreement as to the order in which jobs should be ranked, even though there is disagreement as to the social class to which they should be assigned.

The material dealing with job ambitions is too complicated to be briefly surveyed in an intelligible form. So I shall confine myself to two points. In a sample of adults in two urban areas who were asked what occupation they would like their son to enter, more than a fifth of the working-class subjects chose a profession and less than 8 per cent. a clerical job; the commonest choice (about 36 per cent.) was for a skilled trade. The figures are not complete, as a good many said their

7 Report of the National Union of Teachers: *Transfer from Primary to Secondary Schools*, p. 20.

son must choose for himself. In the middle-class section of the sample, clerical jobs were even less popular, and the total vote for independent business was practically negligible. A similar dislike of the sound of clerical and office jobs was found by Dr Jahoda among school-leavers in Lancashire—that is to say, among the boys. The girls put office work at the top of the list. When boys were asked what jobs they most definitely rejected, office work was the one most often chosen, but half of those who named it did so because they did not think they were qualified for it.[8] It would be very rash to jump to conclusions from such fragmentary evidence, but it does seem possible that office work is losing its charm. It is often described as dull and monotonous, and perhaps the rise in wages for manual work and familiarity with conditions of full employment are robbing it of some of its other former attractions.

The second point of interest is the clear evidence, at present confined to one area, that working-class boys who get into grammar schools have very high expectations that they will rise in the world, while middle-class boys in modern schools are inclined to expect to fall below the position of their parents. No less than 63 per cent. of the boys of lower working-class origin in grammar schools expected to rise at least two steps on a five-point status scale above their fathers; only 12 per cent. of their comrades in the modern schools were equally ambitious. But, if we measure the rise by the boys' own estimate of it and not by objective standards, the percentage falls from 63 to 21. This inquiry was reported in Dr Himmelweit's article in *The British Journal of Sociology*, June 1952. It suggests that the boys themselves feel that selection for secondary schooling has a decisive effect on future careers, and that boys from the humbler working-class families who get into grammar schools may overrate their chances without fully realizing how ambitious their success has made them. So long as this is the case, 'parity of esteem' is hardly possible.

[8] *Occupational Psychology*, Vol. XXVI, pp. 132–4.

Effects of Social Distance

My last point relates to the possible effects of social distance on life in a grammar school. Grammar schools, one might say, have a tradition, an educational atmosphere, and contacts with the world outside which have for some time past belonged to the way of life of the middle classes. And the middle classes are over-represented in the school population, even though the skilled working-class families may supply the largest absolute numbers. If, then, we introduce boys and girls from outside this circle, can they fit in? Can they become sufficiently assimilated to enter into the life of the school and get out of it what it has to give, and yet retain enough of their identity to break down, in the course of time, any class barriers which exist, and thus make the way easier for their successors, and for the Welfare State? Much study is needed before this question can be fully answered. We have evidence to show that middle-class boys in grammar schools (in the area studied) do better on average in class examinations in pretty well all subjects than working-class boys, and that, when teachers are asked to rank the boys in their class in terms of such things as industry, responsibility, interest in school affairs, good behaviour, and popularity, the middle-class boys do definitely better than the rest. And working-class boys are inclined to care less about their marks and to take less part in general school activities, and yet, as we have seen, they expect great results from their grammar school status when the time comes for them to get a job. On the other hand may not a school have an assimilating influence and mould its members into a more homogeneous group than they were to start with, thus producing in reality the category of children which until then existed only in the imagination of the selectors? That is a question which points the way to a fascinating piece of research which has hardly yet been begun.

The Americans have similar problems today, and there is much evidence of status-consciousness in the high schools of the United States. The book, *Who Shall Be Educated?*, by Lloyd Warner, Havighurst and Loeb (1946), is a revelation on this point. We hear a junior high school principal say: 'You generally find the children from the best families do the best work. The children from the lower class seem to be not as capable as the others', and on this the authors comment that 'this correlation holds true. There is a strong relationship between social status and rank in school.' A teacher then says that there is a lot of class feeling in the school. 'Sections [i.e. streams] are supposed to be made up just on the basis of records in school but it isn't [*sic*] and everybody knows it isn't. I know right in my own A section I have children who ought to be in B section, but they are little socialites and so they stay in A', and there is much more in the same strain (p. 73). But the problem there is allocation between streams or courses, rather than between schools.

It was on this general question that Sir Cyril Burt made one of his most challenging remarks. 'A realistic policy', he wrote, 'must take frankly into consideration the fact that a child coming from this or that type of home may as a result be quite unsuited for a type of education, occupation or profession, which lies at an excessive "social distance" from those of his parents and friends.'[9] Whereupon Dr Alexander descended on him like a ton of bricks, saying that no Authority could act on the view 'that the present social circumstances of a child should be a criterion limiting his future opportunity'.[10] Undoubtedly he is right. No Authority can act on the principle that social circumstances must limit educational opportunity, but in fact they do, and the accepted methods of educational selection cannot wholly prevent this. The remedy lies in the reduction of 'social distance'.

[9] *The British Journal of Educational Psychology*, Vol. xvii, June 1947, p. 67.
[10] ibid., November 1947, p. 123.

Conclusions

I must now try to sum up. The Welfare State, as I see it, is in danger of tying itself in knots in an attempt to do things which are self-contradictory. One example, I submit, is the proposal to assign children to different schools, largely on the basis of general ability, and then to pretend that the schools are all of equal status. If this means that we shall take equal trouble to make all schools as good as possible, treat all the children with equal respect and try to make them all equally happy, I heartily endorse the idea. But the notion of parity of esteem does not always stop there; and I feel it really is necessary to assert that some children are more able than others, that some forms of education are higher than others, and that some occupations demand qualities that are rarer than others and need longer and more skilled training to come to full maturity, and that they will therefore probably continue to enjoy higher social prestige.

I conclude that competitive selection through the educational system must remain with us to a considerable extent. The Welfare State is bound to pick the children of high ability for higher education and for higher jobs, and to do this with the interests of the community as well as the rights of the children in mind. But the more use it can at the same time make of allocation to courses suited to special tastes and abilities the better. It further seems to me that, for the purpose of selection on grounds of general ability, the objective tests are already accurate enough to do all that we should ever ask them to do, while, so far as 'allocation' is concerned, they will never be able to give a decisive verdict in more than a minority of cases, although they can be of great value in helping to decide what advice to give.

So I agree with Sir Cyril Burt that the problem which now faces us is more administrative than psychological. There is less to be gained by trying to perfect the tests and examinations than by thinking how to shape the structure of our educational and employment systems. It is better to minimize the effects of our decisions in doubtful cases than to imagine that, if we only try hard enough, we can ensure that all our decisions in such cases are correct. The word 'correct' has no meaning in this context; it is a bureaucratic fiction borrowed from the office where there is a correct file for every document.

By 'minimize the effects of our decisions' I mean refrain from adding unnecessary and artificial consequences to acts whose real meaning and necessary consequences I have been urging that we should frankly recognize. A system of direction into distinct 'types of secondary school' rather than 'courses of secondary education' (to use the titles I quoted earlier) must, I think, intensify rather than minimize the consequences. I am aware of the educational arguments on the other side, but do not intend to enter into a controversy for which I have no equipment. The other point at which artificial consequences may be added is the point of passage from education to employment. The snobbery of the educational label, certificate or degree when, as often, the prestige of the title bears little or no relation to the value of the content, is a pernicious thing against which I should like to wage a major war.

There is another matter on which the Welfare State can easily try to follow contradictory principles. It relates to occupational prestige, social class and the distribution of power in society. All I can do is to throw one or two raw ideas at your heads as a parting gift.

Although the Welfare State must, I believe, recognize some measure of economic inequality as legitimate and acceptable, its principles are opposed to rigid class divisions, and to anything which favours the preservation or formation of sharply distinguished culture patterns at different social levels. The segregation when at school of those destined for different social levels is bound to have some effect of this kind and is acceptable only if there are irrefutable arguments on the other side. Further, a system which sorts children by general ability and then passes them through appropriate schools to appropriate grades of employment will intensify the homogeneity within each occupational status group and the differences between groups. And, in so far as intelligence is hereditary and as educational chances are influenced by family background (and I have produced evidence to show that they are), the correlation between social class and type of school will become closer among the children.

Finally, the Welfare State, more than most forms of democracy, cannot tolerate a governing class. Leadership and power are exercised from many stations in life, by politicians, judges, ecclesiastics, business men, trade unionists, intellectuals and others. If these were all selected in childhood and groomed in the same stable, we should have what Raymond Aron calls the characteristic feature of a totalitarian society—a unified *élite*.[11] These leaders must really belong to and represent in a distinctive way the circles in and through which their power is exercised. We need politicians from all classes and occupational levels, and it is good that some captains of industry should have started life at the bench, and that trade unions should be led by genuine members, men of outstanding general ability who have climbed a ladder other than the educational one. It is important to preserve these other ladders, and it is fortunate that the selection net has some pretty big holes in it. It is fortunate too, perhaps, that human affairs cannot be handled with perfect mechanical precision, even in the Welfare State.

11 *The British Journal of Sociology*, March 1950, p. 10.

CHAPTER XIII

THE WELFARE STATE AND THE AFFLUENT SOCIETY

There is an area of modern literature about social questions through which the reader travels with the help of neatly simplified maps, guided by signposts which tell him in clear and incisive terms exactly where he is and where he will get to by whichever road he chooses to take. It is the area in which popular sociology and high-class journalism meet, mingle and are amalgamated. Among the names to be found on the signposts are some which immediately enable him to identify and put in their place the people he encounters on his journey—the white-collared or black-coated, the status-seekers, the establishment. Others refer to different types of social culture, like Meritocracy, or Subtopia, or the two I have chosen for the title of this lecture, the Welfare State and the Affluent Society. Since it must be apparent that catchwords of this kind are fraught with perils for the unwary, my first task must be to explain with what degree of respect I propose to treat them.

I intend neither to accept them as offering us the truth, the whole truth and nothing but the truth, nor to reject them as being no better than a pack of lies. I shall choose a middle course and treat them with respect, but with no more respect than they deserve. The fact that they have become current in the societies to which they refer is in itself enough to entitle them to be taken seriously. It means that they reflect in some way the conception which people have formed about themselves and their environment, and that is a significant fact.

But when we have decided to pay serious attention to these catchwords, there are two dangers which we must be careful to avoid. The first is to imagine that the nature of the social systems can be revealed by a subtle analysis of the names which have been given to them. If we were to apply this treatment to the 'Welfare State', we might soon find ourselves confronted by a picture of benevolent totalitarianism very different from the society to which the term originally referred. The second danger is that of treating these phrases as if they stood for general concepts of universal application. It makes no sense to ask whether France, or Sweden or the United States is or is not a Welfare State, nor can we construct an ideal model of the Welfare State, in all its complex totality, and use it as a standard against which to measure the achievements of particular societies. There are too many different ways in which a State can pursue the end of social welfare, and too many possible combinations of all the methods which might be adopted for this purpose. And there is no scientific procedure by which to determine what, in an ideal Welfare State, would be the relation between government action on the one hand and individual liberty on the other. So we must be content to tie these labels only to pieces of concrete historical reality, at least until we know rather more about them.

This being so, my problem is as follows. The label 'Welfare State' was tied by somebody or other round the neck of British society in the 1940's, and the name stuck. Was it really appropriate, and if so why? Then our sociological journalists borrowed the label designed by Professor Galbraith for the United States, the 'Affluent Society', and fastened it to British society in the 1950's. Was *this* a sensible thing to do, and if so why? And finally, does this change of labels at that particular point of time provide a clue to the interpretation of contemporary history?

When we find men proclaiming a revolution every few years, and when we see that it is always the same revolution, we may be sure that what is happening is a continuous evolutionary movement in one unchanging direction. From the 1880's to the 1940's people were constantly expressing amazement at the social transformation witnessed in their lifetime, oblivious of the fact that, in this series of outbursts of self-congratulation, the glorious achievements of the past became the squalid heritage of the present. Let me give you some examples. In the 1890's an elderly Registrar of Friendly Societies testified that, as regards the standard of living of the working class, 'I think the change in public opinion on that subject has been something perfectly marvellous. I cannot express it sufficiently.' In 1948, he went on, 'we were considered heretics and revolutionists' for trying to bring adults to the level of understanding now reached by children when they leave school.[1] Next, listen to Lloyd George. In 1908, when he was launching his social programme, he told his audience that he had been reading some 'excruciating letters' about the sufferings of the poor. 'The day will come,' he said, 'and it is not far distant, that this country will shudder at its toleration of that state of things when it was rolling in wealth.' (So much for the Registrar of Friendly Societies.) And when his measures had safely passed through Parliament, he boldly proclaimed the arrival of the millennium. 'In hundreds of thousands of cases there is penury, privation, everything going from the household, nothing left unpawned, except its pride. On Monday next an Act of Parliament comes into operation that abolishes that state of things for ever.'[2]

But seven years later Seebohm Rowntree could see no evidence at all of improvement achieved, or even attempted. 'The presence in our midst', he said, 'of masses of ill-paid labour, and millions of human beings living in slums, bears melancholy witness to our indifference in the past to the true welfare of the state.'[3] So it was time for another revolution, and it was announced by Neville Chamberlain in 1925. Since

[1] Royal Commission on Labour, *Final Report*, 1894. Evidence, Question 1852.
[2] Herbert du Parcq: *Life of David Lloyd George*, Vol. IV, pp. 642 and 792.
[3] Asa Briggs: *Seebohm Rowntree*, p. 156.

1897, he said, there had been effected, in a short space of time, 'a profound and almost revolutionary change in the status of the worker in this country'.[4] But that was not the end either, for in 1942 came Beveridge exclaiming that 'a revolutionary moment in the world's history is a time for revolutions, not for patching',[5] and he proceeded to provide the blueprint for the next one. This does not mean that the progress which men thought they had made was illusory. It means that the standards by which that progress was assessed were constantly rising, and that ever deeper probing into the social situation kept revealing new horrors which had previously been concealed from view.

Perhaps I could have found even earlier examples of this sense of guilt expunged by revolutionary achievement, but I rather doubt it. Plenty of pricks were administered to the sleeping social conscience of the mid-Victorians, by Shaftesbury, Chadwick, Dickens, Disraeli and others, but it was not fully aroused. The men who lived in what Trevelyan has called 'the two mid-Victorian decades of quiet politics and roaring prosperity'[6] believed that theirs was an Affluent Society. And, in a sense, it was, judged by the standards of the time. It had emerged from the pioneering struggles of the Industrial Revolution as a going concern governed by logically intelligible principles; out of the flux of change had been born a stable social system, or so most of them thought. And it was well endowed with the things of this world. They agreed with Patrick Colquhoun about the distinction between poverty and indigence. Poverty was a natural and necessary element in society, because it was the spur of poverty that induced labour to create riches. But indigence, or the lack of the means to live, was an evil which must be cured, or at least relieved. The poor were the common soldiers in the economic army, and were adequately equipped, so they thought, for their task; the indigent were the casualties who must be carried off the field and treated by a separate service. Their presence on the

[4] H. E. Raynes: *Social Security in Britain*, p. 200.
[5] Report on *Social Insurance and Allied Services*, para. 7.
[6] G. M. Trevelyan: *History of England*, p. 650.

periphery of the Affluent Society need not disturb the life of the whole. They could be left in the good hands of the Guardians of the Poor, and of the charitable, and forgotten. If this is too harsh a judgement, then how can one account for that series of revolutions in social policy and in the social conscience which I have just described? It represents, in my view, the beginning of the attack delivered by the Welfare State on the Affluent Society; and we are today witnessing the attack of the Affluent Society on the Welfare State. But I anticipate.

Mid-Victorian complacency received a series of shocks, the story of which is so familiar that I will merely recapitulate the headings. The strikes of match girls and dockers and the widespread sympathy they evoked; the demonstrations of unemployed in Trafalgar Square and the record fund subscribed for their relief; the alarming, if exaggerated, tales of the low physical condition of the recruits to the army in the South African War; the path-breaking, even if not very exact, studies of urban poverty made by Booth and Rowntree, and the campaign for Tariff Reform which suggested (but failed to persuade the electorate) that the 'workshop of the world' could no longer face its competitors. Although the facts did not fully justify the conclusions drawn from them, the effect they produced was quite real. It had been shown, first, that the foundations of the Victorian Affluent Society were not as solid as had been imagined; they needed attention. And secondly that the Affluent Society was not really affluent. A considerable proportion of the poor, it seemed, were in fact indigent or, to revert to my military metaphor, large numbers of the common soldiers were really casualties—casualties not of enemy action, but of the military system itself. Poverty and squalor, in short, were central and not peripheral features of the society.

The clue to the spirit of the social policy which these events and discoveries evoked, which is, as I believe, the spirit of the Welfare State, is to be found in the use of the word 'socialism' and the arguments which centred on it. It is remarkable how often this word crops up in the political speeches and writings of men of all parties at the turn of the century, considering how relatively few self-styled socialists there were at that time. We find something called 'socialism' being simultaneously denounced as a damnable heresy and accepted as the orthodoxy of the day even by members of the same party. The explanation of course is that the word had at least two different meanings. On the one hand there was what we might be tempted to call 'real socialism', but that involves a value judgement, so let us call it Socialism A. It includes all schools of thought which set out to transform the social and economic system by abolishing capitalism, whether by violence or by peaceful penetration. It covers the Marxists and near-Marxists, and the figure of John Burns in Trafalgar Square, waving a red flag and crying, 'when we give the word for a rising, will you join us?'[7] It also covers the Fabians in their early phase, when they propagated such doctrines as 'public property in land is the basic economic condition of Socialism', and 'the answer of Socialism to the capitalist is that society can do without him, just as society now does without the slave-owner or feudal lord'.[8] They believed that Socialism would create a new kind of Affluent Society in which indigence would not merely seem to be, but really would be, only a peripheral problem. And so they paid very little attention to welfare policy, at least at first. Graham Wallas, for example, having outlined the shape of the new society, dismissed the welfare question with the words 'there would always remain the sick, the infirm, and the schoolchildren, whose wants could be satisfied from the general stock without asking them to bear any part of the general burden'.[9] Everybody else would be able to pay for what he received, even when it was provided by the State. This kind of Socialism was anathema to Tories, Liberals and Radicals alike.

The other kind—shall we call it Socialism B—was a milder and less alarming affair. It had in it the humanitarianism associated with the so-called Tory Socialists, combined with

[7] Godfrey Elton: *England Arise!*, p. 126.
[8] *Fabian Essays* (Jubilee Edition), pp. 24 and 92.
[9] ibid., pp. 135–7.

some emergent principles of social policy developed by the more advanced Liberals, and a readiness to rely on government action which had a definitely Socialist, or as Dicey would say, 'collectivist', flavour. It was to this hybrid that Hubert Bland referred, in the Fabian Essays, when he said that today 'no popular speaker will venture to address a public meeting without making some reference of a socialistic sort to the social problem'. And that explained why 'that extremely well-oiled and accurately poised political weathercock, Sir William Harcourt, pointing to the dawn', crowed out that 'we are all Socialists now'. To Bland, of course, Harcourt's socialism was completely bogus, nothing but a 'rhetorical falsehood',[10] but Joseph Chamberlain openly insisted that the Radical programme of 1885 was full of Socialism, and that it was none the worse for that. But his conception of Socialism was vague and imprecise, since for him it included the Poor Law, the Education Act, municipal enterprise, and 'every kindly act of legislation by which the community discharges its responsibilities and obligations to the poor'.[11] It is clear, however, that he regarded progressive welfare legislation and socialism, not as alternatives, but as belonging to the same order of things, an attitude typical of what I have called Socialism B. Whereas Balfour, with his eye fixed on Socialism A, took a different view. 'Social legislation', he said, 'is not merely to be distinguished from Socialist legislation, but is its most direct opposite and its most effective antidote.'[12] That is what Bismarck thought too. Winston Churchill, destined to play a leading part in the first phase of Liberal social reform, took a middle course. He was strongly opposed to Socialism A, whether Marxist or Fabian, but admitted that no hard and fast line could be drawn between collectivism and individualism, and that the role of collectivism in society was bound to grow. What was Socialism to Chamberlain was the new Liberalism to him, and he recommended his followers not to be scared of discussing its proposals 'just because some

---

[10] *Fabian Essays* (Jubilee Edition), p. 194.
[11] S. Maccoby: *The English Radical Tradition*, pp. 201–2.
[12] E. Halévy: *History of the English People*, Vol. v, p. 231.

old woman comes along and tells you they are Socialistic'.[13]

Obviously the political philosophy of the Welfare State was born in an atmosphere of confusion. It belonged, in fact, to that area of politics in which the proximate wings of all the parties meet and overlap. It appealed to enlightened Tories, progressive Liberals, most Radicals and moderate Socialists. And this may help us to understand how it was that a movement initiated by Lloyd George and Churchill as the message of the new Liberalism, carried forward by Neville Chamberlain on behalf of the Conservatives, and enlarged and refurbished by another distinguished Liberal, Lord Beveridge, could receive its finishing touches from the Labour party, and be treated by them as a stronghold of Socialism for which they were ready to fight in the last ditch. There was, I believe, the same kind of confusion about the principles of the Welfare State in 1950, when the structure had been completed, as there had been fifty years earlier, when the foundations were being laid; possibly rather more.

For in those early years there was one clear and definite aim of policy which it is easy to identify, namely the break-up of the Poor Law. It was here that the reformers saw the blot that must be rubbed out. Those who discuss this familiar matter are too much inclined to treat it as a bright idea which occurred to Beatrice Webb while she was sitting on the Royal Commission. And they do not sufficiently distinguish between two things to which the phrase may refer. The first is the breaking up of the category of pauper and of the actual company of paupers, by extracting from it whole sets of people and incorporating them in the general body of the free and independent working class, protected and sustained by their basic rights as citizens. This process had been in full swing for some twenty years before the Royal Commission was set up. The second is the breaking up of the administrative machinery of the Poor Law, which had to deal with the residue of paupers, by abolishing the Guardians and transferring their functions to another more appropriate agency. It was

13 W. S. Churchill: *Liberalism and the Social Problem*, pp. 79–81.

over this that Beatrice Webb fought her greatest personal battle, and it was not achieved till 1929. I am concerned here with the first rather than the second of these two developments. The groups which were extricated from the gloomy company of paupers and relieved of the stigma of pauperism were, as everybody knows, the old, the sick and the unemployed. Their emancipation was marked by the passage of the Old Age Pensions and National Insurance Acts in 1908 and 1911. I need not repeat the story, but I have a point I want to make about it.

The central problem of social policy was how to reduce to a minimum the class of persons who were not merely poor, in Colquhoun's sense, but destitute, or on the verge of destitution. And there were three theories current as to how this could be done. One, which we may call the conservative theory, with a small 'c', was that the reduction could and should be brought about by the free play of forces in the economic market. In other words, in the Affluent Society based on competitive capitalism the destitute would be only the incapacitated (who were always with us) and those who fell by the wayside because they were unable to make the grade or unwilling to try. It had been revealed that Victorian society had not been truly affluent in this sense, but it was believed that twentieth-century society could become so. 'While the problem of 1834 was the problem of pauperism,' said Alfred Marshall, 'the problem of 1893 is the problem of poverty.' And the Royal Commission on the Aged Poor to which he made this statement in evidence was optimistic about the future. It based its optimism, and its recommendations, on 'the remarkable growth of thrift' among the working classes which, it believed, would 'greatly aid in the solution of the problems of old age poverty as well as of general pauperism'.[14] Similar views, differently worded, are being expressed today.

The second theory was that of the real socialists, adherence of Socialism A, who rejected this gross misunderstanding of

[14] *Royal Commission on the Aged Poor*, Vol. xi, Question 10358 and Vol. xiv, p. lxxxvii.

the nature and destiny of capitalism, but believed that the desired result could be attained in a socialist society in which nobody would fall by the wayside in the competitive struggle because there would be no competition, and there would be only the immature and incapacitated to care for. So they were not much interested in, and were even suspicious of, social welfare programmes. The third theory was that of Socialism B. It denied that a free market economy could solve the problem however affluent it became, because of its inherent incapacity to satisfy all the needs of civilized man, in particular his need for security. Economic and social values, it held, are distinct and independent things which may coincide by chance, but do not do so of necessity. Social policy was not something inferior to economic policy, a helper-up of the economic system or cleaner-up of its minor messes. It stood above it, representing a higher authority by which the inherent deficiencies of the market economy could be corrected. It was therefore a permanent part of a civilized industrial society. It recognized individual rights not created or measured by the market value of a man, but derived from his status as a citizen. It was in this sense that the principle of the Welfare State rejected the philosophy of the Affluent Society. Naturally the adherents of Socialism A maintained that it also rejected socialism, and that its effect would be to bolster up the capitalist system by means of palliatives, and this issue is still very much alive today.

Now I must ask you to join me in a flying leap from the dawn of the century to the Second World War, the Beveridge Report and the decade that followed it. Here we meet the Welfare State in its full maturity, and here we find it once more engaged in a drama in which its rival is the Affluent Society. The nature of the present attack was expressed very clearly, almost crudely, by a Conservative Member of Parliament who said, referring to the Beveridge Report, that 'to continue applying it in 1960 is to swallow the drug after the disease has gone. For primary poverty has now almost disappeared. Full employment has lifted the mass of our working population to a level of affluence unprecedented in our social history.'[15] More subtle is the approach of the Liberals. They not only question the two principles of universal benefits and free services, but they also, in a more or less official publication, declare that 'the whole Welfare State apparatus must be regarded as a passing phenomenon'.[16] It is true that they give it another fifty years to run, but this delayed death sentence is pronounced by those who claim at the same time to be the parents of the condemned man. I quote these remarks to show you how profoundly the atmosphere has changed in recent years. Is this because the Welfare State of the 1940's, of which Beveridge and Bevan were the chief architects, was not the logical fulfilment of the long movement of social reform which I have been describing, but something quite new and fundamentally different? If so, this might explain why the successors of those who launched and supported that movement should now repudiate its bastard child. Or is it that the Welfare State is in truth the legitimate child of its parents, but that a profound change in the circumstances of our society has caused that long movement to be checked, challenged and brought to a halt? I believe that this second explanation is the true one.

It cannot, I think, be denied that the Beveridge Report and the legislation based mainly upon it had the character of a revision and consolidation of previous measures and administrative devices. This, after all, was what the original Beveridge Committee was appointed to do, and it was done. But by insisting that the Report should be a personal one, Beveridge gained the power to do more. Secondly, the principle underlying the recommendations on social security was the same which had inspired previous legislation, namely that the number of those dependent on State charity should be reduced to a minimum by the creation of social rights vested in the citizen, the rights to an acceptable standard of economic welfare, to health and, one might add, to education. Beveridge was acutely conscious of the collapse in the inter-war

[15] Charles Curran, M.P., in *Crossbow*, Autumn 1960.
[16] Letter in *The Times*, 20 October 1961, and G. Watson (ed.), *The Unservile State*, p. 100.

period of the machinery he had helped to set up to deal with unemployment. Insurance, he said, had been replaced by 'a general system of outdoor relief to the able-bodied'.[17] The process of reducing the number of those dependent on State charity had been reversed. To retrieve the position and prevent a repetition of this disaster it was necessary, first to have a general economic policy of full employment, and secondly to ensure that everyone who was exposed to the risk of being reduced by circumstances to a state of destitution should be guaranteed the right to receive in such circumstances an income at subsistence level. The principle of the subsistence level had not, I think, been explicitly adopted before. Certainly nobody had imagined that Old Age Pensions at 5s. a week would provide subsistence. But things had moved in that direction when the pension rates were raised and when the Poor Law was finally broken up, leaving a Public Assistance authority to deal with what it was hoped would be exceptional cases only. Neville Chamberlain came near to it when, in introducing the Pensions Bill of 1925, he said that it was not intended that pensions should supersede thrift, but they were meant 'to provide a basis so substantial that it will encourage people to try and add to it and thus achieve complete independence for themselves'.[18] It is not a very long step from a 'substantial basis' to a 'subsistence level', and I think we can regard the Beveridge subsistence principle as a logical conclusion of the previous trend. However, as we all know, it was the one item which proved to be too much for the economy to bear and was never fully put into effect.

In the Beveridge Report subsistence was linked with universality. This is how he summarized the central principle of his policy—'unified universal contributory insurance to ensure at all times to all men a subsistence income for themselves and their families as of right; that is to say without any form

17 W. H. Beveridge: *The Past and Present of Unemployment Insurance*, p. 36.
18 Gertrude Williams: *The State and the Standard of Living*, p. 179.

of means test or inquiry about what means they had'.[19] Was this principle of universal benefits without a means test an innovation or a fulfilment of past trends? In trying to answer this difficult question I would say first that contributory insurance is incompatible with a general means test, and that when such an insurance covers the whole wage-earning class and a bit more, benefits will already be being paid to people who are not in urgent need. And, as Beveridge said in his Report, 'many persons working on their own account are poorer and more in need of State insurance than employees; the remuneration limit for non-manual employees is arbitrary and takes no account of family responsibility'.[20] So if one turns away in horror from the idea of an individual means test, one is driven almost inevitably to the principle of universality as the only way of covering—to quote the carefully worded phrase I used just now—everyone who is exposed to the risk of being reduced by circumstances to a state of destitution. For this kind of risk is not exactly correlated with a particular level of income or with membership of any particular social or economic class. But some ten years later this principle of subsistence-cum-universality was being vigorously attacked as the outstanding innovation of the Welfare State. It is interesting to observe the language used by the critics. *The Economist*, as quoted by Beveridge in the House of Lords, said it was extravagant, under any social system, to give money to people who did not really need it and who had any money of their own. So we should give up the whole of insurance and benefits as of right in favour of assistance subject to a means test for everybody.[21] This, you see, is an appeal for a return, not to the *status quo ante* Beveridge, but to the *status quo ante* Lloyd George. This lends support to the view that the Beveridge principle did not in itself amount to a complete innovation.

But that, of course, is not the real point about the principle of subsistence-cum-universality. The real point is that, what-

[19] *Hansard*, House of Lords, 1953, Vol. 182, pp. 675–6.
[20] Report on *Social Insurance and Allied Services*, para. 4.
[21] *Hansard*, House of Lords, 1954–5, Vol. 190, pp. 535–6.

ever may have been its political antecedents, it expressed a
spirit that was definitely new. Its source was the common
experience of the war, when the welfare needs which had to
be met by government action had little or nothing to do
with personal income or class distinctions, but sprang from
the fortunes to which all the people were exposed. 'It was
increasingly regarded as a proper function of government',
writes Professor Titmuss, 'to ward off distress and strain
among not only the poor but almost all classes of society.'[22]
But more important than this was the psychological effect of
the collective effort in face of the common danger. The British Welfare State is unique because it was born in circumstances that were unique. No other country in the world
passed, solid and united, through the whole series of experiences—resistance to attack, onslaught against the enemy, victory in the field and, without any break in continuity (except a change of government), post-war scarcities and reconstruction. In such circumstances any restriction of social
services to a particular class seemed almost as unthinkable as
their limitation by a means test, for 'class' had become for
the moment an improper word. It was so obvious that the
mutual service society of the war should become the mutual
benefit society of the peace that Beveridge devoted little
space to arguing in favour of the principle of universality.
But other countries looked, and still look, at what we did
then with puzzled amazement.

Remembering what I said earlier about the mixed origins
of the policy which led eventually to the Welfare State, let
us look a little more closely at the mixture in the completed
article. How much was Liberal and how much Socialist—in
the sense in which those terms were used at the beginning of
the story? As regards the principle of universality-cum-sub-
sistence, Beveridge once said, 'my Report as a whole is intended to give effect to what I regard as a peculiarly British
idea; the idea of a national minimum'.[23] He admitted the
debt to the trade union idea of the minimum wage, but

[22] R. M. Titmuss: *Problems of Social Policy*, p. 506.
[23] W. H. Beveridge: *Pillars of Security*, p. 143.

claimed that the broader concept was non-party and national in character. Although it had a definitely Socialist flavour, it carried with it a Liberal corollary which he has frequently stressed, namely that the guaranteed minimum leaves the individual free to advance his position as much as he can by his own efforts, so that he can enjoy more than the minimum. The 'collectivist' element in social insurance is the interference with the market. Beveridge saw this operating only up to a strictly defined limit above which the market was to rule supreme. Below the line was welfare and above it competition. This has turned out to be an unrealistic picture of society. On the one hand, as we shall see, some sections of public welfare policy operated very definitely above the base line of subsistence. On the other hand the ways in which a man can get more than the minimum for himself are not confined to his individual efforts in the labour market. They include collective bargaining, directed more by conventional standards of consumption and traditional differentials (which are a species of welfare) than by claims based on productivity, and also private pension schemes and 'fringe benefits'. So the welfare principle functions above the line as well, though operating through different institutions.

One respect in which the structure of the British Welfare State bears a stronger Socialist stamp than some comparable systems elsewhere is the heavy share given to the government, and the taxpayer, in administering and financing the scheme. We retained and extended the tripartite system by which the State is a full partner with the two classes of contributors, whereas in many other countries the State may either not contribute at all to a particular service, or else give limited support, as it were from outside, at the points that need it most. And we decided to run the whole health insurance and medical service through public bodies, whereas in some countries this is done through mutual benefit societies (as at first with us) and a more autonomous medical profession. Obviously the greater the share of the cost borne by the taxpayer, the stronger the objection to paying benefits to people who do not need them.

But most important of all, perhaps, was the recognition that welfare measures and institutions were not just pieces of machinery specially designed to cope with problems of the moment, not merely means to an end, but in a certain sense ends in themselves, a much-to-be-admired feature of our society and the embodiment of the British way of life. The Beveridge Report came out during the war and was greeted as a declaration of the country's peace aims, which gave us something positive to fight for. Two weeks after its publication the Gallup poll found that 19 out of 20 adults had heard of it and that an overwhelming majority were in favour of it.[24] 'It has become in the minds of the people and the nation', said James Griffiths in the House of Commons, 'both a symbol and a test. It has become first of all a symbol of the kind of Britain we are determined to build when victory is won.'[25] This attitude towards measures of social welfare is characteristic of what I have called Socialism B, and it was accepted by Liberals from Lloyd George to Beveridge. But, as the passage I quoted just now shows, it is no longer generally accepted by the Liberals of today for whom the Welfare State has become a passing phase. A bifurcation has become apparent in the historic stream of social policy.

This should not surprise us, for there were incipient contradictions within the structure of the Welfare State itself. Beveridge's conception of a minimum above which individual effort must be free to create individual differences, outside the scope of welfare policy altogether, did not blend any too easily with the different ideas embodied in the Health Service, in public education, in housing policy and in free or subsidized school meals. In health and education the State undertook to meet fully the needs of the citizen regardless of his economic status. It did not offer a basis for private enterprise to build on, but a complete alternative to what could be obtained from private sources. In housing too the public authorities made every effort to satisfy family needs in the order of their urgency and to offer more than a bare minimum

[24] W. H. Beveridge: *Power and Influence*, p. 319.
[25] Janet Beveridge: *Beveridge and His Plan*, p. 128.

in doing so, while there was nothing resembling a subsistence minimum about school meals. The philosophy expressed in these services differed significantly from that of the National Insurance Act, and was akin to the Socialist philosophy of 'fair shares'. For a time it dominated the scene, because of the circumstances attending the birth of the Welfare State. It was born at a time when the sense of national solidarity created by the war coincided with the enforced restraints on consumption and the régime of sharing imposed by post-war scarcity. I cannot escape the conclusion that the Welfare State reigned unchallenged while linked with the Austerity Society and was attacked from all sides as soon as it became associated with the Affluent Society.

Austerity lasted a good deal longer than most people now remember and it was in full command of the situation in the years in which the Welfare State was conceived and brought into the world. The end of the war was followed by a world economic crisis during which no major relaxation of controls was possible. In fact some new ones were added, such as the rationing of bread. Wages and prices were fairly stable till 1947, and then serious signs of inflation appeared which led to the appeal by Stafford Cripps early in 1948 for what we should now call a 'pay-pause'. Unlike his present-day successor in office he received immediate promises of co-operation not only from employers but even more emphatically from the Trades Union Congress. The response truly reflected the spirit of voluntary restraint that went with the policy of austerity, but the truce was brief, and in 1951 a new crisis occurred and the Government fell. The lifting of controls began seriously in 1949, during the short-lived truce. In that year clothes-rationing ended and the termination of labour controls was announced for the following year. Milk, jam and all the goods on the 'points' system were freed in 1950, in 1952 tea came off and the utility goods scheme—the very hall-mark of utility—ended. Sugar, sweets and eggs were de-rationed in 1953, and butter, margarine, cheese, bacon and meat only in 1954. And that was the end. While all this was happening a peace reigned in industrial relations which was almost complete. The largest number of working days lost by stoppages in any year never exceeded 2½ million, and was generally much less; this figure should be compared with the 35 million working days lost in the first year after World War I. By 1956 the psychological as well as the administrative restraints on consumption had been cast aside, the inflationary urge reappeared, and in 1957 8½ million working days were lost by stoppages. The new atmosphere was one of unrestrained freedom in which each is entitled to have whatever he can get, because it is assumed that there is enough for all and to spare. The Affluent Society had made its entry on to the stage.

I am using this concept broadly in the sense in which I understand Professor Galbraith to use it and which gives it a definitely derogatory flavour, and differs somewhat from the sense in which I used it to refer to the mid-Victorian age. It does not mean simply a rich society, nor one that has abolished poverty. The Affluent Society is certain to be, in some sense, the former, and may be, but is not necessarily, the latter. It should not be defined as either. The term denotes a standard of values rather than a level of living. The Affluent Society, according to Galbraith, worships at the shrine of production, but its most significant feature is the consequent artificial stimulation of consumption in order to absorb the products. 'As a society becomes increasingly affluent', he writes, 'wants are increasingly created by the process by which they are satisfied.' The desires of the individual are 'synthesized, elaborated and nurtured by advertising and salesmanship', and driven forward by the spirit of competition, or emulation of the standard of expenditure of one's neighbour.[26] This is the aspect of life in the Affluent Society most directly relevant to the fortunes of the Welfare State, because it is the antithesis to the latter's emphasis on the satisfaction of genuine needs, the justification of income differences by their social legitimacy, and the principle of 'fair shares'. Consumer competition in the Affluent Society tends

[26] J. K. Galbraith: *The Affluent Society*, pp. 2 and 124.

to forget about the services by which incomes are earned and
to concentrate only on the getting and spending of them,
however come-by. In its more hysterical and perverted form
it ceases to care whether the reward is logically related to
productive labour at all or to any service whatever. It looks
eagerly for windfalls, whether they come through speculation, capital gains, bogus expense accounts, football pools,
premium bonds, or, at the lowest level of all, the shady business of spivs and Teddy Boys. What these latter saw around
them, says Mr Fyvel in a recent book, was 'a life of recurring
boredom where nothing mattered but money and the smart
thing at all times was to give as little as you could for as
much as you could get; in short, as they saw it, a distorted
materialist society without purpose'.[27] Their view, of course,
is a caricature, but it has in it a modicum of truth. The Teddy
Boys, Drape Boys, Bohemians and the rest, with their cherished twenty-guinea suits, are the modern working-class practitioners of conspicuous consumption, the inverted, negative
version of which is the conspicuous non-consumption of the
Beatniks.

The Welfare Society was based on the opposite principle.
It did not reject the capitalist market economy, but held that
there were some elements in a civilized life which ranked
above it and must be achieved by curbing or superseding the
market. It did not desire a dead level of consumption for all
alike, but believed that the inequalities should be explicable
and defensible in terms of legitimate claims. In the matter of
welfare it saw society as a sort of mutual benefit club in
which consumption was rendered co-operative by the pooling
of risks and the sharing of resources. It was a kind of capitalism softened by an injection of socialism, and many socialists disliked or mistrusted the mixture. The Welfare
State, says Mr Crossman, is the 'adaptation of capitalism to
the demands of modern trade unionism',[28] and as such only
a step, though probably a necessary one, on the road to socialism. But Mr Crosland, true to the tradition of Socialism

[27] T. R. Fyvel: *The Insecure Offenders*, p. 16.
[28] R. H. Crossman in *New Fabian Essays*, p. 6.

B, sees more in it than that. It is for him a new kind of society, inspired by a new spirit. 'No one would argue', he writes, 'that in the contemporary Welfare State the dominant ideology was one of self-help or aggressive individualism. . . . Nor does anyone now much believe in the over-riding rights of private property.'[29] And this, he considers, is characteristic of a socialist type of society. But he wrote this in 1956, before the Affluent Society had taken over.

In the clash between the two opposed ideologies, the Welfare State was at a disadvantage throughout. First, it was associated with the Austerity Society, which nobody liked or wanted to preserve. It was easy for the critics to maintain that the Welfare State yearned to get back to it. Secondly, the Welfare State had not been true to itself. Inflation caused the principle of the subsistence level to be abandoned without ever having been really put into effect. The role of National Assistance (or Poor Law under another name) grew once more, and the ideal of the national mutual benefit club was lost. For this the Welfare State was attacked by its disappointed friends. Thirdly, the rise in the standard of living made the principle of universality sometimes look rather silly. Socialist critics said that all it had done was 'to provide free social services to the middle class',[30] while middle-class critics pointed to the injustice of prosperous working-class families living in subsidized Council houses. And it was difficult to convince a society turned materialist that the case for the principle of universality did not rest on materialist arguments at all. Fourthly, as the Affluent Society expanded, the benefits offered by the Welfare State seemed to lose, not only part of their value, but in a sense their dignity also. To quote Mr Fyvel again, 'Through the irresistible mass attack of this new artificial culture, everything else appeared suddenly pushed into the background, reduced in size, dated.'[31] That, I think, describes very well the atmosphere which encouraged

[29] C. A. R. Crosland: *The Future of Socialism*, pp. 64–5.
[30] B. Abel-Smith: 'Whose Welfare State?', in *Conviction*, ed. Norman Mackenzie, p. 57.
[31] op. cit., p. 205.

people to think of the Welfare State, recently so deeply respected, as a back number. Fifthly, and closely related to this, the balance of the contribution to welfare began to shift from the public to the private schemes, powerfully assisted, as Professor Titmuss constantly insists, by tax concessions. This is most conspicuously true in the matter of pensions, and not at all true of the health service. Sixthly, the Welfare State had been unfortunate in its education policy. The system of selection for the three streams of secondary schools was intended to be free from the taint of competitive rivalry, and inspired by the idea of 'parity of esteem'. I think I had good grounds, when writing about this just thirteen years ago, to doubt whether the ideal would be realized. In fact educational competition has never been more intense, and it is associated directly in the public mind with the class barriers which break up the unity of our society. The power of the schools to curb the growth of aggressive individualism has been weakened.

Finally, looked at with the cold eye of economic rationality, some of the devices of the Welfare State for collecting contributions and distributing benefits appear cumbersome, illogical and pointless. It taxes the well-to-do citizen and then gives him back in return benefits or services which he does not want. It retains the essentials of a market economy in which rewards are adjusted to output and to market value, and then takes steps to equalize real incomes by means of devices like free services, family allowances, rent control, steeply progressive taxation and, in times of special difficulty, rationing and price fixing. It was this that Professor Robbins once described as 'somewhat *simpliste*'. I ventured to challenge this judgement because I thought this might be the only way of balancing economic and social values and of upholding the social rights of the citizen within the framework of an otherwise free market economy. I believed it could work in the conditions of the immediate post-war world, with the philosophy of the Welfare State to justify and sustain it. But, I said, 'This phase will not continue indefinitely. It may be that some of the conflicts within our social system are becoming too sharp for the compromise to achieve its purpose much longer'.[32]

That phase has ended, as it was bound to do. The British Welfare State of the 1940's was, as I have tried to explain, the culmination of a long process which began in the last quarter of the nineteenth century, a process during which, as Mr Crossman puts it, 'capitalism has been civilized'.[33] But it was also the product of an explosion of forces which chance and history had brought together in Britain's unique experience in the war and in the transition to a state of peace. As this situation dissolved the society changed, and the thing to which we had first given the name of 'Welfare State' passed away. Its institutions, practices, procedures and expertise are still with us, but they are operating in a different setting and without the original consensus which welded them into a social system with a distinctive spirit of its own. A mutual aid society must be based, as regards its fundamental aims and principles, on unanimity and not on a majority vote. You can no more have a Welfare State than a Democratic State that belongs only to the programme of the party in power at the moment. From this I conclude that, if we are to preserve the essential spirit of the Welfare State, and not merely the bits and pieces of its machinery, we need to develop a new model so adjusted to the conditions of the time that it may once more become a central part of a social system accepted by all. That is why I began this lecture by insisting that 'Welfare State' cannot serve as a general concept or an ideal type. To use it as such is bound to falsify the issue by suggesting that there is one structural pattern which is, so to speak, the orthodox or correct one. Whereas in fact the pattern must change with the times.

But, if it is necessary to remodel the machinery of the Welfare State to fit the conditions of the Affluent Society, it is equally essential to change the spirit of the Affluent Society to fit the principles of the Welfare State. And it is the spiritual element in politics that is the most elusive. 'The Liberal

[32] See p. 133.
[33] op. cit., p. 6.

Party is once more in trouble about its soul'; so wrote Sidney
Lowe in 1899.[34] It found a new one a few years later and
presented it to the Welfare State in its infancy. The Labour
Party, said Anthony Crosland in 1956, has been for five years
past 'furiously searching for its lost soul',[35] and the hunt is
still on. It is the one it gave to the Welfare State in its maturity. These troubles are recurrent in political philosophies
and need not worry us too much. What is more disturbing is
that the Affluent Society does not appear as yet to have a soul
at all, either to lose or to look for, and it is unaware of what
it lacks. It is imperative that it should acquire one, and it is,
I contend, only in the body of a refashioned Welfare State
that it can hope to find it.

[34] *The Nineteenth Century*, 1899, Vol. XLV, p. 10.
[35] op. cit., p. 79.

CHAPTER XIV

THE WELFARE STATE—
A COMPARATIVE STUDY

It is the business of sociologists to classify social phenomena and arrange them in categories. They base their operations on concepts which have been rigorously defined and purified to the point at which they resemble prime numbers. The practice has not unnaturally spread into that intermediate area of literature which can be called either popular sociology or intellectual journalism according to taste. But there it is used for tying labels round the necks of highly complex social systems—like 'Welfare State', 'Affluent Society' and 'Meritocracy'. This is likely to make the purist shrink and shudder. All generalizations are dangerous, and those cunningly expressed in tabloid form are the most dangerous of all. They pass into the language of common speech as familiar truths, instead of being quoted as propositions offered for discussion. One can hardly avoid using a term like the 'Welfare State', and one cannot, when using it, introduce a qualifying parenthesis, since there is no room for parentheses in a catchword. One must either accept it or discard it.

It would be a great pity to discard it. Any catchword which has been widely used by people in speaking about their own society must tell us something about that society, for current beliefs about the contemporary world are themselves part of the situation to which they refer, like the self-portrait of an artist. Of course they must be treated with care and not be credited with possession of the ultimate truth. This should not be too difficult. More subtle is the problem of deciding exactly what it is to which they refer. When somebody points at the landscape and exclaims 'it is beautiful', you know that he is expressing a genuine experience and you understand what he means, but you may not be quite certain what he is pointing at. Is it the shape of the hills, the colour of the fields or the effect of sunlight breaking through the clouds? And he may not be quite sure himself. So it is with the Welfare State. We know that those who introduced the phrase and those who quickly adopted it were expressing a genuine experience and we can understand the sentiment they meant to convey, but we may still be in doubt what was the exact combination of circumstances in Britain in the 1940's which evoked that cry of 'Eureka!' and what precisely they were pointing at when they emitted it. And this is a serious matter, because social phenomena, unlike museum pieces, do not retain unchanged the character they possessed when they were first labelled, and there is a chance that the label may be left on when it has ceased to be appropriate.

Professor Briggs, in his illuminating historical essay,[1] is as much concerned with this question of identifying the object we are talking about as with that of assessing the significance to be attached to it. He explains—and with justice—that the Welfare State was not the culminating achievement of the lone efforts of the British Labour Party nor simply the result of the proddings of the Liberal conscience. He finds its origins in many streams which began to flow in the nineteenth century and became strong rivers in the early years of the twentieth. And he asks whether the end product, whatever it was, is still with us or was only flashed briefly on to the screen of our consciousness in the 1940's and early 1950's and is already passing away or changing into something else. That there have been important changes during the past decade is beyond doubt, but we cannot tell exactly what we have lost until we have decided what it was that we earlier

[1] The references to Professor Briggs, Boettcher and Reynaud are to the contributions of these authors to the number of *The European Journal of Sociology* in which this article originally appeared.

acclaimed. The view has altered, but it may still be beautiful.

At one point Professor Briggs says that conservative social reformers like Ashley and Oastler would have considered the twentieth century breach with *laissez faire* more significant than the capitalist breach with the past in the Industrial Revolution. For from their point of view 'the Welfare State was the true historic state'. And the Fabians would have agreed with them. This raises two very important points. The first is the fundamental question whether we are justified in talking about social systems at all, and if so, in what sense. The second concerns the nature of the vital respect in which it is alleged that British society before the Industrial Revolution resembled British society after the Second World War.

Obviously the first of these questions is much too large to be seriously broached here, and all I shall do is to distinguish between three propositions regarding it. The first is that in all societies which are not in a state of chaos or dissolution social interactions take place which are sufficiently repetitive and predictable to be treated as constituting a social system. This does not imply that all parts of the system interact, nor that nothing happens that is not repetitive and predictable, nor that friction and conflict are not perpetually present somewhere, nor even that change is not taking place in the pattern of the system all the time. I consider that this proposition, or something like it, must be accepted if we profess to study human societies and not merely individual behaviour. The second proposition is that we can identify particular social systems as they occur in human history, and that this is a legitimate and helpful way of interpreting historical data. It implies, not merely that social life is normally systematic, but that particular systems take shape and become recognizable in the life of societies just as particular social situations take shape and are recognized in the life of individuals. If we are to discuss the Welfare State, we must, I think, accept this second proposition either as a truth which we intend to illustrate or as a hypothesis which we intend to test. The third proposition is one about which we may well have more serious doubts. It is that, when we have identified particular social systems in their concrete historical settings, we can construct out of them concepts which are suitable for general application to any or all societies. It is very doubtful whether, or in what precise circumstances, this can safely be done, since social systems are deeply impregnated with the unique influences of the time and place in which they came into existence. It is wiser to speak about 'feudalism' or 'feudal society' than about 'the feudal system'. We can then conceptualize the elements of feudalism and use these concepts in comparing, say, the French feudal system with the English feudal system at specific dates. Similarly we can find useful concepts for the analysis of welfare policy, its measures and institutions, and use these to study the 'British Welfare State' in the post-war period, and to compare it with the welfare systems of other countries. We can leave the question of 'Welfare State' as a valid general concept till later.

It is the purpose of this essay to suggest some lines on which such an analysis and comparison might be attempted, especially with reference to England, France and Germany. I would begin by suggesting that the inquiry should be pursued at two levels. The first is the level of actual practice, of the objective facts about the social mechanism and the way it works. The second is the level of the subjective perception of the system in the minds of the people who have designed it, are operating it, or merely live with it. It involves the difficult question of consensus. If we postulate the existence of social systems, we must also assume that there is a fair measure of conformity to the norms of the systems in outward behaviour. We also realize that this degree of conformity would hardly be possible unless there were also a fair measure of accommodation to the norms in the realm of values and ideas. The second level relates to this accommodation of ideas, or consensus. The questions which particularly interest me are these: are there key points in a social system with regard to which consensus, if it exists, has a particularly profound effect, which may spread as an influence for conformity into areas where consensus in other respects is weak, or at least not explicit? And are there periods in the history of a society during which consensus at these key points is particularly strong? I am here using 'consensus' to mean something more than mere passive acquiescence in the legitimacy of a social order. I am referring to an agreement as to the meaning of the measures and institutions concerned together with positive approval of them as vital elements in the social system.

The separate treatment of these two levels is likely to be helpful because international comparison is considerably easier at the first level than at the second, and full advantage should be taken of this before the complexities of the second type of comparison are introduced. But the inquiry will not be finished until the two results have been combined, since neither is fully intelligible without the other. At that point we can face the question whether there exists in any of the societies we are comparing a social system which has, so to speak, a distinctive, comprehensible or integrated personality. For that is the condition of affairs we presume to be present when we make use of a label like the 'Welfare State'. It is likely to be found, if ever, when an unusually well integrated mechanism is combined with an exceptionally strong consensus at key points, in an historical setting which favours the development of collective self-awareness or—to use the term which so often appears in the French story—solidarity. But we must begin at the beginning.

If, as has been suggested, the British social system after the Second World War resembled in some vital respect the social system before the Industrial Revolution, what is the clue to this resemblance? Professors Briggs and Boettcher both offer what is essentially the same answer, though with a difference in the use of terms. It is the relation between social policy and the free market. Professor Briggs defines a Welfare State as one 'in which organized power is deliberately used . . . in an effort to modify the play of market forces in at least three directions', which can be briefly described as subsistence, security and 'a certain range of agreed social services'. The first two, he says, might be pursued by the Social Service State, but the third is different, because it aims, not at a minimum, but at an optimum. Professor Boettcher uses the terminology current in German politics since the war and distinguishes sharply between the Social Market Economy and the Welfare State. The first refers to the policy of combining an essentially free market system with measures designed to preserve an acceptable social balance. It claims to avoid the defects both of pure *laissez faire* and of socialist planning by preserving the driving and directing forces of the market while making them operate in a social framework. The Welfare State, on the other hand, uses mechanisms which supersede the market. This distinction would leave us with a conception of the Welfare State too narrow to fit the British model, while Professor Briggs' phrase 'effort to modify' seems too weak to cover all the measures we shall have to consider. If we intend to compare the welfare systems of different countries in search of a meaning for the term 'Welfare State', we must include all the measures they have adopted either to influence, to interfere with, or to supersede the free play of market forces in the interests of welfare. I think we can assume that the Welfare State must make use of all these methods.

Turning, then, to my first level of inquiry, concerned with the actual mechanism of social policy, we may begin with measures which strike at the very heart of the consumer market itself, without nevertheless wholly superseding it; I mean measures like rationing, price control, rent restriction and the subsidies that accompany them. All countries have used these extensively in time of war and in post-war periods of reconstruction, but have gradually shed them thereafter. But some of them have survived for a very long time, and may even have left a permanent mark on the economy. In England subsidies are still an important feature in the economic system, but a somewhat obscure one, in the sense that most people know very little about them, and they are not held up for admiration as an achievement of the Welfare State. Housing subsidies and rent restriction are quite another matter. Twentieth century social policy has put the family and the home in the centre of the picture, and has accepted the responsibility of providing houses for the people as one of special urgency. It is also a very difficult responsibility to discharge. Rents behave capriciously when left to the higgling of the market, and they may absorb an extravagant share of the family budget, while real estate is a province in which the contrast between the behaviour of the market and the interests of the public is generally held by the man in the street to be greater than anywhere else. Nevertheless it is hard to say which particular measures for coping with this problem have been permanently incorporated into the machinery of social policy. General rent restriction might in time be replaced by special allowances of the type given in England through National Assistance. But action to stimulate the building of houses is likely to continue as a part of either social or general economic policy. I lack the knowledge to make a comparison between the three countries on this point, but I would hazard the guess that the British system of subsidized building by Local Authorities, followed by letting at uneconomic rents to tenants, chosen by reference to their needs and not their means goes further in the direction of not merely interfering with the free market but superseding it than corresponding measures in other countries. And I am sure that it is more hotly debated, and more loudly acclaimed by its supporters as an essential social service and a matter of principle not merely of expediency, than elsewhere.

As my second illustration I will take the area of social insurance, which in certain of its forms operates by compulsorily inserting conditions into contracts of employment, an invasion of the freedom of the market by which Dicey was particularly alarmed. Measures of this kind are used everywhere, but not always in quite the same way nor for exactly the same purposes. I suggest that three questions be posed about this field of policy. First, as to the uses to which social insurance is put; secondly, as to the closeness with which public insurance copies the model of private insurance; and thirdly as to the extent to which it is controlled and financed by the state.

As regards the uses to which insurance, or finance by compulsory contributions, is put, we may note that family allowances in France, and the more limited scheme in Germany, are both financed in this way, whereas in England the cost is carried by general taxation. This is interesting. Family allowances can be regarded as a form of supplementary wage, earned by labour and paid by employers. This was the first approach in France, and there was a faint suggestion that they represented a kind of employers' liberality and not merely an employers' liability. But France was also concerned about its declining birth-rate and looked to the allowances as a means of checking it. This political aim gave to the allowances the character of an extra-budgetary tax, or what has been called a *taxe parafiscale*. Finally the emphasis came to be laid on the simple issue of family needs, and the allowances assumed the form of *une aide sociale à la famille*, or a measure for the redistribution of income in order to maximize social welfare.[2] In this sequence of events the method of insurance became less and less appropriate. It was odd to treat children as a risk, to be placed to the account of the employers, when they were being welcomed as a national blessing, and the coverage of the scheme had to be extended far beyond the limits of the employed population. But France has not wished to replace the form of insurance by that of a general welfare service, or kind of national assistance. Britain had no such inhibitions.

The second case in which the use of compulsory insurance differs is that of unemployment. The clearest contrast is that between the early policy of France (followed by Belgium and the Scandinavian countries) to rely mainly on subsidies to voluntary insurance schemes, supplemented where necessary by non-contributory assistance, and the policy adopted from the first by Britain and eventually by Germany of establishing a state scheme of compulsory contributory insurance. Assuming that subsidized voluntary schemes assist the market, compulsory insurance interferes with it and non-contributory assistance supersedes it, we could say that the French approach paid more respect to normal market mechanisms than the

[2] André Rouast and Paul Durand: *Sécurité sociale* (1960), pp. 417–23.

British. But this ceased to be true as the assistance element came to outweigh the aid to voluntary agencies, until at the end of 1958 a massive collective agreement between organizations of employers and workers to set up a contributory scheme throughout industry and commerce, endorsed and encouraged by the government, brought the voluntary element to the fore again. A third difference of pattern is that the medical services in France and Germany are an integral part of sickness insurance, whereas in Britain they are quite separately administered. This point can more conveniently be taken later.

On the question of the degree of fidelity to the model of private insurance, I must confine myself to two or three points only. In France and Germany great emphasis is laid on the principle that social insurance is a mutual arrangement between employers and employed, and is administered by autonomous organs (e.g. the *Caisses* and the *Krankenkassen*) elected by the parties, though the corresponding bodies are nominated in the case of German unemployment insurance. This principle implies the limitation of the beneficiaries to employed persons and, although coverage has sometimes been extended, especially in Germany, to other gainfully occupied persons, the extensions are clearly defined and limited. Voluntary adherence may be allowed beyond these limits. For instance, in German sickness insurance a man with his own business may join provided he does not employ more than two insured workers.[3] In a bilateral scheme, presumably, men who are primarily employers cannot sit on both sides of the table. In the British tripartite plan of universal coverage, on the contrary, an employer, while contributing to the insurance of his employees, must also fill up his own card as a self-employed person.

Another example is the linkage of contributions and benefits with the rate of earnings. In France and Germany (and commonly elsewhere) the basing of insurance on a percentage relationship with wages is regarded as a principle of funda-

[3] Paul Caesar: *Sozialversicherung* (1958), p. 65.

mental importance, not merely of political expediency. It is expressed in the following comment of a German authority on the 1957 pension plan:

> The pension will be a fair one, because it will be individually assessed. It will be assessed on the individual merits of each case, reflecting as it were the varying development of the wage or the salary of the person concerned throughout his working life, and the varying periods for which he may wish to insure himself.[4]

The same principle is praised by a French authority, not only because it is just, but because it provides an incentive to greater activity in the labour market:

> This system has in addition the advantage of encouraging workers to attain a high level of living during their active life by guaranteeing that, if rendered incapable of work, they will continue to receive an income comparable with their former earnings.[5]

A first modest step in this direction has recently been made in the reform of the British retirement pensions, and a more far-reaching application of the same principle figures in the programme of the Labour Party.

My third and last example is the following. Private insurance as conducted in the market is normally concerned with a particular risk, and contributions and benefits are calculated in relation to this risk. Social insurance, fixing its attention on the needs of the individual citizen and his family, is easily drawn into comprehensive, or at least composite, insurance schemes which cover a collection of risks. The British system is highly integrated, the French markedly fragmented, in terms both of risks and of occupational classes, and the German comes somewhere between the two. In both France and Germany it is recognized that the urge to base policy on the concept of social welfare as the final goal is accompanied by a movement for the integration of schemes for protection

---

[4] *Paul Caesar: Sozialversicherung* (1958), p. 91.
[5] Rouast and Durand: op. cit., p. 65.

against social risks. In French terminology *l'assurance sociale* covers certain specified risks, while *la politique de sécurité sociale* gives a general guarantee against all risks.[6] In German terminology, the unification of different types of *Versicherung* in one scheme is a step towards a policy of *Versorgung*, or direct care by the state of those for whom it has a special obligation.[7] As we shall see, *Staatsbürgerversorgung*, or treating all citizens as meriting the care previously bestowed by government only on its military and civil servants, is often considered to be the significant new element in the social policy of the Welfare State.

My last question about social insurance concerns the administrative and financial functions of the State. I have already pointed out that in France and Germany the operative agencies are autonomous and self-administering, within the limits laid down by the government, whereas in England the State now administers the schemes directly through its own organs. At one time there were in France and Germany considerable local variations in the services rendered, just as there were in England under the régime of Approved Societies, but basic uniformity of treatment, with optional supplements, has gradually been imposed. As regards the financial contribution of the State, it is noticeable that in France and Germany the State is not a full partner in the insurance scheme, but stands outside and gives financial aid in the form of a block grant, or by allocating funds to specific purposes, sometimes drawing them from earmarked taxes. The British tripartite system reduces so much the resemblance to commercial insurance that it is often argued that a transfer of the whole burden to general taxation would not make any fundamental difference. It has been estimated that in the middle 1950's the percentage of the total amount devoted to social insurance and family allowances borne by the State was in Britain 26.5, in Germany 15.6 and in France 2.7.[8]

I have now looked briefly at measures for the control of

[6] ibid., p. 29.
[7] Hans Achinger: *Soziale Sicherheit*, p. 43.
[8] J. Henry Richardson: *Economic and Financial Aspects of Social Security*, p. 67.

market prices and at compulsory insurance. There is room to consider only one other type of action, namely the provision of a public social service, such as education or a medical service. The British people are very conscious that they have by no means eliminated market forces from their education system, especially the secondary schools, but they are proud of the fact that their National Health Service is, on the contrary, more completely governed by the principle of welfare than any other. It is available to all, in all major respects free for all, and offers the best service that is to be had with the resources at its disposal. It is financed almost entirely out of taxes, and is thus something that the community as a whole provides for itself. In France and Germany, as already pointed out, the health service is the principal benefit offered by the sickness insurance scheme, as was always the practice of Friendly Societies and similar mutual benefit clubs. This means that the service is, in principle, limited to the insured and their families, and that the doctors are one step further removed from subordination to the organs of public administration than they are in England. In Germany they are paid on the basis of capitation fees, the total sum due in respect of the patients in a region being paid to the local association of doctors for distribution to its members. In France payment is made for each service rendered, which is more like what happens in private practice, and the patient must bear a proportion of the cost known as the *ticket modérateur*. Either he pays the whole fee and recovers the balance, or he pays the amount of the *ticket* and the *Caisse* pays the rest. The doctors prefer the former arrangement, but the latter is spreading. The value of the *ticket* is calculated by reference to a tariff of fees, but usually the tariff is lower than the fees actually charged so that the patient must pay more than the amount of the *ticket*.[9] In this way the 'market' prevails over the 'welfare' principle.

I have tried to show some of the lines along which a comparison could be made of the actual mechanisms of social

[9] Rouast and Durand: op. cit., pp. 262–8.

policy in different countries, and I must now turn to my second theme, the interpretation of the system in the minds of government and people and the degree of consensus at key points in the social system. There can be little doubt that, in England, the first practical steps along the new road of social policy were taken in the first decade of this century, and the ideas which inspired them were developed some twenty to twenty-five years earlier. The crucial fact in the British story is that welfare operations in the nineteenth century were directed to the relief not of the poor but of the paupers, not of the needy but of the destitute. The pauper was marked off from his neighbours by a clearly defined status by which he lost his personal freedom and his right to vote. It was a sacred doctrine of the period that the relief of paupers must take place right outside the market and in a manner which could not interfere with its working. The British Welfare State represents the very antithesis of this conception, and it is because of this antithesis, which figured explicitly in the controversies of the early days, that its personality has become so clearly marked. The tradition in France was, I believe, different, perhaps because of the more prominent part played by the churches and the religious foundations for which relief of the poor was relief of neighbours and parishioners. The Mayor, as President of the *bureau de bienfaisance*, was officially designated as 'representative' of the poor and distributed the proceeds of private charity as well as the smaller municipal grants. An investigator in the 1890's noted that there was a 'traditional horror of anything approaching the English system'.[10] The German tradition was more like the English. Poor relief fell into the category of *Fürsorge* and was kept distinct, as Professor Boettcher explains, from other forms of social policy, and it carried a stigma and loss of the franchise.[11] But in neither country was there the intense reaction against the spirit of the Poor Law that marked the beginnings of twentieth-century social reform in England. In

[10] Emily Greene Balch: *Public Assistance of the Poor in France* (1893), p. 79.
[11] Hans Richter et alii: *Die Sozialfürsorgerecht*, p. 9.

both countries, in fact, relief to the destitute still has something of the multi-purpose character that distinguished the
English Poor Law before it was finally broken up in 1929,
but without its harshness. The French *aide sociale* provides
much more than help in cash or kind to those whose needs
are not fully met by other means. It includes services for the
sick, the old, the infirm and the homeless administered by
special administrative authorities. And the new German *Bun-
dessozialhilfegesetz*, which replaces former federal legislation
about *Fürsorge*, is equally comprehensive in scope. The results look almost like a sort of three-tier system of social
categories composed of those above the insurance level, the
insured, and those below, though one should not equate the
last category with the former English concept of pauper. In
the British system there has been an almost complete fusion
as a result of the Beveridge principle of universal coverage,
following the break-up of the Poor Law in 1929. Now everybody contributes and everybody benefits in a national scheme
of mutual aid, with National Assistance as a supplement, not
as an alternative. The system has much in common with the
German concept of *Staatsbürgerversorgung* which was referred to above. It signifies that the life services of the ordinary citizen to the community are similar to those of the
soldier or civil servant to the state and give rise to similar
claims to care and protection. The idea emerges, as German
writers explain, when social insurance departs so far from
actuarial principles that it might just as well be transferred
to general taxation, and when social assistance has been so
fully freed from taint or stigma that it can be used wherever
needed as a supplementary source of aid and not confined to
any specific category of persons.[12] At that point the fusion,
or integration, takes place. The drift towards it is visible in
Germany in the case of the refugees and in France in the
case of family allowances. In England things have advanced
far in this direction all along the line. Oddly enough Lloyd

[12] Peter Quante: 'Grundsätze der Versorgung, Versicherung und
Fürsorge', in Erik Boettcher (ed.): *Sozialpolitik und Sozialreform*,
pp. 229–36.

George, at the moment when he was preparing his social insurance measures in 1911, foresaw the time when they would pass away and be replaced by a different conception of the rights of the citizen. He wrote in a memorandum:

> Insurance necessarily temporary expedient. At no distant date hope State will acknowledge full responsibility in the matter of making provision for sickness breakdown and unemployment . . . Gradually the obligation of the State to find labour or sustenance will be realized and honourably interpreted. Insurance will then be unnecessary.[13]

Only in the National Health Service has this hope been fulfilled as yet.

It is in this conception of the claims of all citizens, directed not at the state but at one another, that I find the consensus at the key point of the British Welfare State. It belongs to democracy more than to socialism, but the clue to its nature can be found in the history of socialist ideas and the reaction to them. The word was used very broadly in England at the turn of the century. It might refer to a revolutionary working-class movement, inspired by Marxism. In his brilliant book, *The Condition of England* (1909), Masterman said of the upper class, or 'conquerors', that 'its fear today is Socialism; Socialism which it does not understand, but which presents itself as an uprising of the uneducated suddenly breaking into its houses.'[14]

But the threat was not grave enough to make Socialism in all its forms an untouchable idea. It was a label that was attached to, and often accepted by, most groups of ardent reformers, like Tory Socialists, Christian Socialists, Radical Socialists and even on occasion Liberal Socialists. Joseph Chamberlain, having outlined the Radical programme of 1885, went on:

[13] William J. Braithwaite: *Lloyd George's Ambulance Wagon*, pp. 121–2.

[14] C. F. G. Masterman: *The Condition of England*, p. 64.

I shall be told tomorrow that this is Socialism . . . Of course it is Socialism; the Poor Law is Socialism; the Education Act is Socialism; the greater part of municipal work is Socialism; and every kindly act of legislation by which the community discharges its responsibilities and obligations to the poor is Socialism but it is none the worse for that.[15]

This is a crude and early form of the new approach, the essence of which was to abandon the notion of social assistance as something on the fringe of policy dealing with a small class of outcasts, and to substitute the idea that social policy was an integral part of total policy and was concerned with the normal needs of all, or nearly all, the members of the society. As a half-way house between the old and the new we meet phrases like that used by Bismarck when he spoke of 'the right that men have to be taken care of when, from no fault of their own, they become unfit for work'.[16] The implication is that in most cases the poor are to blame for their poverty, but that there are some who have no cause to be ashamed of having been reduced to a shameful state.

The next stage in the advance brings in the idea of solidarity, or social and political integration, and it asks for recognition of claims based on a lifetime of useful work for society. We can hear it voiced by Millerand in 1901 when he spoke of the 'social debt' to the aged and went on: 'It is not possible . . . that the aged who have done their duty in working all their life should at the moment when they are no longer able to work be abandoned by the society which they served so faithfully.'[17]

And this leads on to the statement by the French Minister of Labour in 1922, explaining a Bill for social insurance: 'The essential point is that society as a whole should, in a spirit of solidarity, assist the wage-earners to defend them-

[15] S. Maccoby: *The English Radical Tradition, 1763–1914*, p. 201.

[16] B. E. Shenfield: *Social Policies for Old Age*, p. 103.

[17] C. W. Pipkin: *Social Politics and Modern Democracies*, Vol. II, p. 174.

selves against the dangers by which they are constantly threatened.'[18]

The call is for solidarity to protect one class in society from dangers which threaten that class alone, and which are inherent in the social order and cannot, apparently, be eliminated from it. We are reminded of an earlier example of a similar attitude found among the 'Socialists of the Chair' (*Kathedersozialisten*) in Germany and expressed in the classic literature of *Sozialpolitik*. This, as Professor Boettcher has explained elsewhere, was a cross between an academic discipline and a social policy which aimed, not at any fundamental change, but only at a correction of the defects of the contemporary capitalist system. It started from the conception of society as divided into groups or classes, and sought means for strengthening the weakest class, the wage-earners, in its struggle with the stronger class of employers.[19] But the *Kathedersozialisten* were also for solidarity. Gustav Schmoller, their leading spokesman, said that the task of nineteenth-century government was 'to resolve the conflict between the fourth estate and the classes above it, and to reincorporate the fourth estate harmoniously into the organism of state and society'.[20]

Have we now reached the point at which we can say that the British social system in the 1940's achieved a still closer degree of integration, that this was combined with an exceptionally strong consensus as to the meaning of the system, and that this is the explanation of the phenomenon we call the 'Welfare State'? This is too large a question to be answered here in detail, and all I can do is to indicate some of the evidence which might be held to justify an affirmative answer. First, the legislation of the 1940's finally dismantled the old three-tier system of the independent, the insured and the paupers, and was greeted with acclamation for so doing. This has not yet happened elsewhere. Secondly, the

[18] ibid., p. 196.
[19] Erik Boettcher: *Sozialpolitik und Sozialreform*, Chapter 1.
[20] Gustav Schmoller: 'Die soziale Frage und der preussische Staat', *Preussische Jahrbücher*, xxxii (1873), p. 342.

inspiration which fired the minds of the public when they read the Beveridge Report was drawn from the principles of comprehensiveness and universality rather than from the principle of a guaranteed subsistence. Hubert Henderson maintained that these were very different principles, and in fact that there was no relation 'other than a contradictory relation' between them.[21] Subsistence, or the abolition of want, was the aim of the old system, to be achieved by insurance supplemented by the Poor Law, but universality was quite new. And, as we know, the guarantee of subsistence was never clearly embodied in the legislation, still less achieved in administration; but the popularity of the Welfare State survived. Thirdly, the true symbol of the Welfare State was much more the National Health Service than social insurance, or even family allowances. In a recent inquiry it was found that 92 per cent. of the families questioned said that the Health Service had been of great help, and 82 per cent. said it had been of more help than any other.[22] The Health Service has nothing to do with class relations, poverty, subsistence or the defects of the capitalist system. It typifies humanity fighting against natural ills, as medicine always has done, it suppresses the economic market and replaces it by a calculus of needs, and those who give are distinguished from those who receive, not by superior wisdom, better morals or greater wealth, but by professional skill and knowledge. This, I believe, is what it stands for in most people's minds.

Fourthly, the Welfare State of the 1940's was accompanied by what has been called a 'period of wage restraint' during which 'the T.U.C. took great pains to try to carry the trade union movement with them',[23] and by a very low incidence of disputes. This suggests that, for the time being, the pattern of inequality in the distribution of income could be accepted as intelligible and legitimate, given the social and economic conditions which had emerged from the period of common effort and common endurance during the war. But,

[21] H. D. Henderson: *The Inter-war Years*, p. 207.
[22] P.E.P.: *Family Needs and the Social Services*, pp. 35-6.
[23] *The Times*, January 26, 1961.

if this is significant, then it must be equally significant that the truce was of short duration and soon yielded place to the familiar pattern of annual wage claims and frequent strikes.

Mention of the war reminds us of the important question of the historical setting of the various national welfare systems. The experiences of the three countries have been very different. France, says Professor Reynaud, emerged from the trials of the war with a new solidarity born of the resistance, and adopted social policy almost unanimously; it was *un élan*, and not a compromise. Since then the political scene has been greatly disturbed and the confidence in the wisdom of governments shaken. More than one measure has been defeated by popular or professional opposition. Now, says Professor Reynaud, the period of ideological debate is over, and the issues that provoke discussion are technical and not matters of principle. But it almost seems that this is not because a strong, positive consensus has been achieved, but rather because there is an almost apathetic acceptance of the mechanism of social security, even when it is not very well understood. This may be in part the result of the ever livelier interest shown in problems of economic development, in both the most advanced and the most backward areas of France. Germany, Professor Boettcher tells us, reacted strongly against its experience of totalitarian government, and in fact against almost any governmental interference with the private affairs of the citizens. The mood was one of political and economic liberalism, and naturally of social liberalism also. The Social Market Economy was acceptable, but any move towards the Welfare State was regarded with suspicion. However, the pressure in that direction, associated in particular with the need to provide for the war victims and the refugees, could not be wholly resisted. The result has been, he says, confusion of theory and incoherence of practice. And Germany too, like France, has put its maximum effort into economic development.

In England the story was very different. Solidarity grew without a break through the war and into the first years of peace. The Beveridge Report was a best-seller because it offered, while the war was still in progress, a blue-print of what the nation was fighting for. British war aims were expressed in terms of social justice. The Welfare State could enjoy a ready-made consensus. But the crucial point is, I believe, that the Welfare State was born into a world of austerity—of rationing, price control, coupons, rent restriction, and houses requisitioned for the use of the homeless. It was not that these restrictions on the free market were regarded as good in themselves and desirable elements in the new social order. Some might be so and others not. But they provided as a background to the welfare legislation a society committed to 'fair shares' and to a distribution of real income which could be rationally justified and was not the unpredictable result of the supposedly blind forces of a competitive market, in which everybody was entitled to take as much as he could get. It was as a part of this system of regulated consumption that the trade unions refrained from wage demands.

By the middle of the fifties the Austerity Society had passed away and the Affluent Society was taking its place. The restraints on self-enrichment and competitive consumption were removed, and sensational stories were told of astronomic salaries, limitless expense accounts, and fabulous speculative gains in real estate and elsewhere. Prices rose, wage demands became an annual event, and inflation deprived some of the welfare benefits of their original value; the gap was filled by National Assistance. It was in these circumstances that the basic principles of the Welfare State came under attack. The main objectives of the attack were the principle of universality in social insurance, and the provision of certain welfare services free to all. It was argued that the distribution of a large volume of real and money income through a complicated system of public administration might be justified in times of scarcity, but in times of prosperity increased productivity should enable nearly all the people to meet nearly all their needs out of their own pockets and through the mechanism of the market, thus reducing free or subsidized welfare provisions once more to the level of a peripheral affair. 'To continue applying it (the Beveridge principle) in 1960', said a Conservative M.P., 'is to swallow the drug after the disease has gone', and Lord Hailsham asked whether a system of social services 'determined by the spectacle of Victorian poverty and of under-employment between the wars' was the ideal system 'for a society enjoying full employment in mid-twentieth century conditions'. 'We are not a nation of paupers', said Mr Butler, 'we are a nation of prosperity.'[24]

So it seems that the Welfare State as we knew it in the 1940's, or at least the consensus which sustained it, has been smothered by the Affluent Society. And perhaps we should conclude that France and Germany pressed on into the Affluent Society without ever pausing to establish a Welfare State. But this does not mean that British welfare measures will be scrapped. Much has been built which will undoubtedly endure. But there is need for a new model. Perhaps one feature of this model is foreshadowed in the graduated pensions scheme of the Labour Party, which mirrors the arrangements of private enterprise and sets out to beat it at its own game. Perhaps some of the public social services will become more like nationalized industries, trying to balance their budgets by means of contributions from their clients. Or perhaps failure to defeat inflation will cause a return to some of the restrictive measures associated with the period of austerity. Or perhaps, finally, we shall embark on one of those interludes which occur between the periods in which clear-cut social systems appear with recognizable personalities of their own.

[24] *Crossbow*, Autumn 1960, p. 25, and Summer 1959, pp. 57–8.

CHAPTER XV

THE AFFLUENT SOCIETY IN PERSPECTIVE

Adam Smith, you will remember, observed that 'China has been long one of the richest . . . countries in the world', but 'the poverty of the lower ranks of people in China far surpasses that of the most beggarly nations in Europe'.[1] Riches of this kind have nothing in common with the affluence with which we are concerned. Our affluence must be widely distributed through the society and be an attribute of the great majority of the population. But this is not all. The concept of the 'Affluent Society' as developed (not always under that name) in recent years by historians, economists and sociologists implies not merely that affluence should be present but that there should be a certain common attitude towards it. The concept refers to motives as well as to achievement, to ethical as well as to material values.

I said, in parentheses, that this concept appears under several different names. I mean that, in spite of some differences of emphasis, the 'Affluent Society' of Galbraith corresponds to the 'Age of Abundance' of Jessie Bernard, the 'Stage of High Mass Consumption' of Rostow, the 'People of Plenty' of David Potter, and the 'Phase of Incipient Decline' of Riesman; and early traces of the same ideas occur in the well-known work of the Lynds. So we see that our concept has moved in very respectable company. All agree that the central feature of the Affluent Society is a system of large-scale production sustained by mass demand at a high and ever

[1] Adam Smith: *The Wealth of Nations* (1880), p. 55.

rising level. As Jessie Bernard puts it, 'In an age of scarcity
the existence of a class of Haves depends on the existence of
a large class of Have-nots. . . . In an age of abundance, on
the other hand, the existence of a class of Haves depends,
not on a large deprived class, but on an expanding class of
Haves.' Abundance 'creates Haves and Have-mores rather
than Haves and Have-nots'.[2] One might criticize the phras-
ing, but one sees what she means. All agree, too, that the
Affluent Society is distinguished by an extraordinary (in the
literal sense of the word) emphasis on consumption. With
the arrival of abundance, says Potter, 'at once the vital nature
of the change will be apparent; the most critical point in the
functioning of society shifts from production to consumption.'[3] Rostow uses almost the same language: 'The balance
of attention of the society, as it approached and went beyond maturity, shifted from supply to demand, from problems of production to problems of consumption, and of welfare in the widest sense.'[4] Riesman naturally expressed the
same thought in his own peculiar terms: 'While the other-
directed person's tremendous outpouring of energy is channelled into the ever expanding frontiers of consumption, the
inner-directed person's energy was channelled relentlessly
into production.'[5] The other-directed person is, of course, the
typical inhabitant of the affluent society.

Galbraith, however, arrives at the emphasis on consumption by a different route. He sees it as a secondary phenomenon derived from the basic phenomenon of the glorification
of production. Efficient production, he says, came to be the
universally accepted measure of economic achievement. Progress meant simply producing more—and ever more and more.
'Production', he writes, 'remains central to our thoughts.'[6]
But one cannot treat production wholly as an end in itself;
the product must be consumed. So consumption becomes, at

[2] Third World Congress of Sociology, *Transactions*, Vol. III, p. 27.
[3] D. M. Potter: *People of Plenty*, p. 173.
[4] W. W. Rostow: *The Stages of Economic Growth*, p. 73.
[5] D. Riesman: *The Lonely Crowd*, p. 79.
[6] J. K. Galbraith: *The Affluent Society*, p. 97.

one remove from the epicentre, the chief immediate preoccupation of those running the economic system. It is their *chief* preoccupation because, with productive capacity constantly above the level of output, it is easier to increase production than to stimulate consumption. Thus we arrive at the situation in which, as Galbraith puts it, 'wants are increasingly created by the process by which they are satisfied', that is to say new products, as they filter into the pattern of social life, become objects of desire to those striving to emulate their neighbours, and the whole process is immensely fortified by advertisement, public relations campaigns, and hire purchase credits.[7] Percival and Paul Goodman, writing a few years earlier than Galbraith, were even more explicit about the consequences of this situation. 'Hand in hand with a planned expanding production', they wrote, 'there must be a planned expanding demand'; it would not do to leave this to the advertisers. Production had suffered because the urges to 'emulation, ostentation and sheer wastefulness' had not been strong enough, until the demands of war restored the balance. 'Then, let us reverse the analysis and suggest how, even in peace time, men can be as efficiently wasteful as possible.'[8] This somewhat fanciful and eccentric presentation of the case agrees as regards the historical sequence of events with the picture drawn by Rostow. The first steps towards high mass consumption were taken in the United States during the boom of the 1920's, but they were checked by the depression. The movement was restarted by the exceptional demands of the war and continued in the post-war boom, gathering strength all the time. The beginnings were noticed by the Lynds in Middletown. 'Today', they wrote, 'Middletown lives by a credit economy that is available in some form to nearly every family in the community.' And they drew attention to the subtle effect this had on the way of life of the business class, inducing them 'to vote the Republican ticket, to adopt golf as their recreation, and to refrain from "queer", i.e., atypical behavior'. As early as 1890

[7] J. K. Galbraith: *The Affluent Society*, p. 124.
[8] *Communitas*, pp. 61–2.

the local press had said that 'advertising is to business what fertilizer is to farm', but the transformation of the function of advertising from that of attracting demand to that of creating demand still lay in the future. But there is a definitely Galbraithian ring about the statement of the leading local paper in 1925 that 'the American citizen's first importance is no longer that of citizen but that of consumer. Consumption is a new necessity.'[9] This need not alter our judgement that the Affluent Society, in its full maturity, is a post-war phenomenon.

We arrive at the same judgement if we look more closely into the question of the motives that inspire consumption. We see at once that there is a sharp distinction to be made between the conspicuous consumption of Veblen and the high mass consumption of Rostow or the similar picture drawn by Galbraith. It is the difference between the distinctive attribute of the few and the typical behaviour of the masses. One might, in fact, almost say that what prevails in the Affluent Society is inconspicuous consumption, meaning by this that the effort to consume springs from a desire to be like our neighbours, not conspicuously unlike them. There is, at least, enough in this idea to make us question the commonly expressed view that modern American society—and British also—is outstandingly competitive in character. Of course salesmanship, operating through high-pressure advertising, is competitive. But is consumption competitive too? Potter, I am sure, meant that it was when he said that 'the American character is in a large measure a group of responses to an unusually competitive situation'.[10] But he was thinking of long-term influences and not only of post-war society. Riesman, deeply concerned to pin-point the significance of the passage from the dominance of the inner-directed to that of the other-directed personality, draws subtle distinctions regarding the propensity to consume. 'The conspicuous consumer', he writes, 'is engaged in an externalized kind of

[9] R. S. and H. M. Lynd: *Middletown*, pp. 46, 47 and 88.
[10] op. cit., p. 60.

rivalry, as indicated by Veblen's use of such terms as "ostensible", "emulative", "conspicuous", and the rest of his beautifully ironic thesaurus. The other-directed consumer *may* compete in what looks like the same way, but only to the degree that the peers impel him to. His desire to outshine, as we should expect from his mode of peer-group socialization, is very much muted.'[11]

However, as Riesman is careful to admit, this does not entirely eliminate the element of competitive rivalry from the situation. There is a fringe area of 'marginal innovation' in which a modicum of differential consumption is not only permitted but is rewarded with increased popularity. More generally, too, it may be said that a passionate desire to be in the swim, to possess all the outward and visible signs of belonging, and also to step up one's level of consumption when others do so, though in origin a mass-produced motive is in operation an individualistic one. It can evoke a mercenary selfishness and a spirit of rivalry in trying to grab whatever is going before others can get it. And one must not forget that the Affluent Society is also a socially mobile society, and that even its other-directed inhabitants are often determined not only to keep up with the Joneses but also to catch up with the Robinsons.

In our society incomes are extensively standardized by means of wage and salary scales drawn up by central and local government for their hordes of employees, or fixed by collective bargaining between employers and trade unions; it would be surprising if this accent on personal gain did not foster a disposition to look for ways of picking up additions to what the standardized systems of payment prescribe. One way of doing this is by shift-work bonuses and overtime. Ferdynand Zweig, in his recent study, *The Worker in an Affluent Society*, observes that the attitude to overtime is the resultant of two contradictory forces, represented by the statements: 'Everybody cares for overtime; the extras make all the difference'; and 'Nobody really likes overtime; it's a social

[11] op. cit., p. 123.

evil.' Both are true, but the first refers to 'extra money' and the second to 'extra work'. And a couple of pages earlier he has remarked that today 'it is money, money all the time'.[12] Other, and perhaps even more popular, ways of achieving the same result are speculation and gambling, including premium bonds and football pools, or various forms of fiddling, some just inside and others definitely outside the frontiers of legality.

Evidence of this kind of acquisitiveness is found at all levels of the social hierarchy. Douglas Jay, in a chapter entitled 'The Windfall State',[13] describes the ways in which members of the business world expect to receive manna from heaven in the form of capital gains and other bonuses which fall so indiscriminately into their outstretched hands today that they cannot be regarded as rewards for exceptional services. This has provoked at least one member of the right wing of the Tory Party to fulminate against devices which manage 'to achieve a standard of living bearing no relation to the income on which tax is paid', thanks to 'capital gains; expense accounts; free cars and petrol; cash out of the till; subsidized house purchase; members of the family in bogus employment as anything from directors to clerks; houses registered as offices; household staff carried on the firm's books; free telephones; bogus business trips abroad—the list is endless and even the advertisements now say ". . . plus free car and usual fringe benefits".'[14] And in a recent survey of saving and investment it was found that those asked why they bought shares rarely mentioned dividends as an attraction. They spoke of 'capital gains', 'tax-free profits', 'making money', or just 'for the gamble'.[15]

Ferdynand Zweig, looking at a lower level in the social scale, says that 'the most striking trend is the rise in acquisitive instincts as expressed in shop-floor behaviour. Money-mindedness plays an ever-increasing part in a man's attitude

[12] op. cit., p. 70.
[13] *Socialism in the New Society*, Chapter 21.
[14] Letter in *The Times* from H. J. Hickey, March 27, 1962.
[15] *The Times*, March 21, 1962.

to his work.' This is the result of 'the revolution of rising expectations', with its focus on durable consumer goods. And he concludes with the following impressive passage: 'The acquisitive society has succeeded in expanding its frontiers and converting its natural antagonists to its own creed. It seems as if the acquisitive society has only now come into maturity, reaching a uniformity and regularity which could hardly have been foreseen a generation ago.'[16] Finally Mr Fyvel, in his fascinating study *The Insecure Offenders*, stepping outside the boundaries of normal respectable society, finds among the Teddy Boys and their successors the same acquisitive spirit. It is consumption that eggs them on, typified by their expensive and frequently renewed suits of clothes, a form of consumption which, though conventional to the group, is conspicuous enough to the outsider.

Do these investigators exaggerate? Are they seeing life today with jaundiced eyes? It may be so, but their observations should not be too lightly brushed aside. It is not only in the works of British writers that one finds these references to a moral issue. In the United States, in the middle 1950's, the Federal Council of Churches sponsored a series of studies on the theme 'Ethics and Economic Life'. One of them, edited and introduced by Elizabeth Hoyt, opens with the sentence: 'Americans are faced by a new kind of issue—the rapid increase of income', and it is evident that the subject of the series is the ethical dangers of affluence. I do not wish to suggest that the Affluent Society is a happy hunting-ground for the devil in which men fall victim to temptation as ripe fruit falls from the tree. But I do believe that it would be wrong to belittle the ethical issue. Anthony Crosland said recently that Socialists 'may justly attack the vulgar bias towards unregulated private interest which is one of the characteristics of our prosperous society. They must not, however, attack this society root and branch . . . Any normal socialist will whole-heartedly rejoice at the spread of material affluence.' So far I can agree with him. But when he says that

[16] op. cit., pp. 68, 206 and 212.

this affluence favours personal freedom, social justice, an egalitarian society, democratic anti-paternalism,[17] I find I have reservations. These blessings will not flow automatically from affluence. In fact I believe that the ethical conflict between public policy and private acquisitiveness permeates some of the most important social problems of our age.

So far I have been looking at the Affluent Society in the perspective of some of the literature—mostly American—to which the concept owes its existence. Before I go on to examine it in a different perspective, I want to fix in your minds three points arising from what I have said which will have a prominent part to play when we apply the concept to the subject that most deeply concerns this Conference, namely the social problems of our own country.

The first arises from the alleged concentration of the Affluent Society on the satisfaction of needs which, by definition, are not basic, since they are in large measure created by the productive process itself, aided by high-pressure advertising. This state of affairs, and the attitude of mind that goes with it, must be compared and contrasted with the preoccupation with the poverty line, basic subsistence, and the minimum standard which dominated much of our thinking about social policy from the days of Booth and Rowntree and the early Fabians to the time of the Beveridge Report and the Welfare State. This approach now seems to be out-of-date, and there is a danger that we may, in discarding it, repudiate at the same time the whole apparatus of which it was the original foundation, instead of seeking to adapt it to the new circumstances. There are also, of course, subtle ways in which the change of emphasis affects the system of priorities that directs our judgement, and our general way of looking at things. I have recently noticed in statements supporting a claim for increased wages or salaries, that what is stressed is not so much the miserable pittance received by those at the bottom of the scale as the oppressively low ceiling that marks the maximum height to which those at the top can climb. It

[17] C. A. R. Crosland: 'The Future of the Left' in *Encounter*, March 1960, p. 12.

is as though one first decided on the top figure and calculated the rest of the scale from there.

The second point comes from the gospel according to Galbraith. He argues, as I explained, that production remains central to our thoughts in the Affluent Society, and that the need to stimulate consumption arises when productive capacity outstrips effective demand. This view is advanced as an historical observation, not a theoretical deduction. It describes what happened in the United States. In that rather curious book from which I quoted earlier, Percival and Paul Goodman maintain that, in the decade before the war, 'the American industrial plant ran frequently at less than 50 per cent. of its productivity; nevertheless, the production was in excess of even generous minimum standards of consumption'.[18] I find it a little difficult to accept this estimate, but the fact remains that, in the American picture of the rise of the Affluent Society, production is seen as outrunning consumption, whereas we in this country are constantly being told that we are getting into serious trouble because, in *our* Affluent Society, consumption persistently outruns production.

The third point is the ethical one. It is alleged that as our national affluence increases, the values that govern our thoughts and actions become more materialistic; also many of us fall a prey to self-seeking and acquisitiveness. It is not my intention to pass judgement on the moral virtues or failings of my fellows. My interest in the matter is rather different, and more precise. It is a question of legitimacy versus a mild form of *anomie*. If, for a moment, we made a rudimentary use of the technique of the 'ideal type', we can envisage a society in which all rewards received for work done, services rendered or money invested are determined by reference to principles which are generally accepted. It follows that income differences and wage differentials are also so regulated. In such circumstances all claims to wealth or welfare would have to establish their legitimacy before they were met. Sud-

[18] *Communitas,* p. 60.

den outbursts of conspicuous consumption, indicative of sudden increases of income or property, would be regarded, not with envious admiration, but with deep suspicion. Maybe some windfalls would be permitted as legitimate, but they would be few and of minor importance. Undoubtedly such a system—and I am thinking of a democratic, not a totalitarian society—would involve some redistribution of income by the State and a generous provision of welfare services. Adding all this together, and slipping surreptitiously from the 'ideal type' to the Party programme, we could call it a system of fair shares and mutual aid.

Now compare this picture with the other, the picture of mild economic *anomie*. Here we find a social order based on the major premise that free competition and individual enterprise are the highest goods, and that, provided there is no open and demonstrable breach of the law, the title to everything gained by these means is a legitimate one. The mottoes of such a society are: 'finding's keeping', 'what I have I hold', 'I can do what I like with my own', and so on, all implying that the mere fact of acquisition (again assuming formal legality) is proof both of right and of merit. What is lacking is the concept of legitimacy based on a principle of social justice. Sudden outbursts of conspicuous consumption are not only individually admired, but collectively regarded as sure indices of national prosperity. I call this economic *anomie*, because in its more extravagant forms the distribution of wealth defies logical analysis, makes no sense and conforms to no defensible pattern. It is 'mild', because social life goes on in the main in an orderly way, and the bulk of the population may be having a hell of a good time.

Having pointed the contrast, let me now destroy a large part of it. Since the first type of society is a free democratic one, with a wide range of incomes and a hierarchy of social status, while the second is on the whole orderly and law-abiding and makes provision by public services for the needs of the economically unsuccessful or unfortunate, the outward and visible differences between their respective conditions of life may seem small. But, I believe, the differences between their philosophies of life are large and significant. And they are the differences between the philosophies of the Welfare State and the Affluent Society. I am not suggesting that the Welfare State can never be affluent, or that the Affluent Society makes no provision for welfare. My point is that many difficult problems arise when you try to marry the two contrasted social philosophies in a society which is regarded by half its inhabitants as a Welfare State and by the other half as an Affluent Society, when in fact it is neither.

And with that pregnant but somewhat elusive thought, let me turn to my second perspective, that provided by British history. I shall begin by going back a hundred years or so to the time of the mid-Victorians. This was a period which, according to Asa Briggs, possessed 'a real unity of its own'. Its mood, he says, was conditioned by five main influences: prosperity—'the skies were rarely clouded'; national security—'Britain ruled the waves'; trust in institutions—'never seriously shaken'; a common moral code—'based on duty and self-restraint'; and belief in free discussion and inquiry.[19] In terms of the categories I am using, it could be classed as a society which believed itself to be an Affluent Society but was mistaken. The country was rich and powerful by the standards of the time, though without the wide diffusion of wealth and the spendthrift habits of the present age. It was the workshop of the world, the home of freedom and democracy, and a haven of internal peace. Of course there were the poor, but we know on the best authority that they are always with us. There were also the paupers, but they represented to the people in those days only a peripheral and, it was hoped, a temporary problem. Most of them were assumed to be the victims of their own failings, and there was no reason why these should be passed on to the next generation. A stern Poor Law, they thought, and spreading habits of thrift, aided by the opportunities that prosperity brings, should prevent this.

But what impresses one most is their stubborn resistance to

[19] A. S. Briggs: *Victorian People*, pp. 16–17.

the growing volume of revelations about the widespread misery, cruelty, squalor and destitution which crawled in the basement of their grandiose and luxurious building. Only the belief that theirs was a society of a new type, for which these things were but a minor and temporary anxiety, could have sustained their confidence so long in face of the evidence that disproved its basic assumptions. They shuddered as each disclosure struck them, pronounced the situation it revealed 'intolerable', appointed committees of inquiry, and even passed some usually ineffectual laws, but they made no serious attempt to incorporate new elements into the fabric of the social system with which they were so well satisfied or to modify the creed by which their thoughts were guided. When I say 'they', I mean the bulk of the public and the politicians. As Oliver MacDonagh has pointed out in an important article, a 'revolution in government' was taking place in face of considerable opposition, within the administrative system, which finally led to the replacement of the belief that social evils could be cured by legislation alone by the realization that you must have continuous, long-term action by a permanent, professional executive staff. He calls this a 'new and more or less conscious Fabianism', and says that it had already brought into existence a modicum of collectivism before 'the catastrophic and very general collapse of political individualism in the last quarter of the nineteenth century'.[20] Asa Briggs expresses the same general opinion when he says that the unity of the mid-Victorian period is deceptive. It concealed cracks and friction which in due course destroyed the mood of confidence. Finally revelations of wider import and incidents carrying graver threats to their peace of mind shattered the complacency of the Victorians and opened the door to radical reformers. Looking back down the perspective of history, we can see that the policy which went into action after 1906, inspired by ideas which took shape in the previous quarter of a century, started the movement which led eventually to the legislation of the 1940's. Thus the first pseudo-

[20] Oliver MacDonagh: 'The Nineteenth Century Revolution in Government', in *The Historical Journal*, 1958, pp. 60–3.

Affluent Society wilted before the attacks of the Welfare
State, which now, in its turn, is facing the attacks of the
second, less pseudo, but still not quite genuine, Affluent Society of the 1950's and 1960's.

A notable feature of this story is the vigorous swing of the
pendulum from side to side. The self-satisfaction of the Victorians strikes us today as overweening. But the triumphant
cries of the architects of the Welfare State were also somewhat immoderate. Take, for example, this passage from a
speech by Lloyd George, delivered shortly after the passing
of the National Insurance Act. He was, of course, speaking in
Wales. 'I can see the Old Age Pension Act, the National Insurance Act and many another Act in their trail, descending like
breezes from the hills of my native land, sweeping into the
mist-laden valleys, and clearing the gloom away until the
rays of God's sun have pierced the narrowest window.'[21]
This sounds quite ludicrous to us, and we dismiss it as typical
of the oratory of a past age. But when we move on to the
Beveridge Report and the final establishment of the Welfare
State we may be equally amazed, though not in the same way
amused, by the dramatic presentation of the programme and
the deep emotions that it aroused. The Report is, without
doubt, a technical masterpiece, but that alone cannot explain
why it was hailed as the manifesto of a new social order. It
was a best-seller both here and on the Continent, it was offered to the troops to show them what they were fighting for,
and hastily withdrawn on the orders of the War Office
(which, according to Beveridge, sealed the fate of Churchill
at the general election) and, as Lady Beveridge tells us, it
was described by the Archbishop of Canterbury as 'the first
time anyone had set out to embody the whole spirit of the
Christian ethic in an Act of Parliament'.[22] But what did it
contain, apart from plans for tidying up the jungle of social
administration? A cynic might reply that it promised to every
man, woman and child in the country that, if for any reason

[21] Herbert du Parcq: *Life of David Lloyd George*, Vol. IV, p. 80.
[22] W. H. Beveridge: *Power and Influence*, p. 332, and Janet Beveridge: *Beveridge and His Plan*, p. 135.

whatsoever they fell on evil days, the State would give them the wherewithal to continue balancing on the tightrope of the poverty line until their circumstances righted themselves. But of course the Report meant much more than this.

Undoubtedly the sincerity and enthusiasm of Beveridge himself, and his colourful language about the attack on the five giants of Want, Disease, Ignorance, Squalor and Idleness, helped greatly to give the Report its remarkable impact. But that is only part of the explanation. First we must add to the measures of social insurance which were fully elaborated in the Report the three assumptions on which the proposals were explicitly based, namely family allowances, a national health service and full employment. And then we should, for good measure, throw in the Education Act as well. Add all these to the universal, test-free subsistence minimum, and you have something very substantial indeed, something that could legitimately be regarded as ushering in a new phase of our social history. But on top of all this we must recognize that the impression of a new adventure was fostered by the common experiences of a nation united in a supreme war effort, and determined that it should not have been made in vain. Whatever happened, peace would initiate a new phase of some kind. And on top of that we must remember that the measures described or foreshadowed in the Beveridge Report were put into effect during a period of scarcity, when Britain can best be described as an Austerity Society. I use this term to denote a society which, when faced by scarcity, imposes on itself a régime which demands self-denial in the common interest. If properly administered it becomes a society governed by the principles of fair shares and mutual aid, and what I have called legitimacy of economic rewards. I am not suggesting that these principles can only be applied in an Austerity Society, but rather that they *must* be applied there, if the society in question is a democratic, law-abiding and united one. So we may say that Beveridge's language was justified, because he was announcing the take-off into a Welfare State compounded of his own insurance plans, all the other measures I have listed, plus the quite exceptional national spirit bred by the war and the situation that followed it. The popular mood was as important in the 1940's as it had been in the 1850's.

And now the pendulum swings again and voices are calling on us to scrap the lot. It is obvious that our social problems today must derive much of their character from these oscillations from one side to the other—from the inflated self-satisfaction of the mid-Victorians to the exaggerated glorification of radical social reform and the machinery of the Welfare State, and from this again to the unfounded belief that we have now at last become a fully-fledged representative of the Affluent Society, in which poverty is really only a peripheral phenomenon. We set up the Welfare State as an idol to be worshipped—or some of us did—as a monument showing the five giants of Beveridge being toppled off their pedestal. And now some of us have started to worship another monument crowned by an object which is beginning to look like a golden calf. The antithesis between the two objects of worship was certainly sharpened by the association of the former with the period of austerity—which might be thought to be an historical accident—and the abruptness of our leap forward to embrace the latter. But the clash between the principles governing the two systems, between legitimacy and acquisitiveness, is, I believe, a real one. And yet the situation cannot possibly be resolved by the total victory of one over the other. We are not going to return to austerity nor to abandon welfare. The oil and vinegar for our political salad need to be combined to form a palatable dressing, and I hope this Conference[23] may help us to find a suitable mixer for the purpose.

I have now looked at the Affluent Society in two different perspectives, that provided by the literature, mostly American, in which the concept was evolved, and the other given us by the panorama of British history. I shall conclude by making a few consequential observations about the problems with which this Conference is concerned, remembering al-

[23] A conference of the British Sociological Association at Brighton in March 1962.

ways that my business at this point is to pose questions and not to confuse the issue for the contributors of papers by trying to answer them in advance.

I mentioned one circumstance which is likely to affect all, or nearly all, our social problems when I said that ours is not a genuine Affluent Society. This is because, as I have explained, it took a short cut and missed one of the important preparatory phases. As Alan Peacock pointed out at an earlier Conference of this Association, economists during the war laid great emphasis on 'the maintenance of effective demand as the main problem of the post-war situation', and regarded improved social security measures as one way of achieving this. But the effect was to impede the investment in industry needed to step up production.[24] Now we have many of the typical features of the Affluent Society, full employment which maximizes effective demand, high-pressure salesmanship to spur it on, social forces urging ever greater consumption either in competition with or in imitation of our neighbours and peers, with the familiar result of regularly repeated organized claims for higher wages or salaries. This is all very fine if, as in the Galbraith model, it is a high and even a surplus productive capacity that gives the push that starts the wheel spinning, but with us it is not. We seem to have decided to behave like an Affluent Society on the consumer side—we felt we earned this by our war service—but we have not bothered to do the same on the producer side. The result is a chronically inflationary situation which Governments must try to curb, by exhortations, pay-pauses and the like, while tax-payers clamour for a reduction of public expenditure, including that on education, health and social services. The latest development is a bold attempt to reintroduce the principle of legitimacy into our acquisitive society through the operations of a mixed National Economic Development Council.

All this is very familiar, and I must not labour it. The questions that arise for us here are: How deep are the effects

[24] 'Economic Aspects of Contemporary Social Policy', in Report of the Conference of the British Sociological Association, 1953, p. 4.

of this situation on the political attitudes and activities of the various classes of the population? Does the fact that the Government is bound to intervene, or at least to nag, make *it* rather than capital the target for the assaults of organized labour? And is the character of class alignments, as distinct from status groups, at all affected by the fact that the bombardment of the Government by claims for higher incomes comes from every quarter of the society, from university teachers, civil servants, school teachers, engineers, railwaymen —everybody? It looks as if we were all in the same boat, and that it is not quite the luxury liner we thought it would be. Is there a tendency for the economic interest groups which we are wont to refer to as classes to become more and more detached, both in composition and in spirit, from the stratified layers of the status system? In the article to which I have already referred, Jessie Bernard quotes a remark by Richard Hofstadter which bears directly on this point:

> We have at all times two kinds of processes going on in inextricable connection with each other: *interest politics*, the clash of material aims and needs among various groups and blocs; and *status politics*, the clash of various projective rationalizations arising from status aspirations and other personal motives. In times of depression and economic discontent . . . politics is more closely a matter of interests . . . In times of general prosperity and well-being on the material plane, status considerations among the masses can become much more influential.[25]

In our rather bogus situation we have both the status aspirations of affluence and some of the economic conflicts associated with depression. So what is the effect of all this on our political behaviour?

And now, what is the effect of affluence, or of an affluent pattern of consumption, on the status system itself? I have quoted Ferdynand Zweig's conclusions about the new acquisitive society. They may well be challenged. They are based on

[25] Jessie Bernard: *The Age of Abundance*, p. 38.

a small and not wholly representative sample, drawn from five large-scale and well-conducted enterprises belonging on the whole to prosperous and expanding industries. But his observations are interesting and helpful, provided they are treated as hypotheses rather than as statements of established fact. He finds that saving by wage-earners has spread but is still exceptional. When it occurs, the amount involved may be large. The purchase of a house provides one of the most powerful incentives and, if achieved, has a deep effect on social attitudes. I think he would say that there is now a recognizable model of the saving working-class family which is having an influence on the atmosphere in working-class neighbourhoods. 'The term class', he writes, 'was invariably linked with snobbishness but rarely, if at all, with class struggle.' And in general class consciousness, and class sub-consciousness, were on the decline. Of particular interest is his observation that class was often regarded as something that belonged inside the factory only. 'I am working-class only in the works, but outside I am like anyone else', said one man. 'Here I am a worker, but outside I am a human being', said another.[26] It is not altogether easy to combine these various comments and to draw from them a consistent general picture. But it may be that there is a consciousness of working-class status in the factory, in the sense of recognition of a common interest derived from a common function, but that this is rarely linked with the idea of the class struggle—it is more localized and less bitter than that. In the world outside there is plenty of status aspiration, but it does not generally crystallize into a consciousness of belonging to a particular social group. How much truth is there in this? And is it one facet of the dissociation of economic interest groups from social status positions? These questions are worth asking.

The imperfect character of our Affluent Society also affects the problems of poverty and the social services. Two obvious examples are the trouble caused to social insurance by inflation, and the rapid spread of private and occupational wel-

[26] op. cit., pp. 134–5.

fare schemes, especially for pensions. The question of how to balance or to integrate these with the public schemes is crucial and urgent, and it figures very definitely in current political programmes. There is much popular education needed on the subject of the expenditure on services like health and education. When I was lecturing recently in Berlin, a young American asked whether it would not be better to transfer expenditure from unproductive use in the National Health Service to productive use in the manufacture of armaments. An argument followed, but he was quite incapable of seeing that either medical services must be cut down absolutely, or else the cost merely transferred from the taxes paid by the citizen to the fees paid by the citizen, which would not of itself directly alter the distribution of national resources. In a recent letter in *The Times* advocating cuts in expenditure on education and health, the writer explicitly stated that this would give the doctors more time for really important work and prevent education being wasted on pupils who could make no use of it.[27] There is much confused thinking on this point, and a failure to distinguish between proposals to change the way of collecting the money to pay for a service, and proposals to apply a discriminating (it is hoped) deterrent to prevent wasteful use of it.

There is also confused thinking about the alleged abolition of poverty by the Affluent Society—or, to be fair, I should say the almost complete abolition of primary poverty. The introduction of the adjective 'primary' has a big effect which it is not easy to interpret. The results of Rowntree's distinction between primary and secondary poverty have not been entirely happy, and I wonder how valuable these concepts are today. If we use an extravagantly high standard of careful expenditure, then much of what will be classed as secondary poverty will, by ordinary human standards, be primary. If we set a low standard, then secondary poverty merges into problem families—the really bad managers shade off into the hopeless managers. And perhaps we could do with a new con-

[27] Letter in *The Times* from C. Beattie, March 21, 1962.

cept of tertiary poverty, for the situation in which both the requisite income and the good management are present, but the goods and services are simply not obtainable. I am thinking, of course, particularly of housing, but also of some personal services needed by the old, the sick, the handicapped and those overburdened with large families. Finally, when carrying out the minute analysis of types and causes of poverty which we need so much today, we shall obviously distinguish carefully between poverty caused by insufficient earnings and poverty caused by inadequate social benefits. But we must also look at that different kind of poverty which might be called comparative deprivation. It is bound to be augmented in a situation in which private welfare schemes cover a part only, though a large part, of the population, while quite a lot of people, having at one time been included in them, have subsequently, for one reason or another, dropped out.

I think I have said enough to illustrate how my two perspectives can help us to recognize the problems today. But before I end I want to refer briefly to one other matter which may occupy a place in the background of our thoughts. When I was living in Paris recently, I was amused to find that, in the context of the public transport of that city, the word *affluence* meant the rush hour—the hour at which streams of men and women flow together to create a mob, or mass, which is drawn remorselessly through the network of passages provided for its use. I wonder whether this is symbolic of the affluence we are discussing? Does it, too, herd human beings into a mass? Some time ago I stated categorically that the principle of the Welfare State was the principle of individualism; the cash benefits it offers are claimed by individual right, and in its services of education and health it does its best to give to each what he requires to meet his individual needs. Of course any system that serves a whole nation is bound to contain much that leans in the other direction, towards mass uniformity, but the principle should be strong enough to outweigh this. In the Affluent Society we see again two opposite tendencies. There are mass communication and mass advertising, busily regimenting millions of other-directed souls on the road they want them to tread. But there are also the individual and family aspirations to keep up with or outstrip the neighbours, and to climb towards the top which, as they think, affluence has broadened so as to make room for all. And perhaps there is also a consciousness of individual responsibilities to one's family, one's neighbours and even to the community, responsibilities which force themselves on the attention more insistently as affluence begins to provide the means with which to meet them. What will be the final balance between these different forces? This may well be one of the most important issues for a democratic society in the mid-twentieth century.

CHAPTER XVI

VOLUNTARY ACTION

Voluntary action is a theme whose debate engenders a merry tussle between instinct and reason. 'It will always have a place in a democracy,' says Instinct. 'It represents one of the fundamental and eternal values.' 'Why?', says Reason (as always). 'Your ancestors said the same of charity as they understood it. And yet you now hate that old-world charity and deny its virtue. Will your voluntary action stand better against the criticism of future generations? And what is "voluntary action" anyway?' Challenged in this manner, Instinct tries to reason, and as often as not becomes lost in a maze from which it can only escape by jumping the hedges, borne on the wings of irrational faith and illogical conviction. This does not mean that Instinct is wrong, but it does suggest that we have here a problem to which there is no tidy solution. This is clearly the conclusion reached by Lord Lindsay, who writes:

> Democracy is a form of constitution intended to leave room for and encourage growth and newness and invention. In the modern world that cannot be done without organizations so large that they choke the freedom they are intended to defend. Yet the remedy cannot be anarchy. It is obviously a mixture of tidiness and looseness, or unity and diversity: of statutory and voluntary. For the proper proportions of the mixture there is no recipe. It has to be worked out on the spot all the time.

And again: 'Voluntary work ought to be efficient and yet its efficiency is sometimes its undoing.'[1] What shall we call this: a tissue of contradictions, blind opportunism or practical common sense? There can be little doubt that it is the last of these.

In his latest book,[2] Lord Beveridge wisely refrains from staking his reputation on the discovery of water-tight definitions. He is content to describe his subject in operational terms. 'Voluntary', he says, means 'not under the directions of any authority wielding the power of the State', and 'action' means action 'outside each citizen's home for improving the conditions of life for him and for his fellows' (p. 8). It would be easy, but futile, to pick holes in these phrases if one chose to treat them as definitions. Take them as signposts or boundary marks and they make it sufficiently clear what he is going to talk about. The signposts point, not only to the voluntary social services, but also to the Friendly Societies; not only to the philanthropic motive, but also to the mutual aid motive. And here at once we meet one of the crucial problems of the subject.

Henry Mess, in a book on which he was working shortly before his death and which was completed by others, expressed the view that 'mutual aid is to be contrasted with help rendered by the privileged to the unprivileged . . . It is still implicit in the notion of voluntary social service that some help shall be given by the privileged to the unprivileged.'[3] Lord Beveridge could agree with the first sentence, for he himself distinguishes between the two motives, especially in their historical manifestations. But he would probably wish to qualify the second, for fear it might be taken to imply that the two motives must be kept apart. It is one of his definite recommendations that 'Mutual Aid, in the more equal society of the future, must broaden into philanthropy, into the promotion of social advancement, not simply each

[1] *Voluntary Social Services*, ed. A. F. C. Bourdillon, pp. 305–6.
[2] *Voluntary Action: A Report on Methods of Social Advance* (George Allen & Unwin).
[3] *Voluntary Social Services since 1918*, ed. Gertrude Williams, p. 2.

for himself, but for the whole of society' (p. 300). More specifically he suggests that Friendly Societies might invest part of their capital in homes and clubs for old people and holiday camps for their members (pp. 276, 298). But he returns to the wider vision on his final page: 'So at last human society may become a friendly society—an Affiliated Order of branches, some large and many small, each with its own life in freedom, each linked to all the rest by common purpose and by bonds to serve that purpose' (p. 324). And this implies, not merely that the Friendly Societies as we know them should extend their philanthropic services, but that the voluntary social services, through which help is rendered by the privileged to the unprivileged, should hand over to new associations built on the principle of mutual aid. It is clear that Lord Beveridge regards this Utopia as still remote, for he devotes his attention primarily to immediate measures which do not involve any such revolutionary change.

But is this really such a revolutionary concept? Is it not exactly what has already happened in the statutory social services? The entire citizen body is organized in a great mutual aid society. All contribute, and all are entitled to receive benefits. There is no longer any distinction between the privileged and the unprivileged. And—an important point to which we must return later—those who administer the services are constitutionally responsible to those for whose benefit they are administered. But, it may be said, although the principle is certainly present, a mutual aid society run by the State, with compulsory membership and contributions, and covering the whole nation, cannot have the qualities that Lord Beveridge has in mind when he describes a Friendly Society as 'a fellowship of men knowing and trusting and influencing one another' (p. 27). Such an idea can only be realized within the field of voluntary action.

There is obviously much truth in this assertion, but it would be a grave mistake if, by stressing the special virtues of voluntary action, we were led to neglect the possibilities of developing those same qualities in the statutory services. It is all very well to exalt the one; there is no need to malign the other. There are many ways in which citizens can be made to feel that the public services belong to them, especially when the operative power is vested in a Local Authority. They can participate directly in them as voluntary workers. The elected councillors in local government are themselves an outstanding example of citizens giving voluntary service of a particularly exacting kind. Others, who are not politicians, can play their part as members of special committees. Hundreds more are to be found helping in the management of hospitals and the government of schools. At a humbler level there are the voluntary workers of the L.C.C. Care Committees. Voluntary service is by no means a monopoly of the voluntary agencies. And they, too, employ salaried professionals for work that demands training and technical skill. Links between the citizens and the public services may be forged in other ways as well. Parent-Teacher Associations are a good example of one method. Community Associations and Citizens' Advice Bureaux can serve a similar purpose by helping to bridge the gulf between the public and the bureaucracy. Representative government alone will not create a true democracy if the citizen cringes before the official, or if he sullenly resents his authority. The establishment of a proper co-operative relationship between the public and the bureaucracy is a matter of vital importance, and the statutory services provide the main field of operations. The citizen must learn to respect the authority of the official as something without which he could not discharge his responsibilities, but at the same time to regard him as his friend and his servant. Close co-operation between the statutory and voluntary services is a powerful instrument for the realization of this ideal.

But the problem of management cannot be dismissed without looking at the other side of the picture. It is a curious fact that in none of the recent books on the subject is there any description or discussion of the constitutional structure of the voluntary social service organizations. We are not told who wields the power in them, how the directors of policy are selected and to what constituency they are responsible. No general answer can be given to these questions, because practices vary greatly, but certain aspects of the problem are sufficiently clear. Consideration of them introduces another of the characteristics of the statutory services mentioned above, namely their all-embracing nature. Not only do they cover the whole nation, with considerable decentralization to Local Authorities, but all the various services come under the same ultimate control of the local council or central government. It is this that makes it possible for those who run the services to be responsible to those who use them, that is to say to the whole community whose members will, from time to time, need help of various kinds. But a specialized voluntary society has no such constituency. It cannot be constitutionally responsible to those it serves, because they are a scattered, amorphous and indeterminate body which is constantly changing. Their very need may make them incapable of contributing either money or guidance to the body on which they depend for help. To whom, then, should the management be accountable? There are two obvious groups of people, those who voluntarily subscribe to the funds and those who voluntarily give their services. This, in fact, has been the tradition. But changing circumstances made the situation somewhat anomalous. The increasing volume of grants from public funds has reduced the role of private subscriptions. It is as necessary to satisfy the central or local authorities as the subscribers, and the latter may take as little active part in the affairs of the organization as the shareholders of a joint stock company or the members of a co-operative society. Voluntary workers play an important part, but it is often less important than that played by the salaried employees of the agency. And the recruitment of volunteers is necessarily rather haphazard. Their quality cannot be guaranteed, and they may, by failing to move with the times, outstay their welcome. The system brings into the effective service of the community much of the best that the community has to offer, but there is an inevitable danger that, in a constituency created in this way, the pioneers may be out-voted by the traditionalists. An evolution, such as that of the Charity Organization Society into the Family Welfare Association, may be a long and not entirely painless process.

Here, then, is no tidy picture of a logical clear-cut order of things, but the achievements of the system prove that its merits outweigh its defects. The main need is for constant watchfulness, flexibility and adaptation to change. As the centre of gravity moves from the voluntary supporters to the professional employees of the society the relationship between the two groups is bound to alter. Because there can be no constitutional responsibility to the clients, the moral responsibility is all the greater. It provides the standards by which the service must be judged. It is the general sense of moral duty that urges the volunteers to take the field. It also provides the initial incentive for most paid social workers. But they are pre-eminently in a position to carry things a stage further, by translating the general into the particular —the moral obligation into professional standards. The steady growth of professionalism among social workers should not be regarded merely as evidence of a desire to improve their status and raise their salaries. These aims are legitimate enough, provided status-consciousness does not degenerate into professional snobbery. But professionalism is equally valuable to the employing organizations themselves. It supplies an ingredient whose addition to the mixture of subscribers and voluntary workers can create a constituent body strong enough to defy challenge and criticism. But this implies that the professional workers must rank as members in the sense that they serve on terms of equality with the unpaid on committees and councils. This principle is now widely recognized, but its acceptance is of relatively recent growth and it may well be that there is room for further improvements in this direction.

But developments of this nature do not convert philanthropy into mutual aid. The division between the servers and the served remains, but its significance has changed. It is no longer a division between the privileged and the unprivileged, but between moral and professional duty on the one hand and need on the other. Or one might say between strength and skill on the one hand and weakness on the other. Undoubtedly there has been a movement towards mutuality. Gracious condescension and the charitable dole are things of the past, and the perpetual aim today is to help others to help themselves—to offer a service which hopes for a response, not of gratitude but of effort to face life with new courage. But this reciprocity between server and served, however rich it grows, will not turn the Family Welfare Association into a Friendly Society. Such a transformation would almost certainly destroy a force for social advance which, though it should never claim a monopoly in the field of social service, is right to assert that it possesses unique value. As Lord Beveridge says: 'The Philanthropic Motive is in practice a specialist motive; it drives men to combat a particular evil to meet a particular need that arouses their interest' (p. 125). This special and spontaneous urge to action would inevitably be weakened if all the services that now spring from the philanthropic motive were combined under the direction of an all-embracing community association, run on the principle of mutual aid. Such associations already exist, in local and central government, and it would be hard to duplicate them and still preserve the separate identities of the two parts.

Nevertheless we should be constantly on the watch to see whether there may be, within the present field of operations of philanthropy, some activities in which the division between servers and served, or givers and receivers, is unnecessarily sharp, or even no longer appropriate. In work for the welfare of the blind there is already a strong element of mutual service in that the blind themselves play a large part in the running of the organizations. They can do this because they are a relatively stable community containing persons from all classes and of all ages. A Community Centre may be started by the initiative of a group of those who wish to use it and, when founded, may be managed in all essentials by its members. Dependence on a subsidy need not alter its fundamental character as an enterprise of mutual aid. It is not easy, for obvious reasons, to run a youth club on exactly the same lines. An ever-changing population of juveniles cannot operate in the same way as a stable society of adults. But if the family rather than the juvenile is taken as the unit, a stable and responsible group can be created which could provide, by mutual aid, clubs for its young people. The task is easiest where there is a strong uniting interest such as a religious faith, but there is no obvious reason why the principle should not be more widely applied. Social settlements, says Mr Self, should eventually 'find themselves transformed from charitable organizations into societies for mutual aid and for the promotion of community life'.[4] It is claimed for the Peckham Health Centre that here 'the two together, member-family and Centre, form a zone of mutuality in the living body of society',[5] and the aim is to make subscriptions cover expenses.

This matter of payment is important. The philanthropic motive does not expect payment; the mutual aid principle demands it. But there is a possible half-way house between the two. Even though philanthropy provides the initiative and experience necessary to establish a new service, and even though philanthropy or public funds guarantee its solvency by granting a subsidy, the users may still contribute substantially to the cost out of their own pockets. This can make them, instead of passive recipients of benefits graciously bestowed, active partners in a joint undertaking. Club subscriptions might be adjusted more realistically to what the members can afford, and is there any reason why fees should not be charged for the services rendered by Citizens Advice Bureaux? As the standard of living of the working classes rises and their economic self-sufficiency increases a careful watch should be kept to see where the principle of philanthropy can be diluted by the principle of self-help.

But we have not yet exhausted the subject of the essential differences between the statutory and voluntary social services, and we must return to Lord Beveridge's signposts. Even such an apparently simple statement as that the voluntary

---

[4] Bourdillon: op. cit., p. 248.

[5] Innes H. Pearse and Lucy H. Crocker: *The Peckham Experiment*, p. 291.

services are distinguished by not being under the direction of the State needs closer examination. Lord Beveridge tells us that in 1946–7 grants from central funds to voluntary organizations amounted to £10 million (p. 305). This does not include grants from Local Authorities. Now it is perfectly true that we have in this country evolved a system or tradition by which the grant of public money is not necessarily accompanied by the exercise of public control. We should not, however, assume that, as the sums increase, the control will not increase also. There are signs, even in the case of the Universities, that this is likely to happen. But the important point is that the grants are made because, to quote Lord Beveridge again, voluntary action is part of public policy. There are many voluntary agencies today offering services for the provision of which the State accepts an ultimate responsibility. If the voluntary bodies did not provide them, the State would have to. The State is clearly responsible for the treatment of juvenile delinquents, but most of the Approved Schools are private ventures. The State has formally accepted responsibility for children deprived of family life, but it relies on voluntary organizations to supply a substantial part of the accommodation. The situation has arisen because of the strength of the movement for voluntary action. Private enterprise got there first. These are spontaneous creations taken into partnership by the State. They were not dragged into existence by State pressure. Consequently the value of a genuine co-operation, on all but equal terms, between private and public outweighs the disadvantages of the adjustment the private bodies may have to make to the demands of public policy.

But, as Lord Lindsay says, 'for the proper proportions of the mixture there is no recipe'. The voluntary bodies must be prepared, like any professional association (and professionalism is one source of their strength), to assert themselves, when occasion demands, against the State, but they must also know when it is their duty to submit. They must recognize that, though they are the first guardians of their own standards, voluntaryism is not a guarantee of perfection.

The State cannot waive its right to inspect and approve a service whose efficient discharge is a matter of public policy. The Curtis Committee could both urge that the State should benefit from the example of the best voluntary agencies and also insist that all voluntary homes should be registered with and inspected by the central department. And Lord Beveridge, in spite of his faith in voluntary action, expresses the doubt 'whether the Bill, as first introduced, did not leave the voluntary agencies too much freedom to be antiquated and bureaucratic' (p. 238). But we may feel fairly confident that the mixture will be a success, even without a recipe.

There are, however, two further aspects of the matter to be considered. One is sufficiently obvious to need little comment. Co-operation with the State, especially when it is accompanied by grants of public money, is likely to stimulate the amalgamation of voluntary bodies into large national associations, with all their liability to bureaucracy and remote control. The process is inevitable, and the dangers must be met by the devising of sound internal constitutions. There are other consequences of this process which can better be considered later in a different context. The second aspect of the problem referred to above is related to finance and national resources. In the days of low taxation and unemployment there could be no conceivable objection to voluntary societies raising as much money as they could and spending it as they pleased, by engaging labour, erecting buildings and so forth. Yet even before the war the late Evan Durbin, whom no one can accuse of lack of interest in social advance, sounded a warning note. 'There is therefore a serious danger,' he wrote, 'lurking in the enthusiasm of the public for the social services, and a conflict between the various types of social betterment that they desire—a conflict of which they are not even aware.'[6] He was thinking of the danger that the high taxation necessary to finance social services might 'wipe out social saving altogether, and leave us with a relatively stagnant economy'. Today the situation is different and

[6] The Politics of Democratic Socialism, p. 294.

more serious. With a general shortage of labour and material resources, the Government is responsible for deciding what the nation can afford to spend, and to a large extent on what it should spend it, whether the expenditure is public or private. Even when subscriptions are privately raised, their expenditure involves the diversion of labour and materials from one purpose to another. The voluntary societies can certainly not claim exemption from the restrictions of a national building policy. Subscriptions themselves may be made partly at the expense of the Exchequer, when tax is recoverable by the recipient. Lord Beveridge points out that voluntary action received a severe blow when the Finance Act of 1946 limited the recovery to income tax, excluding surtax. Previously rich men could in effect, by making seven-year covenants, decide how the State should spend a not inconsiderable part of its legitimate revenue. It is difficult now to defend financial autonomy of this kind, and it is not enough to urge on its behalf that the money was devoted to good purposes. The issue depends, as Lord Beveridge rightly says, 'on the importance which the State attaches to independent experiment for social advance' (p. 312). The State must have the final word.

This point has been mentioned as illustrating one sense in which voluntary action is a part of public policy, but the reference to independent experiment brings us back to the big national associations mentioned earlier and through them to a final matter of considerable importance. 'In a free society,' writes Lord Beveridge, 'discontented individuals with new ideas can make a new institution to meet their needs. The field is open to experiment and success or failure; secession is the midwife of invention' (p. 59). But the existence of a powerful national organization may make secession a precarious adventure, or even in effect prevent it. The trade union movement is a case in point. The restrictive effect is enhanced if the national body is the only channel through which grants from public funds can be received, and naturally it is easiest for the State to canalize its subsidies in this way. A Voluntary Service Grants Committee, on the analogy of the University Grants Committee, would, as Lord Beveridge suggests, probably make things worse. The claims are so infinitely varied, that it is better for each Ministry to allocate subsidies in the limited field in which it works and which it knows well enough to recognize the value of the smaller applicants. But the main essential is that the national bodies should ensure that experiment is possible without secession.

It is generally agreed that, if the voluntary societies ceased to encourage variety and experiment, they would lose much of their right to exist. Some writers lay the emphasis on the pioneering function which they have most conspicuously fulfilled in the past and should continue to fill in the future. Mr Barnes, for example, even suggests that voluntary organizations (and he is writing about the Youth Service in particular) 'might well be renamed "pilot organizations" or perhaps "pioneer organizations"'.[7] But this is going rather far. It is quite true that the voluntary bodies provide a field in which there is more freedom for pioneers than in most of the statutory services. But, where public policy is being carried out through a joint partnership between voluntary and statutory bodies, it is absurd to suggest that the voluntary bodies as a whole should keep continually in front dragging the statutory along behind them. The value of pioneer work depends on its quality, not on its quantity. One brilliant educationist trying out his ideas in a single school may initiate a general advance in teaching methods. The voluntary organizations offer great scope for pioneering, but they should not imagine that the statutory services offer none, still less that the results of experiment must be first tried out in the voluntary bodies as a whole before the statutory services can be persuaded to take any notice of them.

It is therefore better to lay stress on variety rather than on pioneering; and if the former is present, the latter is pretty certain to be there too. Pioneering can be relatively concentrated, but variety must range at large and in freedom over wide areas. It is here that statutory services suffer under nec-

[7] L. J. Barnes: *The Outlook for Youth Work*, p. 15.

essary limitations. They need not be rigidly stereotyped, but they must preserve a basic uniformity. Any unorthodox procedure may provide ammunition for party warfare on a local council or provoke a question in the House—a thing which every good civil servant is always anxious to avoid. The activities of public authorities are also limited by the fact that there are some things which, for various reasons, they cannot or ought not to do. Here again the recipe is lacking. Nearly every category one can suggest contains its exceptions. It is sometimes said that statutory bodies cannot do case-work, but there is no more intimately personal kind of case-work than that done by the Probation Officer, nor more difficult than that undertaken by the Mental Health Services or the Civil Resettlement Units—which, incidentally, were pioneer experiments of a very bold kind. Many other examples could be cited to show that there is little that the public services cannot and do not do, but perhaps the most important field in which their action is inappropriate is that where variety is a result, not merely of differences of need, but of differences of taste, belief and deep conviction as to the ways and means by which the need should be met. The history of education is shot with conflict arising from the fact that a state service cannot identify itself with a denominational religious faith. A statutory service for marriage guidance must meet similar difficulties, because a moral code is involved about which there is no unanimity of opinion. In other cases controversy centres round the rival claims of different techniques. As the State takes over more and more the task of providing material assistance, the function of the voluntary organizations will increasingly, as Mr Self has said, be one of education. Not education in the prescribed subjects of the classroom, but education for living. For 'an essential corollary to providing the means of the good life is to teach people how to use them'.[8] This function will remain theirs because it is one in which the State cannot safely meddle. But its retention in

[8] Bourdillon: op. cit., p. 248.

their hands will be justified only if they preserve freedom and variety within themselves.

In this article much space has been devoted to showing that the differences between the statutory and voluntary services are not as great as might at first sight be supposed. This has been done, not because the differences are without significance, but because they are apt to be exaggerated by those who wish to express them in terms of clear-cut principles. It is sometimes even maintained that the statutory services are less democratic than the voluntary. If there is any truth in the charge, it is the duty of a democracy to make them more democratic in the truest sense of that much-abused word. It is tempting to accept their shortcomings as inescapable and to seek to counterbalance them by concentrating on the development of voluntaryism outside their frontiers. But such a course contains the seeds of a rivalry which should have no place where both parties are striving towards the same goal of social betterment.

INDEX

Acquisitive Society, 329–31

Advertising as creator of demand, 327

Affluent Society, 280 ff., 322–23, 324 ff.
  defined, 297–98, 324–28
  in Victorian times, 283–84
  Need to change spirit of, 301–2
  and the status system, 340–41

Allen, C. K., 225

anomie, 33, 333

Argyle, M., 221

Aron, Raymond, 145, 148, 150, 151–52, 279

Ashton, T. S., 4

Asia and the Middle East, 50–53

Askwith, Lord, 122–23

Asquith, H. H., 122

Austerity Society, 296, 322, 337

Aynard, J., 186 n., 200 n.

Balfour, A. J., 286

Barnes, L. J., 356

Barth, Frederik, 63 n.

Bauer-Mengelberg, K., 188 n.

Bendix, R., 211 n.

Benedict, Ruth, 61

Benoît-Smullyan, A., 225, 227

Berelson, R., 144 n., 146 n.

Bernard, Jessie, 135, 149, 154, 325

Beveridge, Lord, 283, 293–95, 346–47, 351, 353, 355–56

Beveridge Report, 290–92, 293–95, 337–38

Birkenhead, Lord, 267

Bland, Hubert, 286

Boettcher, E., 307, 315, 319, 321

Bogardus, E. S., 213 n.

Bonham, John, 146 n.

Booth's Survey of the London Poor, 105, 284

Bourdillon, A. F. C., 346 n., 352 n., 357 n.

Brackenbury, Sir H., 174

Brennan, P., 150

Briggs, Asa, 304, 305, 307, 308, 334, 335

Brodersen, Arvid, 50

Brown, Phelps, 73

Burgess, E., 14

Burnham, James, 145

Burt, Sir Cyril, 264, 276, 277

Butler, David, 146

Butler, R. A., 323